IMAGES
of America

Beardstown Revisited

On the Cover: This photograph, most likely taken from Second Street and Washington Street (or on Washington Street), shows the Beardstown Free Fish Fry in the 1890s, Notice the grand old cars. No one knows what the five ladies were doing, but it seems pretty likely they performed in the bandstand. This was the city square at that time. Attendees got their meals on the right side of the bandstand. This was a grand, all-day affair! (Author's collection.)

IMAGES
of America

BEARDSTOWN REVISITED

Harold Tyson

ARCADIA
PUBLISHING

ISBN 978-1-4671-2987-9

Published by Arcadia Publishing
Charleston, South Carolina

Printed in the United States of America

Library of Congress Control Number: 2018939379

For all general information, please contact Arcadia Publishing:
Telephone 843-853-2070
Fax 843-853-0044
E-mail sales@arcadiapublishing.com
For customer service and orders:
Toll-Free 1-888-313-2665

Visit us on the Internet at www.arcadiapublishing.com

Contents

ACKNOWLEDGMENTS

I would like to recognize the help of Bruce Fischer, who found many of my pictures and identified many more. My son Stan did the manuscript typing and much of the legwork. My wife, Mary, supported my work and helped with the spelling and language. To my many friends through the years who have brought me photographs or allowed me to copy their photographs, thank you! Unless otherwise credited, all the photographs are from the author's collection.

Additional acknowledgments by Stan Tyson: I want to thank many people that helped with the details of these photographs. The most difficult were the sports pictures. We have identified the people as best as we can. Much has changed in the years covered by this book. Some of it I do remember, but much was well before my time. If I misidentified someone, it was my error and I would like to know of it. Looking at these photographs, I can barely recognize Main Street! The ghosts of time are catching up with me. It has been a fun trip!

Introduction

This was published in the Centennial Edition of the *Illinoisan Star* in 1929 and was written by Judge Henry Shaw in 1875:

"The Legend of Monseola"

Far far into the long time ago, and upon the very place
Where Beardstown stands, there lived and loved and died a noble race.
Where pretty lawns and spacious streets and lofty buildings stand,
Monseola's Indian village stood upon the hills of sand.

It was an island then, and round the hills on which it stood
The river ripples wandered in a long continuous flood;
While over all the tall oaks waved in foliage bright and green.
And the trees and tents were mirror'd on the broad and glassy stream.

Three weary moons two Indian tribes had been in a deadly strife,
And Miamis and Muscoutens had yielded many a life:
Till the allies of the Muscoutens had left them all alone,
And the Miamis besieged them upon their island home.

Slowly at night across the waters on the southern side,
The Miamis were paddling their canoes against the tide;
While in advance of every boat there was a branching bough,
Which from the gaze of watching eyes might shield the advancing prow.

Just as the distant glittering beams that led the morning sun
Sat lightly on the yellow knobs of the bluffs of the Sangamon,
A yells of a thousand fiends fell upon the startled ears,
And sleepers woke to sleep again pierced by foeman's spears.

Monesola then, Muscotens Chief raised high the battle cry
And bade his warrior follow him and win the fight or die;
Now on the left, now on the right, his ponderous war club fell,
As many an Indian skull crushed he, and stifled many a yell.

Now backwards borne, now pressing on, Muscotens wavering braves
Proved that the blood that nerved their arms was never meant for slaves;
Till overpowered, and rank by rank fell weltering in their blood,
The brave Monseola fought alone against the crimson flood.

The old chief's daughter, White Wing ran through the rift of spears
Though gentle as a fawn, that day she showed no childish fears;
Pierced to the heart, into his arms she through herself, a shield,
He grasped her lifeless form and slowly bore her from the field,

Where the golden grass was waving on the western shore,
Monseola's birchen shallop touched the flowery bank once more:
There oft before the same proud chief had pushed his light canoe'
With warriors in sinewy keels – three hundred brave and true.

Additional note: This battle took place in the 1600s. At this same time, René-Robert Cavelier, Sieur de La Salle (often shortened to Robert de La Salle), an early French explorer, was building his Fort Crèvecoeur ("broken heart" in French) and trading post on the south bank of the Illinois River at Beardstown. The location of the battle was between Beardstown and Chandlerville. When the farmers started plowing in the Sangamon bottoms, they found rows of skeletons laid head-to-head in the sand. This battle is confirmed in the journals of La Salle. The battle was also confirmed by the Haudenosaunee Confederacy of New York in 2017.

The Native Americans chose the island now known as Beardstown because it was easy to protect and there was an abundance of food. There were all kinds of fish, shellfish, water fowl, small game, and large game close to the river. On the prairie, large game abounded, including deer, elk, bison, and bear.

The French explored the Illinois and Mississippi River bottoms. In the 1600s, when La Salle was building his Fort Crèvecoeur and trading post, he tried to convince the French government that if it would build forts and trading posts at the mouths of each river emptying into the Mississippi, France could control all the trade between the Rocky Mountains and the Appalachian Mountains. France was not interested.

Beardstown was established because of the Illinois River traffic and because there was a need for a ferry to take homesteaders to Schuyler County and the rest of the Military Tract established by Congress as payment to and to provide homes and land for the men who served in the War of 1812.

Beardstown was founded in 1819 but was not incorporated till 1829. Many of the early residents lived in tents until a carpenter could build them a house. In the 1820s, Beardstown shipped a lot of commodities to St. Louis and New Orleans via the river. Commodities included salt pork, honey, apples, flour, and whiskey. It was easier to ship whiskey—and more valuable than shipping the corn from which it is made. Many of these commodities were shipped in barrels.

By the 1870s, the fishing industry and mussel-shell industry were important parts of the Beardstown economy. Fish was later shipped to Chicago via railroad and kept fresh with ice harvested from Mascouten Bay. The mussel shells were eventually turned into buttons that were in high demand in Europe. With an ample supply of trees, Robert Schmoldt, a German immigrant, started a stave mill and lumber yard on the edge of the river near where Schmoldt Park now stands.

In the late 1800s and very early 1900s, ice was harvested from Mascouten Bay and stored in big warehouses near the river and the railroad. In 1907, the area's first ice factory was built, which meant that men no longer needed to harvest it from the river. The production from the several flour mills was 1,500 barrels collectively per year. A hog-packing plant was butchering 75,000 hogs per year.

In the 1960s and 1970s, Beardstown was widely known as the "Fun Capital of Illinois" for its boating, swimming, and hunting. For many years, it has been well known for its watermelons, sweet corn, pumpkins, and other produce. The Illinois River is still a major port for grain via the Archer Daniels Midland, Cargill, and Clarkson grain terminals. The commodities have changed with the times, and Beardstown has changed along with them.

One

TRIUMPHS AND TRIBULATIONS OF ILLINOIS RIVER CULTURE

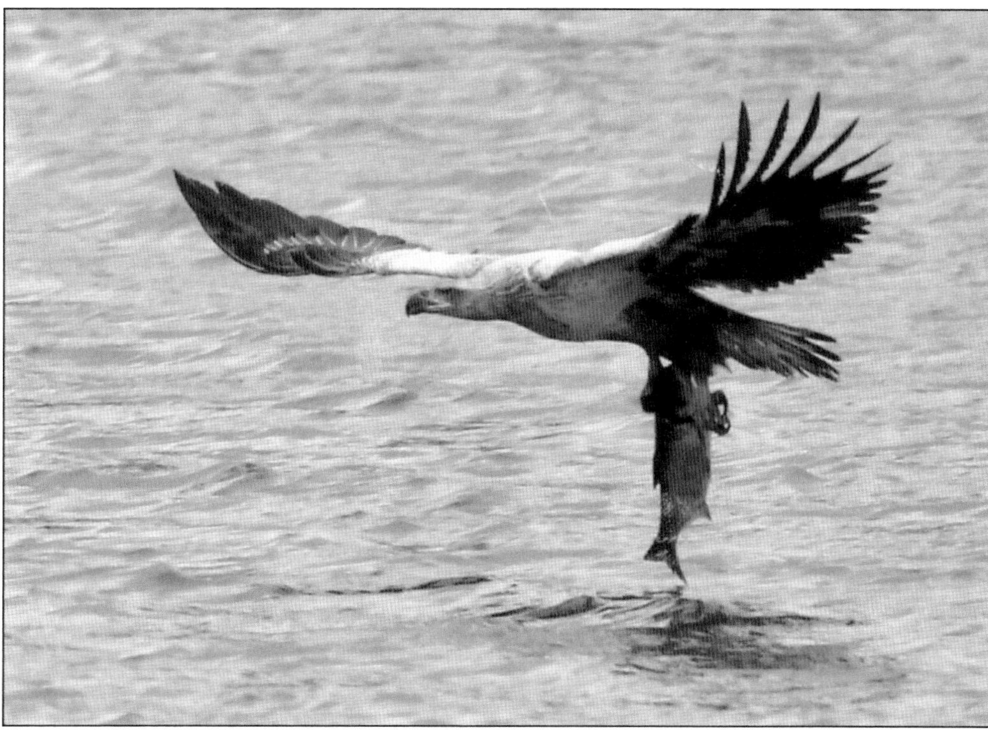

A juvenile bald eagle, about three years old, caught this fish between the two bridges at Beardstown. Brian DeLoche spent many hours hoping to get a good picture, and in March 2017, he got this great picture! (Photograph by Brian DeLoche.)

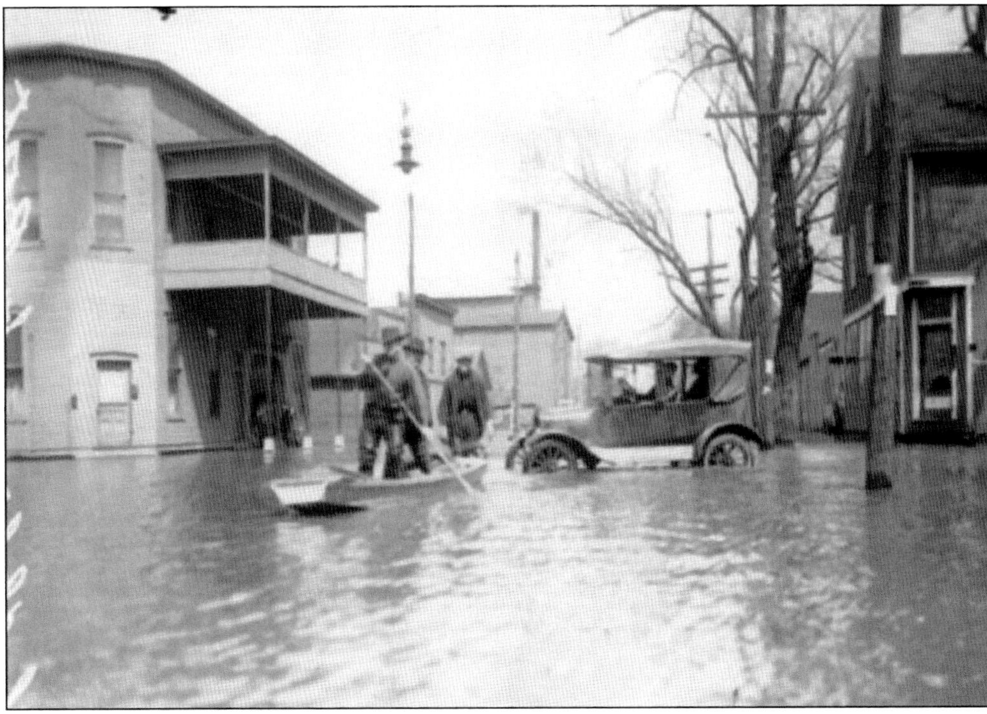

It looks like the boat has the right-of-way. The building on the left is Tice Neff's Tavern, commonly known as the "Crappie Hole." The large building to the left is the Home Mills flour mill. The building on the right is the Palace Hotel and Bar. The hotel bar sold "the best wines, liquors and cigars available." The Palace was reported to be Abraham Lincoln's favorite place to stay.

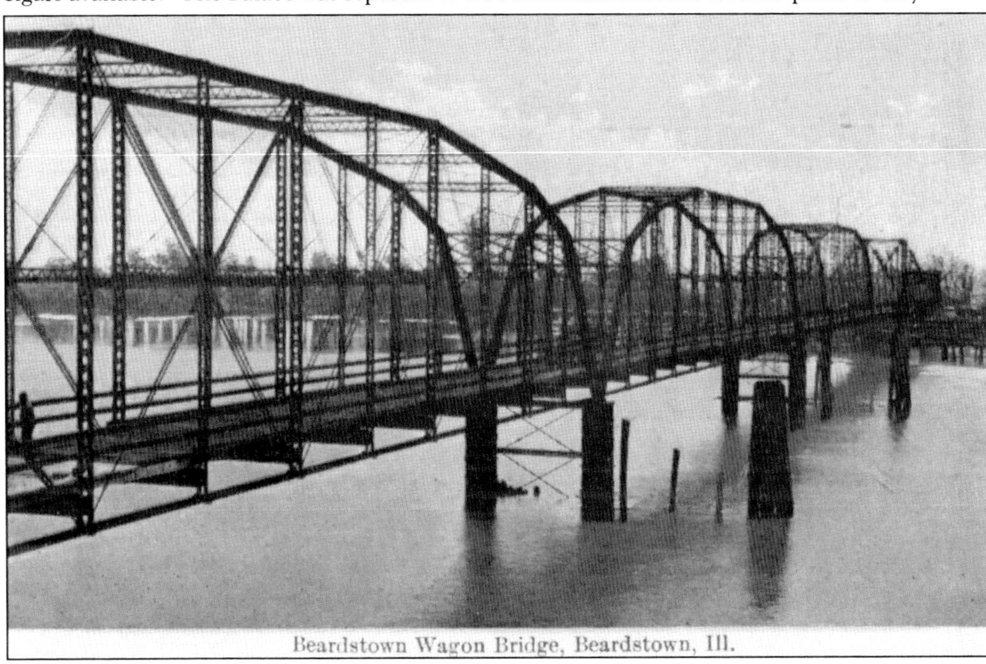

This bridge over the Illinois River at State Street replaced the old wooden bridge in 1880. It was replaced in 1955. The new bridge paid for itself, as it was a toll bridge.

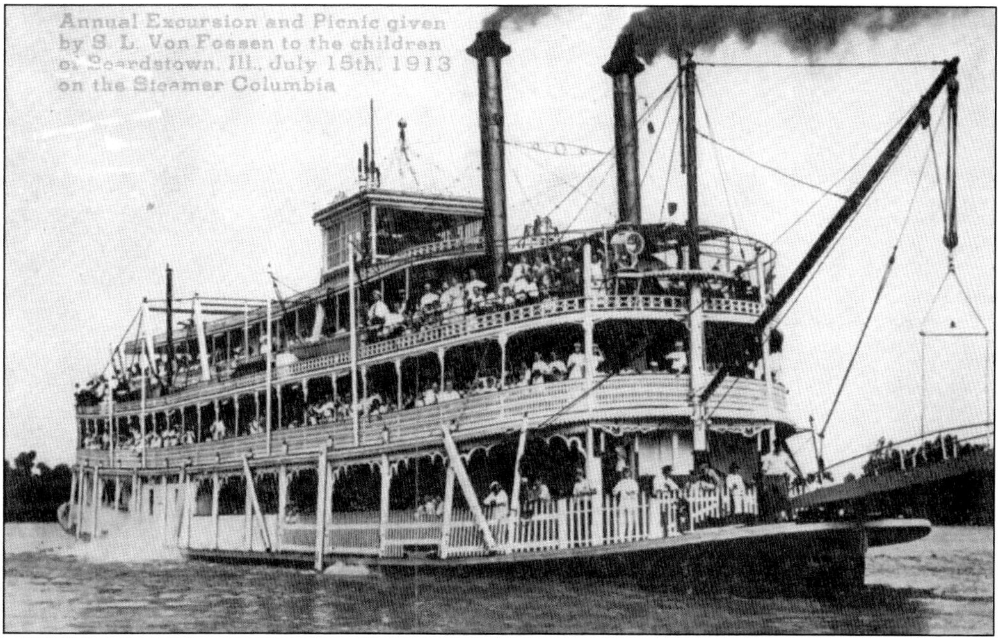

Smith Von Fossen operated numerous businesses next to the river on State Street. As a thank-you to the town, each spring he would take all the schoolchildren on a boat excursion and picnic. This picture shows the excursion held on July 15, 1913, on the steamer *Columbia*. Von Fossen built his home, which still stands, at 1319 State Street.

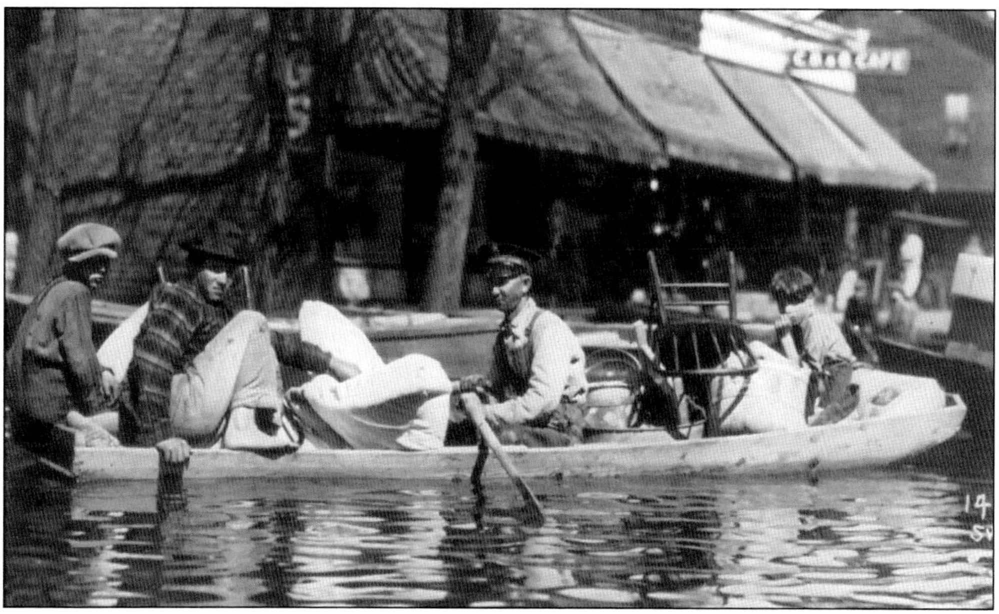

The Spears boys are shown moving out of the high water in 1922. From left to right are Floyd Spears, Bill Spears, unidentified cab driver, and Dan Spears. The picture was taken on Fourth Street next to the Chicago, Burlington & Quincy (CB&Q) Railroad. The CB&Q Café, shown in the background, was located next to the railroad. John Janes's father operated the café, and when John was young, he would take baskets of sandwiches through the train when it stopped at the depot.

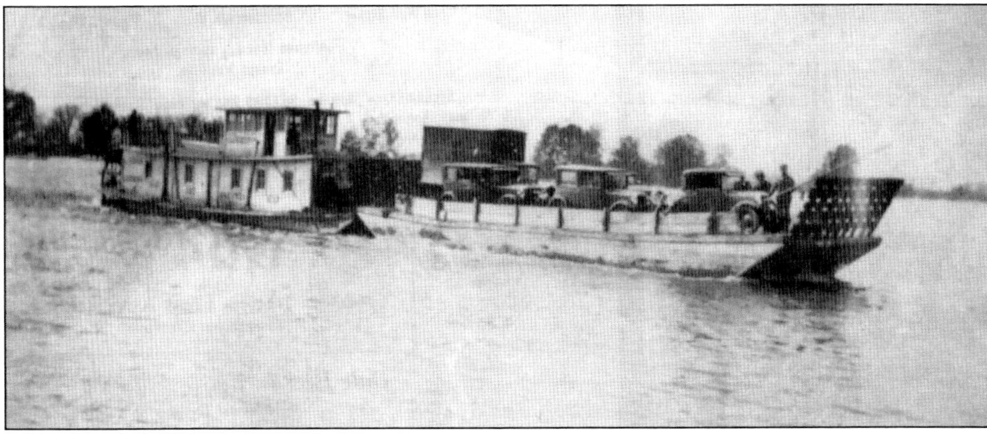

This ferryboat was used in the 1926 flood. It consisted of a paddle wheel push boat and two barges.

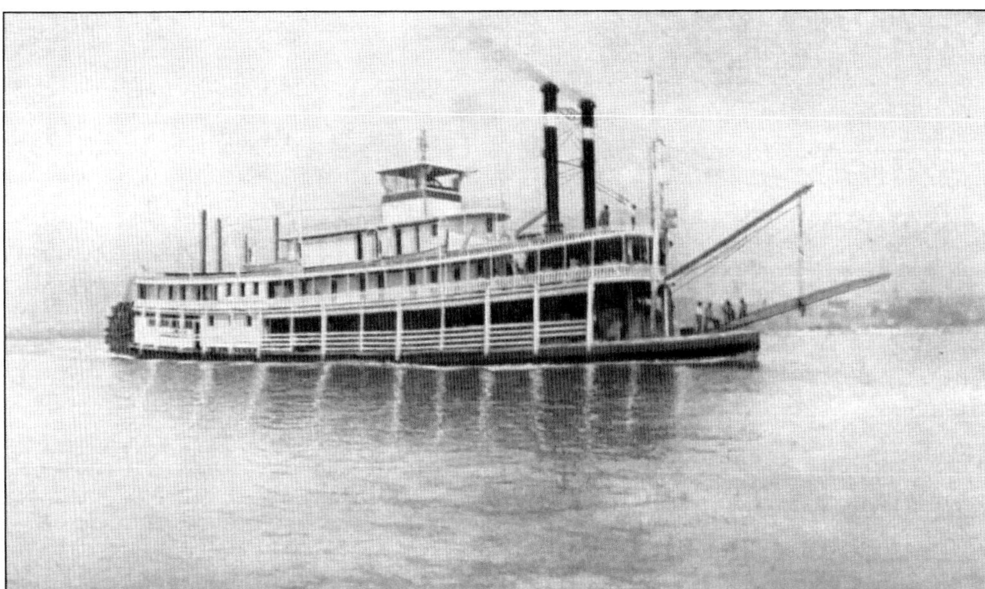

This is the *Helen Blair*, a steam-powered paddle wheeler. Its home ports were in Davenport and Burlington, Iowa. Passengers were upstairs, and animals and freight were downstairs.

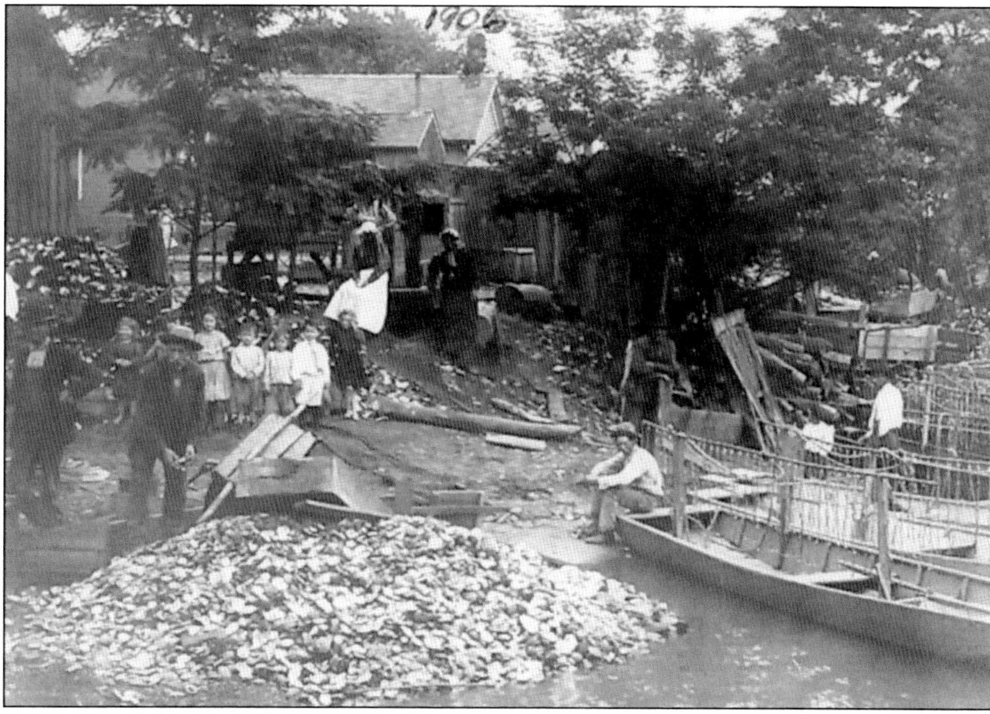

These mussel shells were harvested by dragging wire hooks in the river. The mussel would clamp down on the hook, and this allowed the shell to be hauled into the boat. Cooking forced the shells to open, and the meat would be used for fish bait.

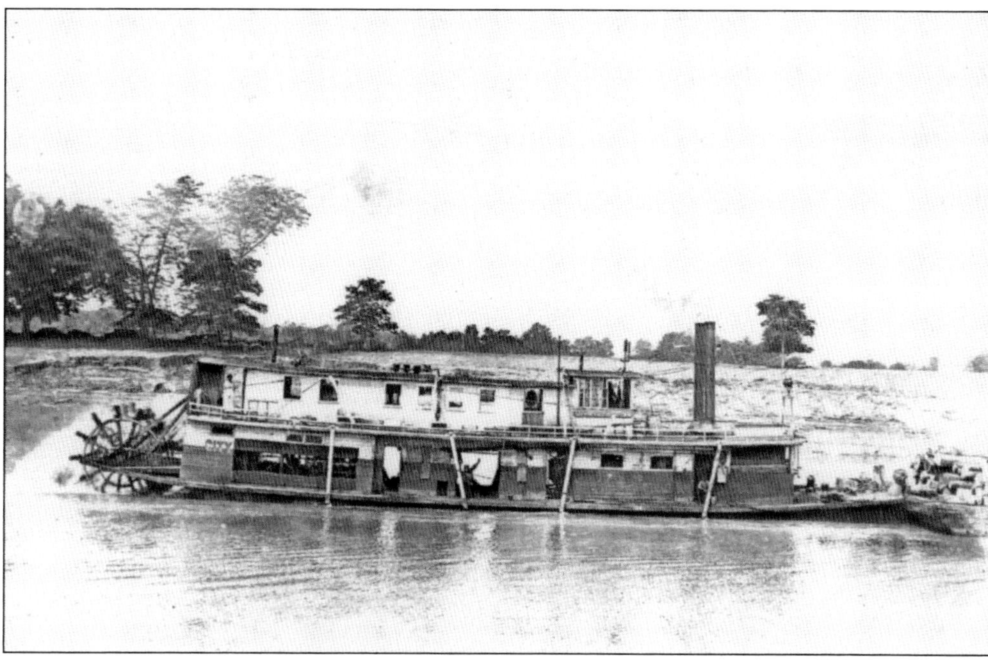

This is a family-owned steam-powered paddle wheeler fired by wood. Notice the woman hanging wash on the upper level of the stern.

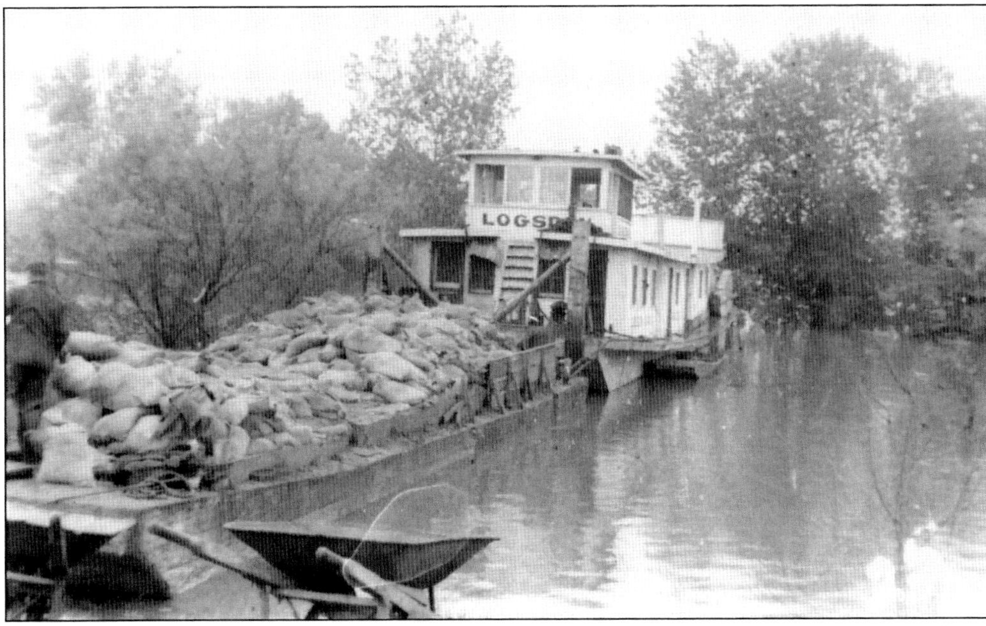

The Logsdon Tug Service steamboat is shown pushing a load of sandbags to shore up the levee during the 1943 flood.

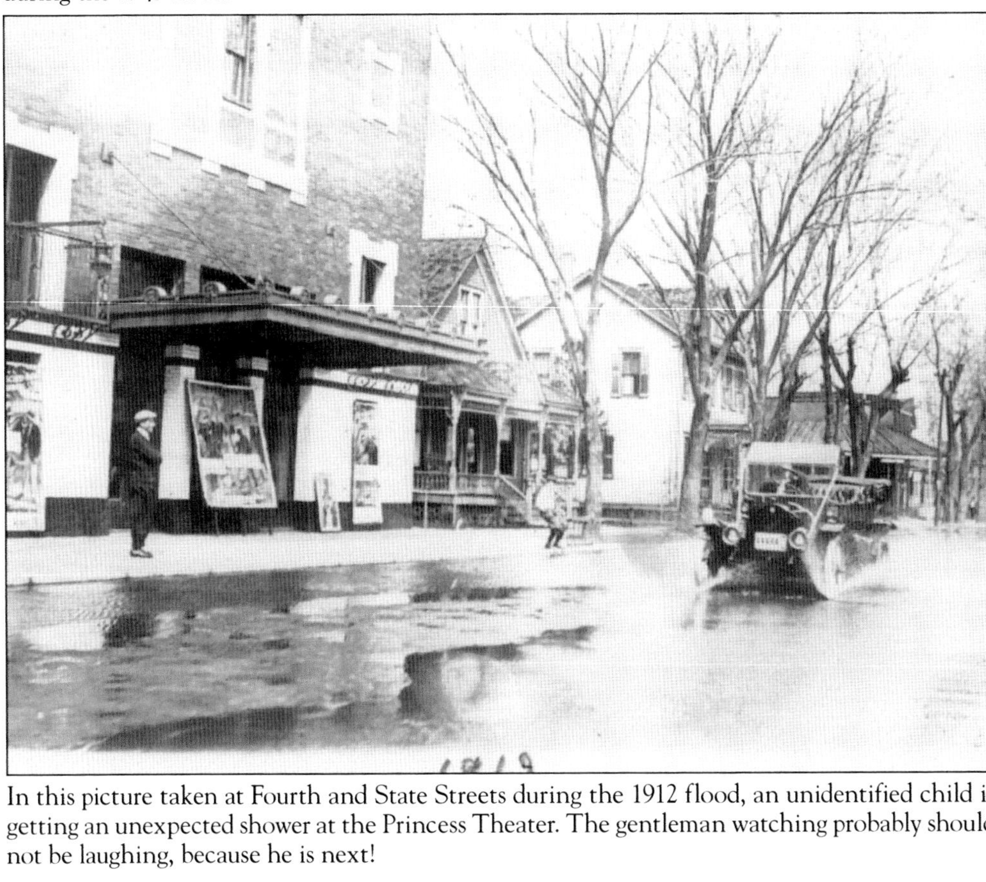

In this picture taken at Fourth and State Streets during the 1912 flood, an unidentified child is getting an unexpected shower at the Princess Theater. The gentleman watching probably should not be laughing, because he is next!

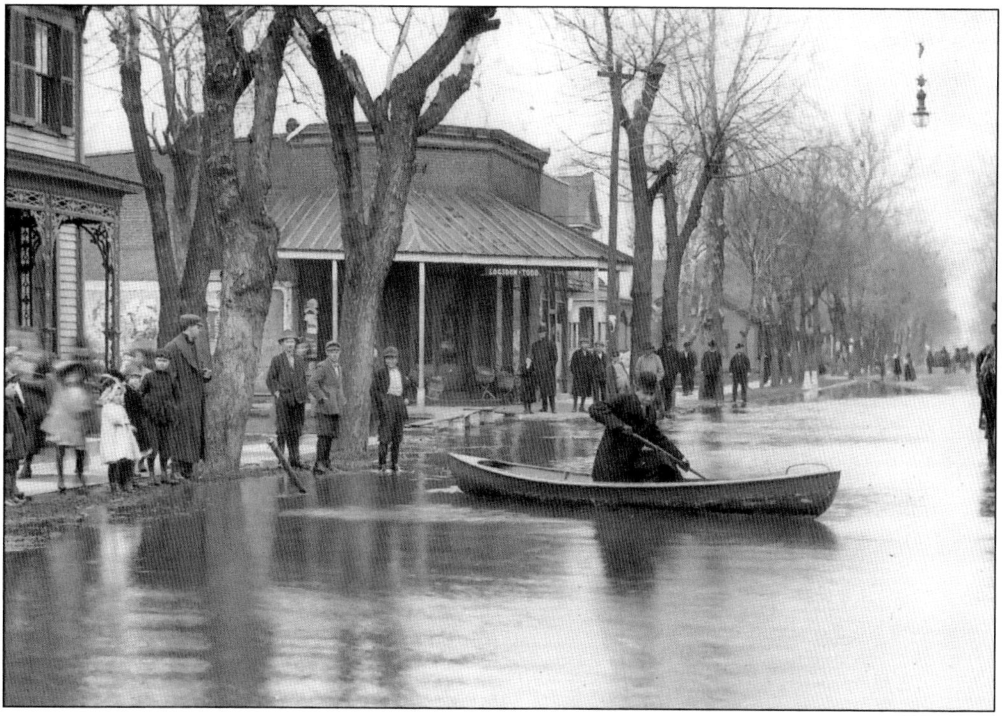

L.L. Logsdon operated this grocery store in 1913. The name of the store was My Store. It was located at the corner of Fourth and Jefferson Streets.

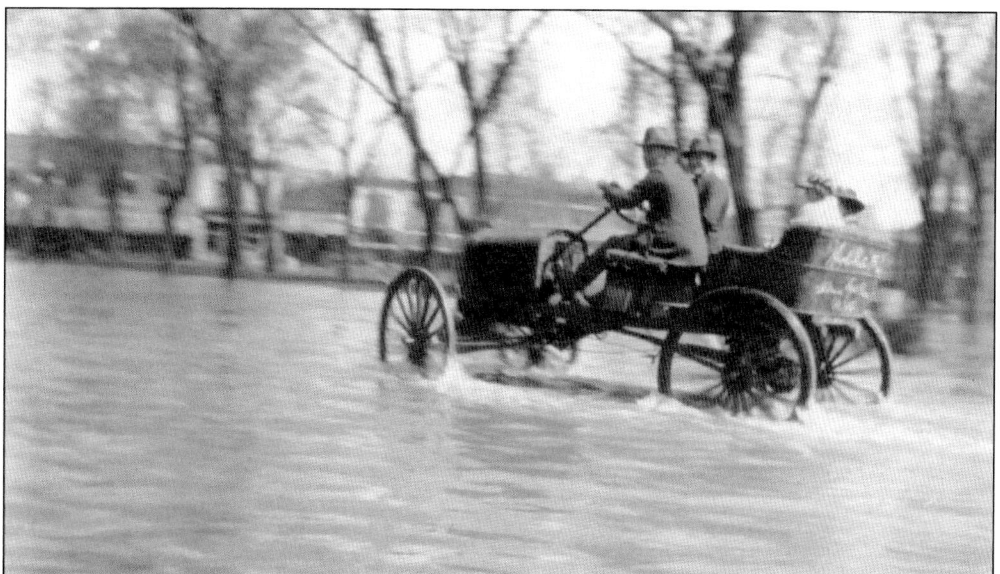

This unusual car was a custom Ford designed to run in high water and was used as a taxi. The low building in the center of the picture is now Tyson's Barber Shop at 212 Washington Street.

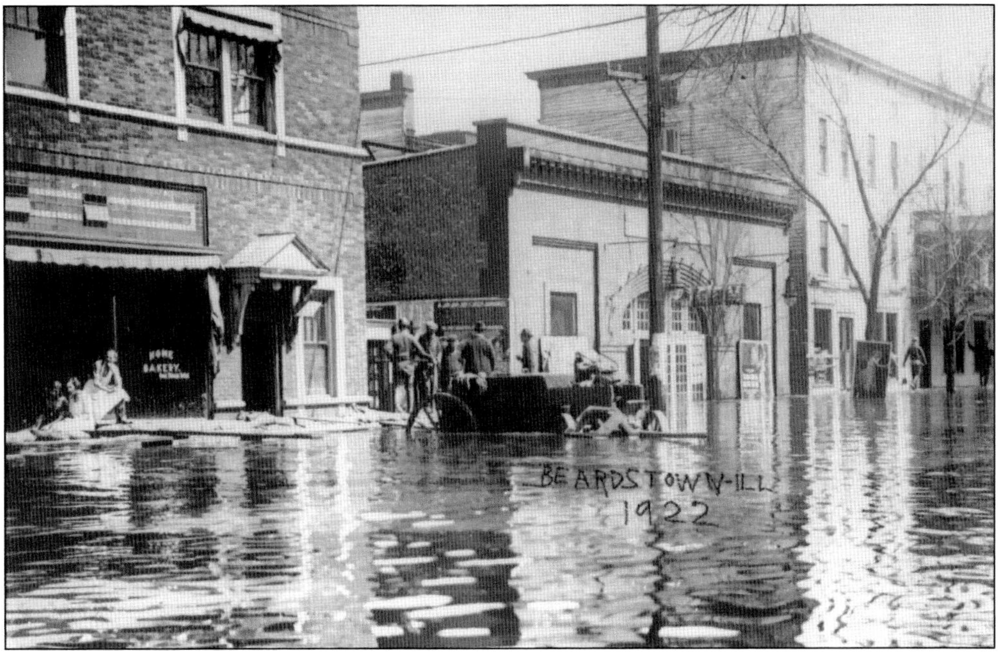

This 1922 photograph shows State Street between Third and Fourth Streets. The Home Bakery (at far left) was operated by Mrs. Harry Musch. The building next to the bakery is the Gem Theater, and next to the theater is the Goodell Hotel, which in later years was the Central Hotel. Note the custom Ford designed for traveling in high water.

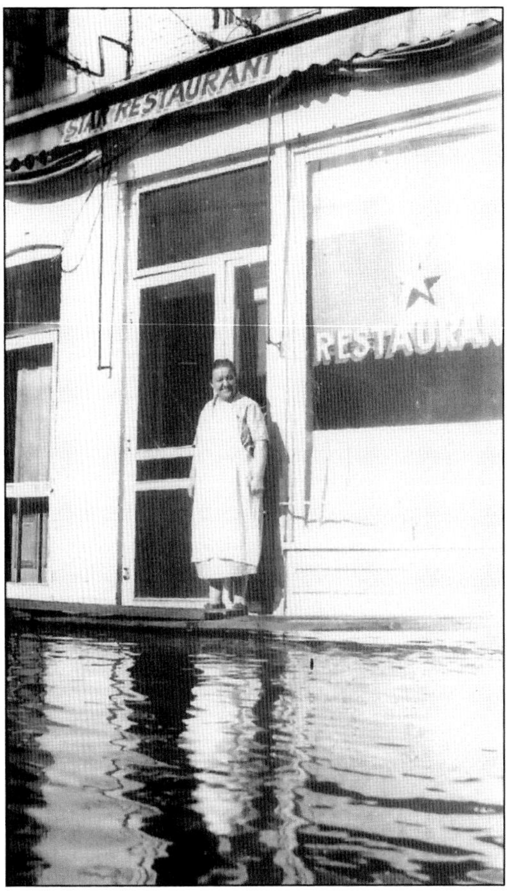

This is the original Star Cafe at 113 State Street. An employee of the café is pictured. It was operated by Spencer Driver and James Bradbury. This photograph was taken during the high water of 1922.

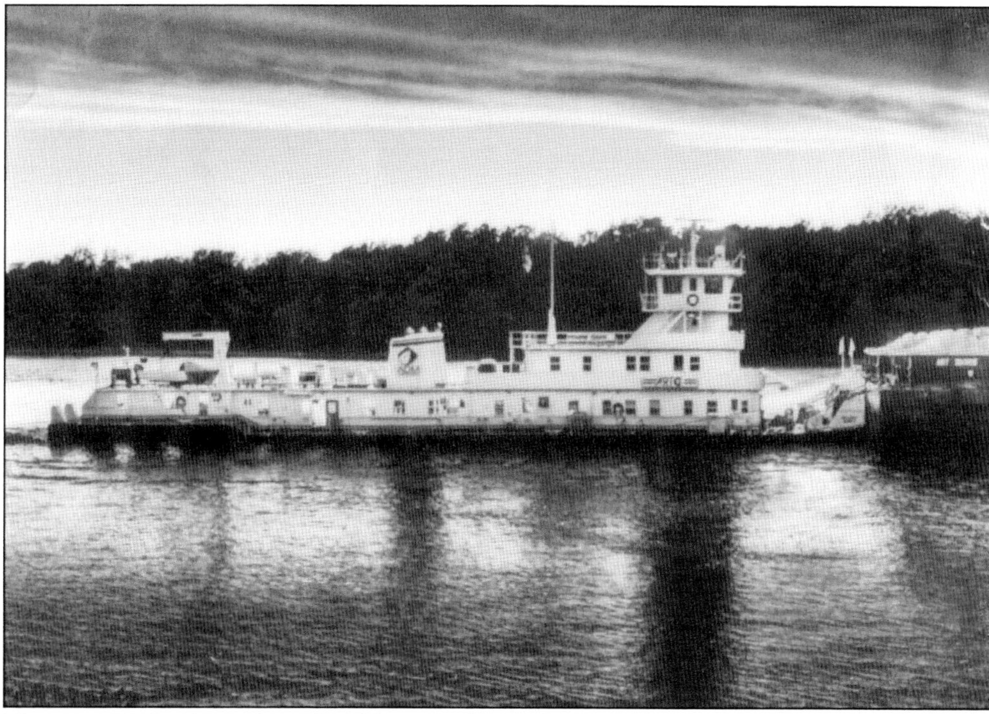

This is an Archer Daniels Midland boat used to push grain barges from one elevator to another. The picture was taken in June 2017 between the bridges at Beardstown. (Photograph by Dale Lovekamp.)

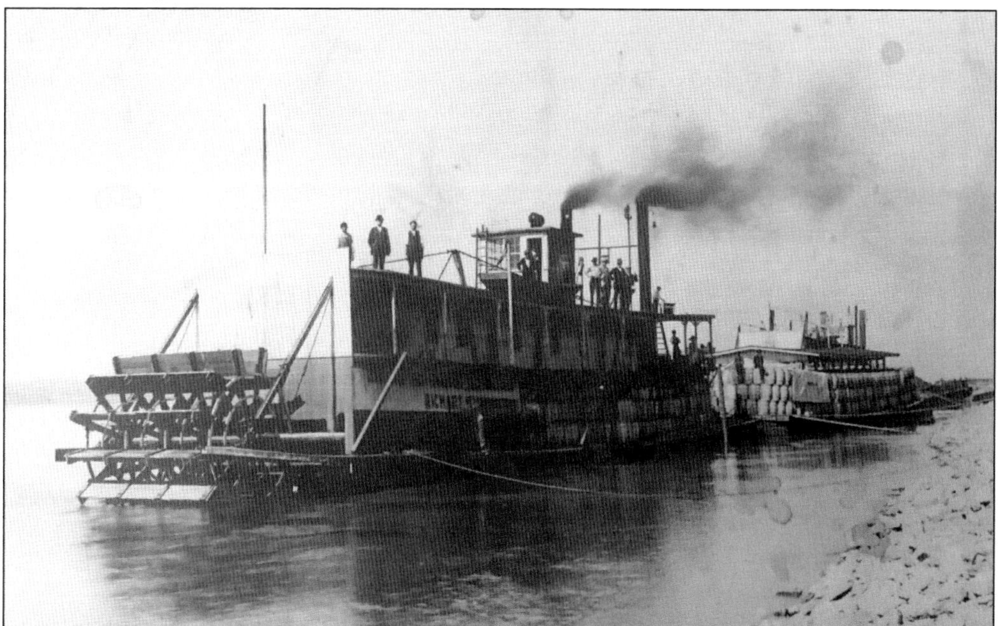

The paddleboat shown here is pushing a packet boat. Note the barrels on the packet boat. Most goods were shipped in barrels to St. Louis and New Orleans. The goods shipped from Beardstown typically included flour, honey, apples, salted pork, and salted fish.

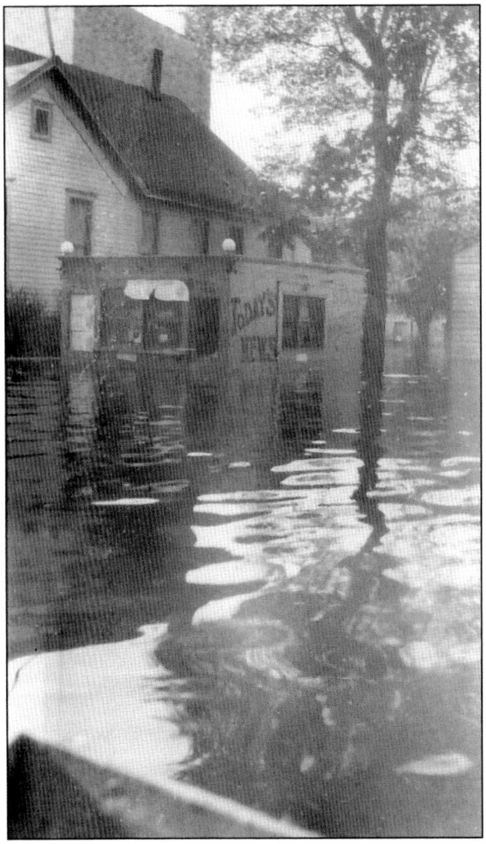

People could get all of the day's news if they did not mind wading in deep water! This is on Fourth Street; the Princess Theater is shown behind the house.

This is the Beardstown Boat Club in its heyday. In 1918, the Army Corps of Engineers did a study that found Mascouten Bay would silt up in 100 years; they were right! In 1954 and 1955, the Corps of Engineers channelized the Sangamon River from Chandlerville to Beardstown. This reduced the outlets of the river from many distribution channels to one. With the fall of the Sangamon River from Chandlerville to Beardstown at 13 feet, Mascouten Bay and the Beardstown Marina filled with the silt load from the river. This photograph was taken about 1956.

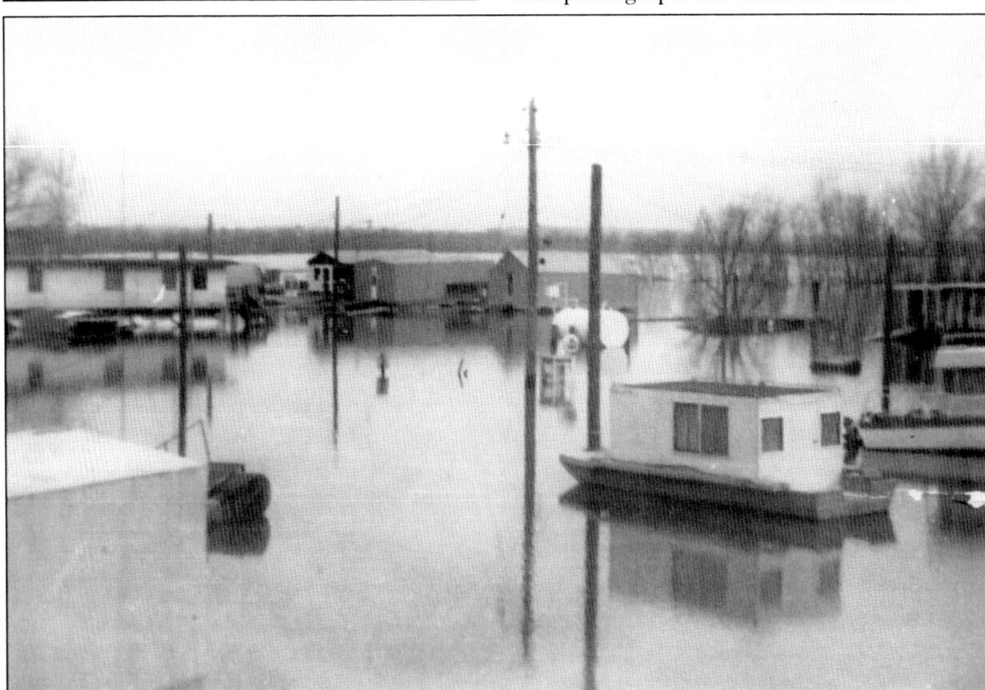

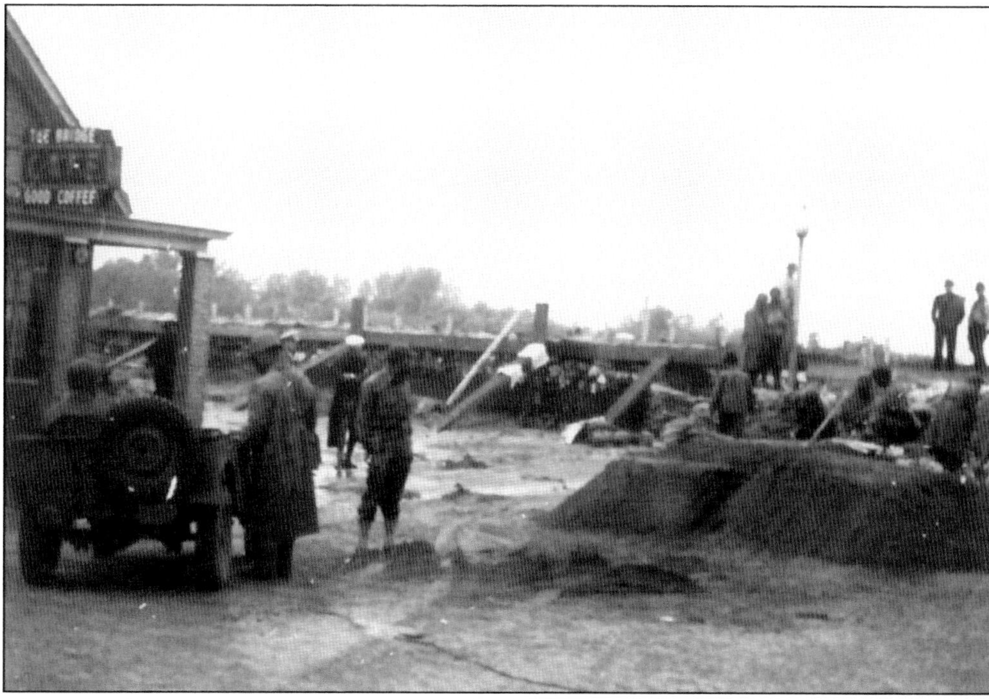

The Bridge Café, on the left, is shown near the bridge during the 1943 dry flood. In the background, workers are strengthening the levee.

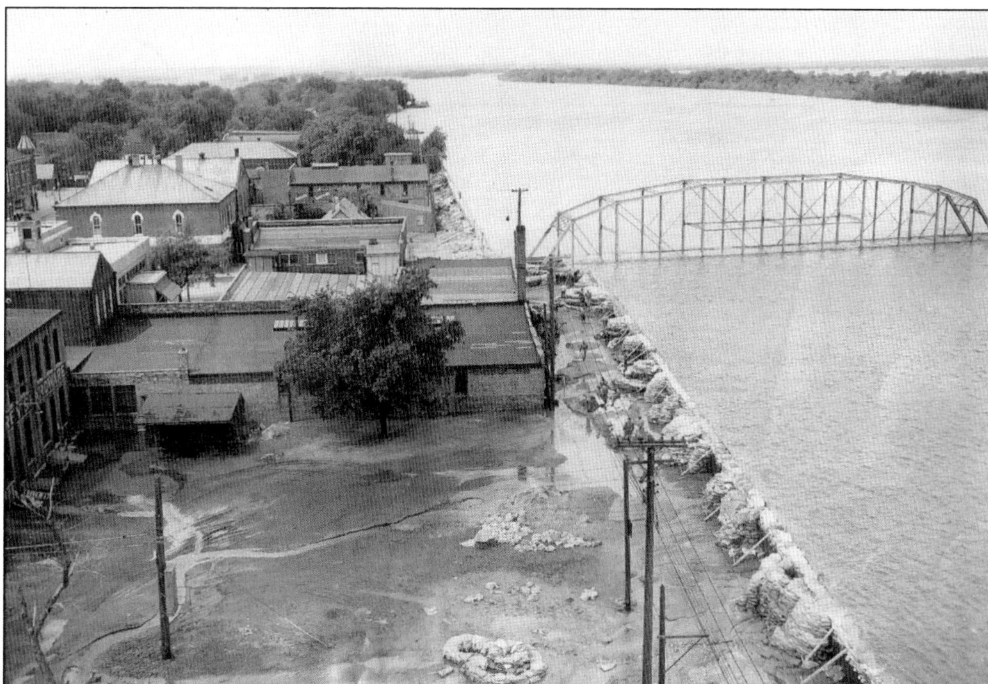

This image shows the "dry flood" of 1943. It is referred to as the dry flood because even though the water was above the levee, workers kept the water out of town. The bridge is at the end of State Street.

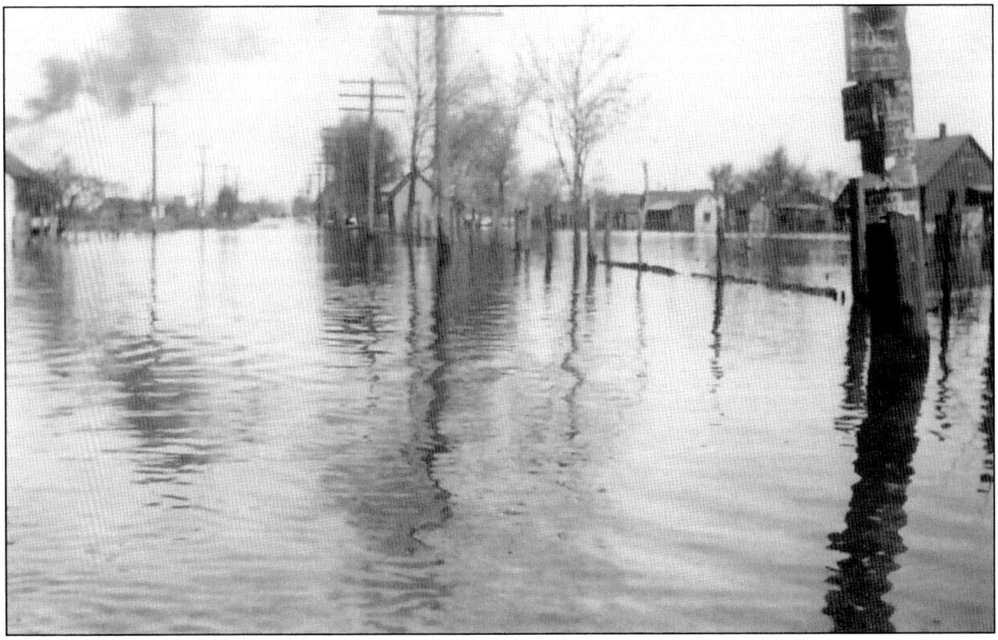

This photograph shows high water in the west end of Beardstown during the 1922 flood. The west end was always the low end of Beardstown and saw a lot of flooding in the early days.

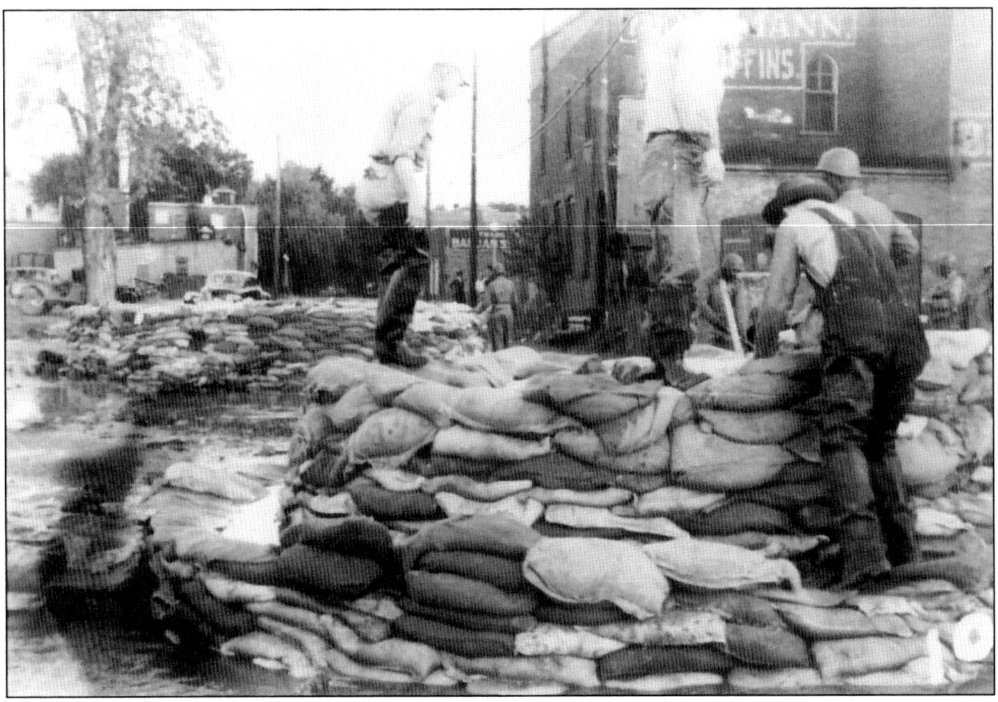

During a high-water event in 1943, workers managed to keep the water out of town. Baujan's Shoe Store, on Second Street, is shown in the background. The building in the foreground is the Mohmann and Cline Funeral Home and Furniture Store.

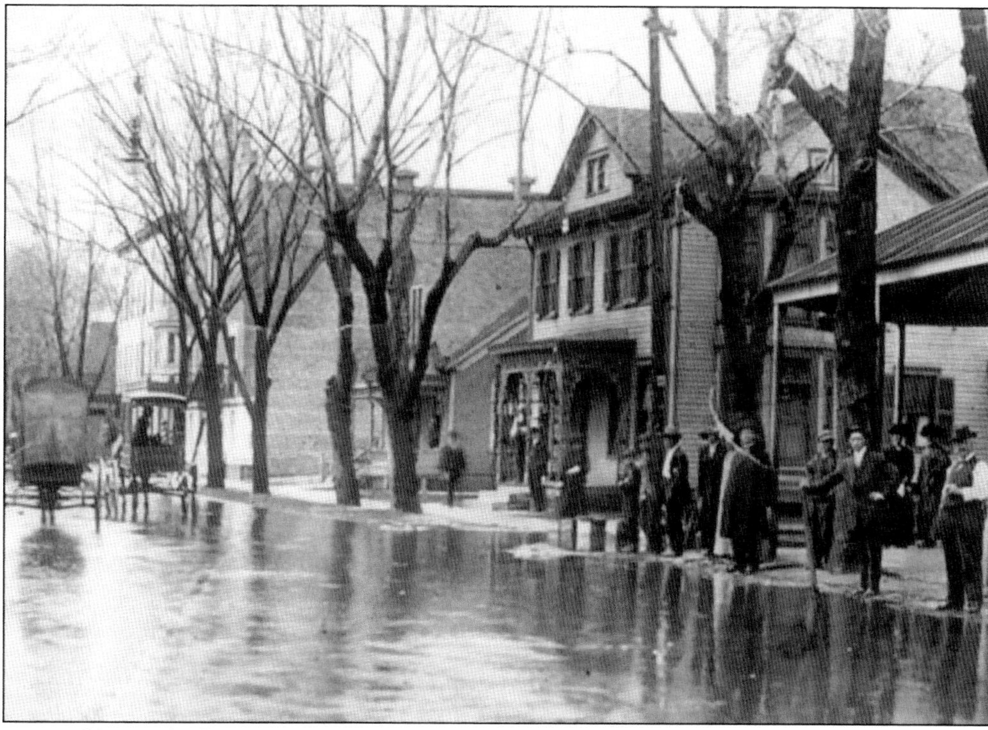

Pictured here is high water on Fourth Street between State and Jefferson Streets in 1913. Shown are, from left to right, the Goodell Hotel (corner of Fourth and State Streets), Princess Theater, and three homes.

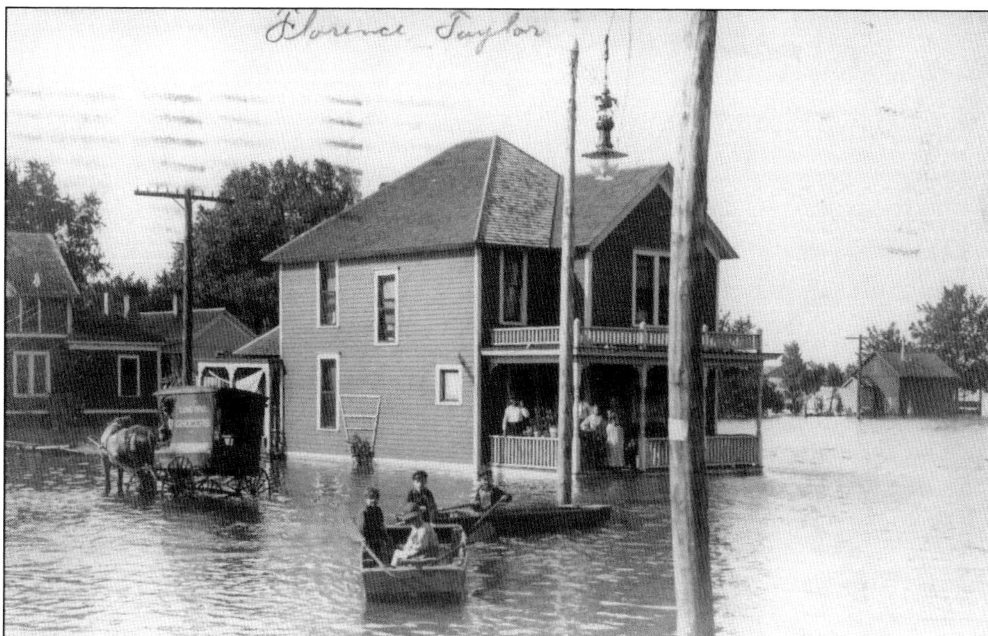

This house at Third and Jackson Streets belonged to Florence Taylor. The picture dates to 1916.

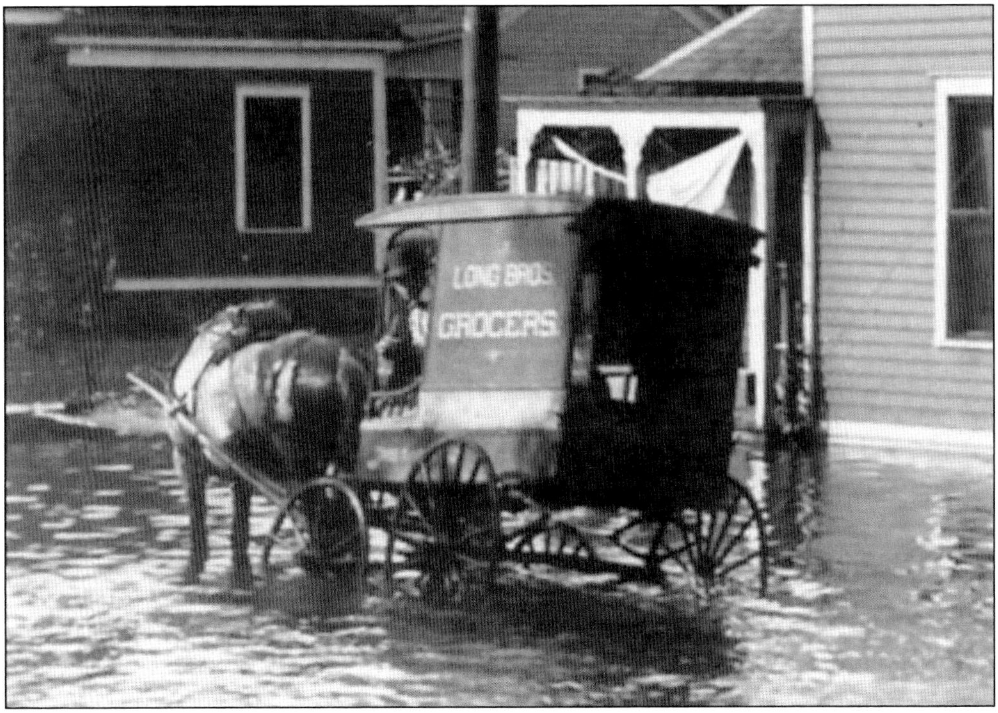

The Long Brothers Grocers delivery wagon is pictured during the flood of 1916.

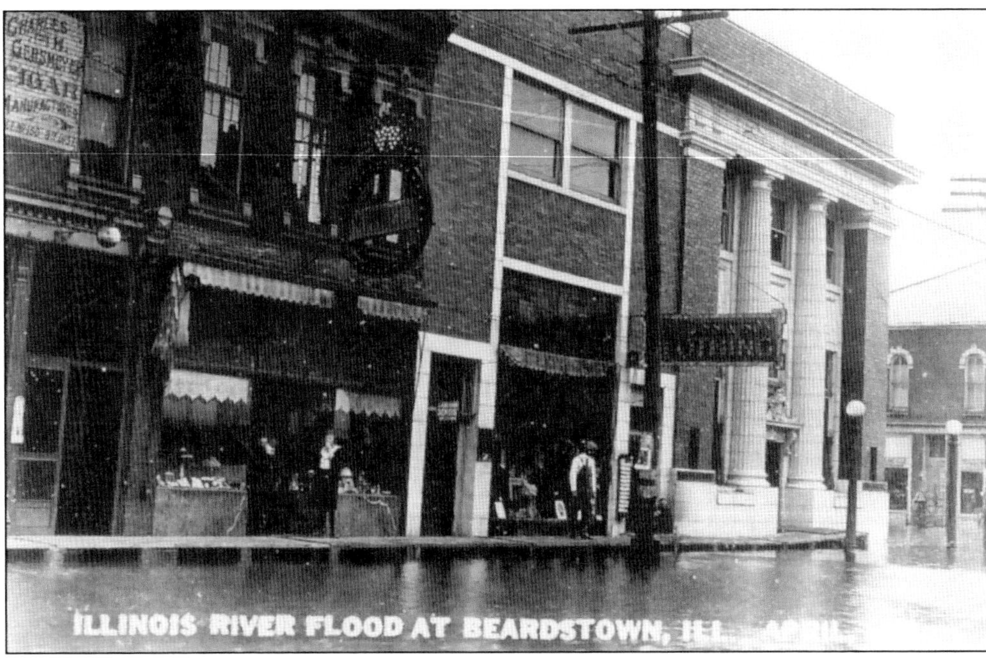

This 1916 photograph shows the store of Charles Gersmeyer, manufacturer of cigars and tobacco products, at 108 State Street. Dryden and Dryden Jewelers is next to Gersmeyer's.

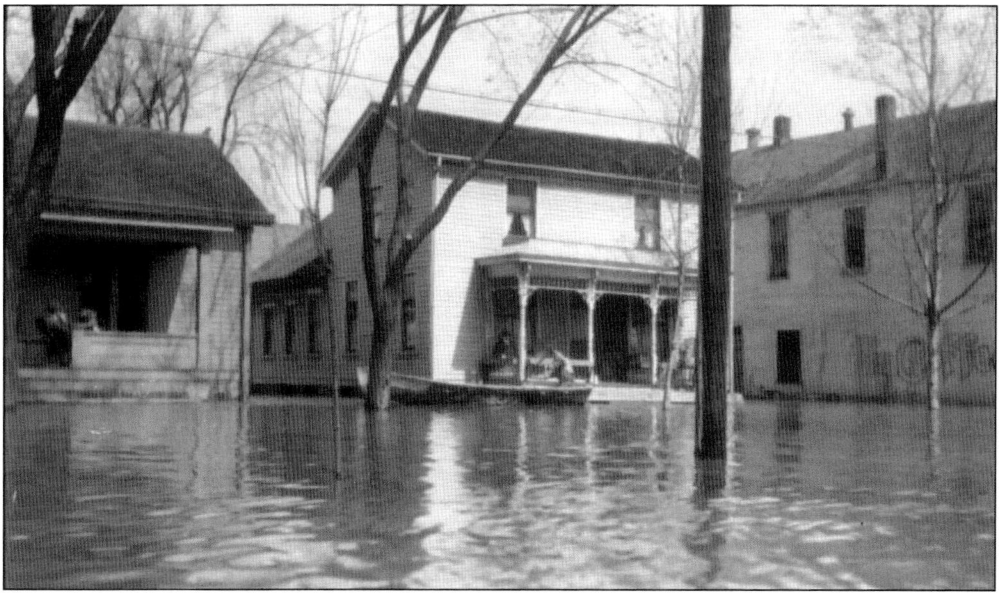

Unidentified people are shown sitting on the front porch watching the river go by in 1922.

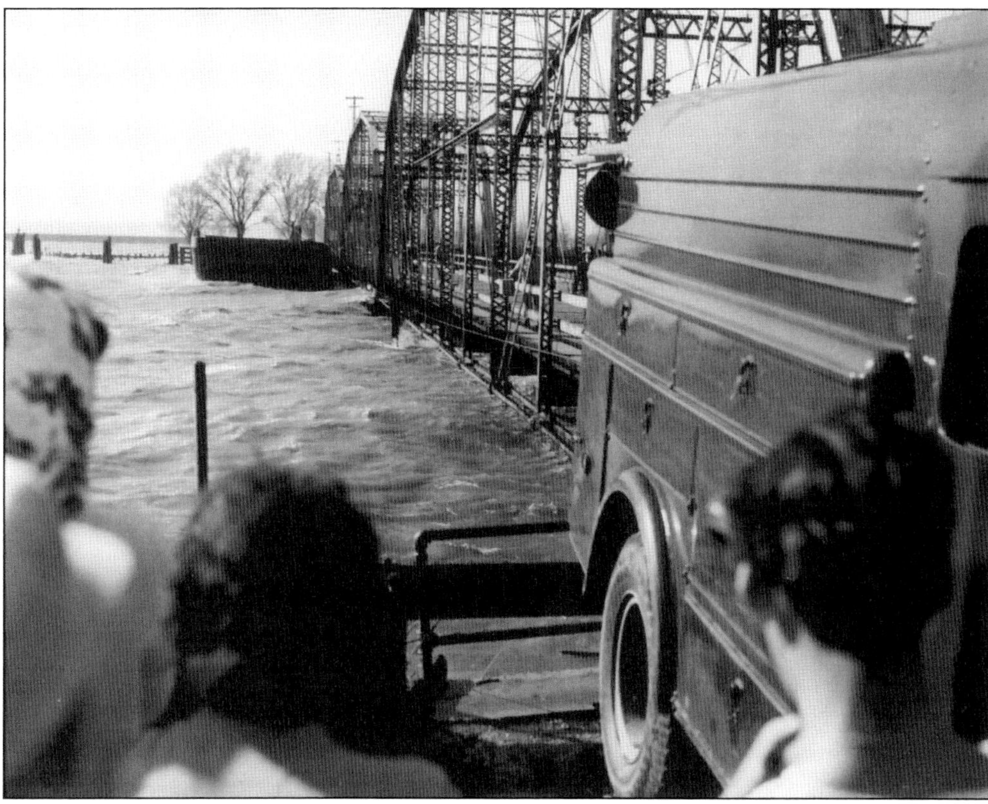

High water reached the bridge deck at the end of State Street during the 1943 flood.

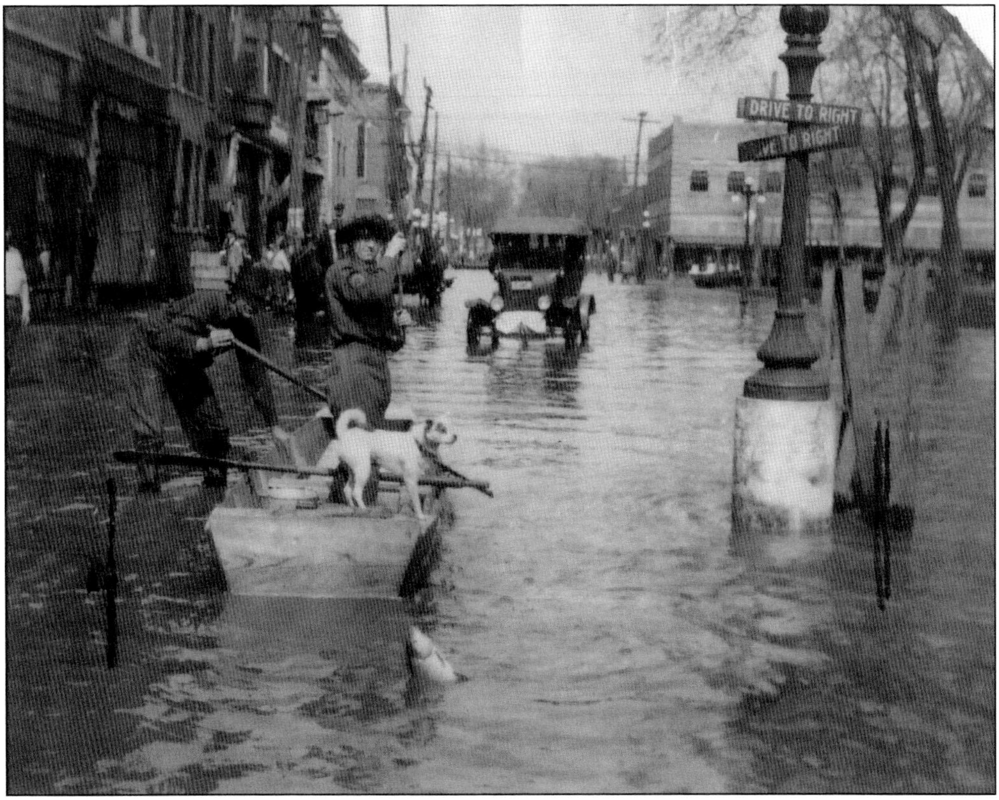

This fisherman caught a nice six-pound carp at the corner of Washington and Second Streets. The large building on the right is Woolworth's. The caption on the back of this photograph—taken on April 17, 1922—reads: "Landing a six pound carp on Beardstown's Main Street. Fishing has ben [*sic*] exceptionally good since high waters began to flow through town."

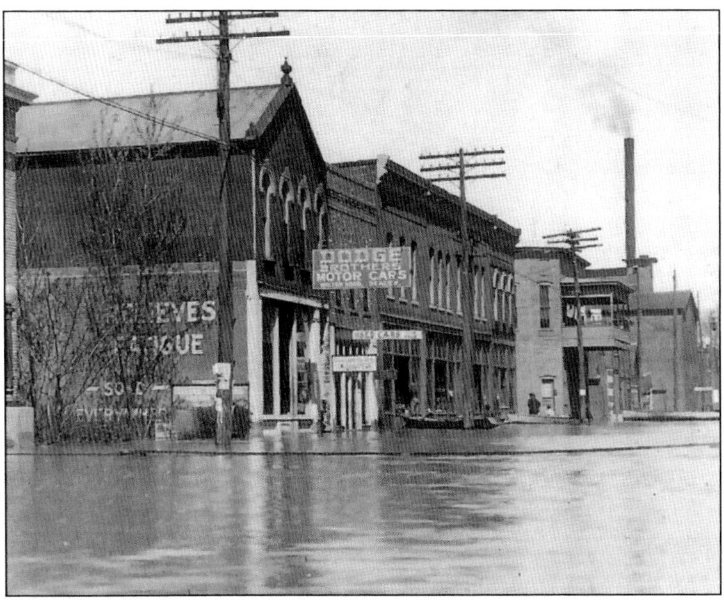

Pictured from left to right are Walter Hood's Used Car Dealership, W.M. Frey Hardware Store, Tice Neff's "Crappie Hole" Tavern (restaurant, grocery store, and boardinghouse), and Home Mills flour mill.

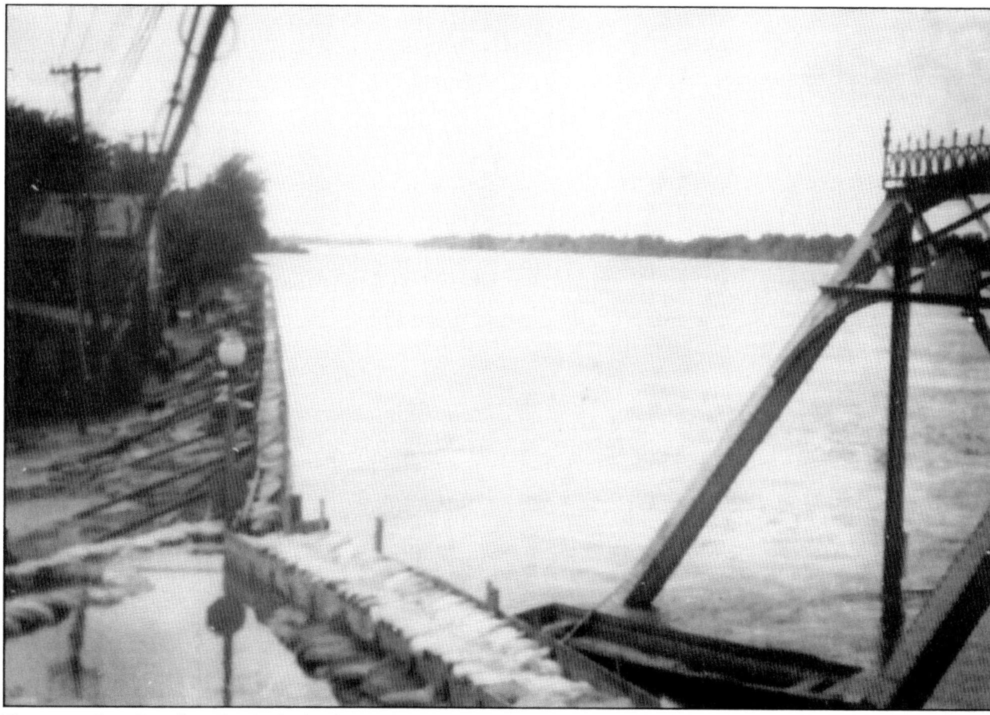

During the dry flood of 1943, the water rose to near the top of the seawall. With the help of plywood, plastic, sandbags, and the military, the town was saved.

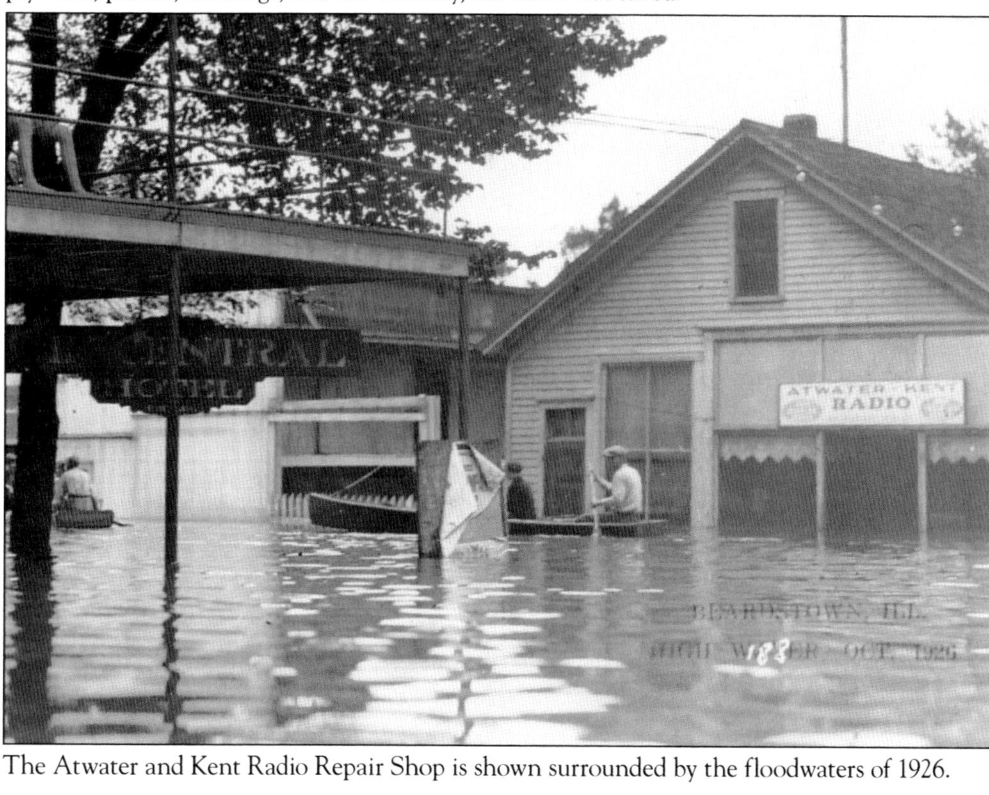

The Atwater and Kent Radio Repair Shop is shown surrounded by the floodwaters of 1926.

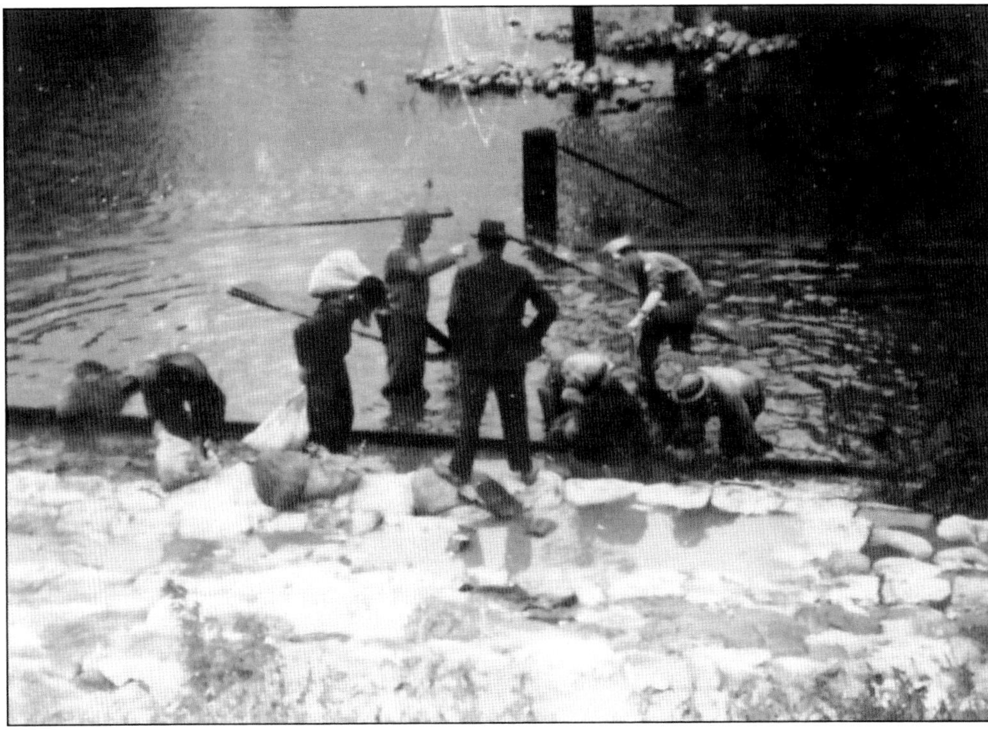

These men are shown placing sandbags along the levee at Schmoldt Park during the 1927 flood.

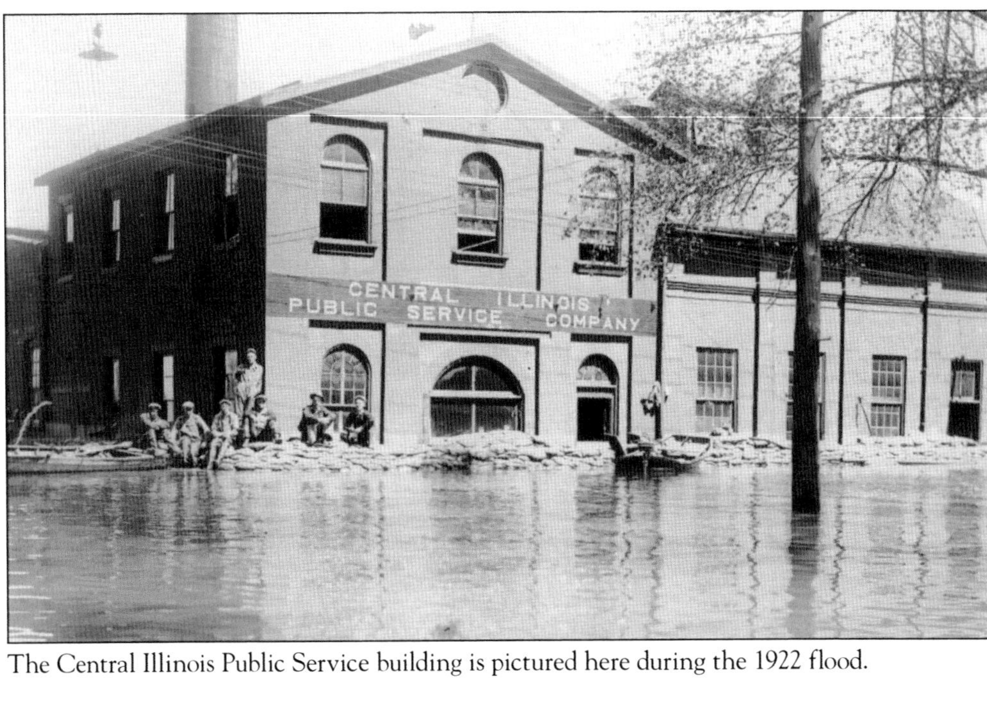

The Central Illinois Public Service building is pictured here during the 1922 flood.

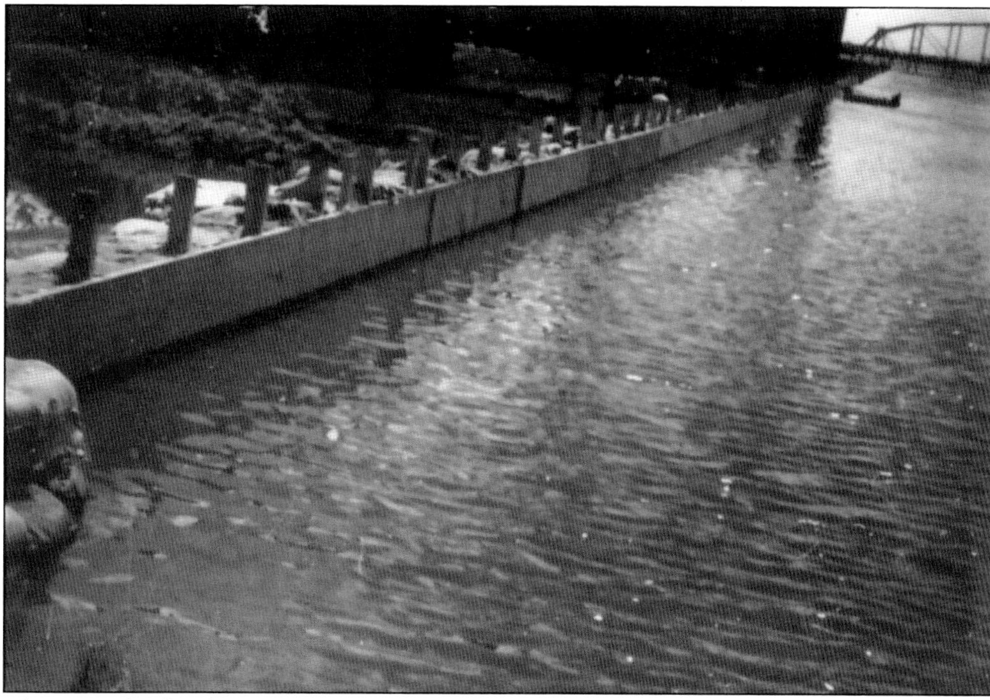

These are the floodwaters in 1943 between the automobile and railroad bridges. The seawall was raised with the help of plywood, plastic sheets, and sandbags. Beardstown was evacuated for safety, but the seawall held.

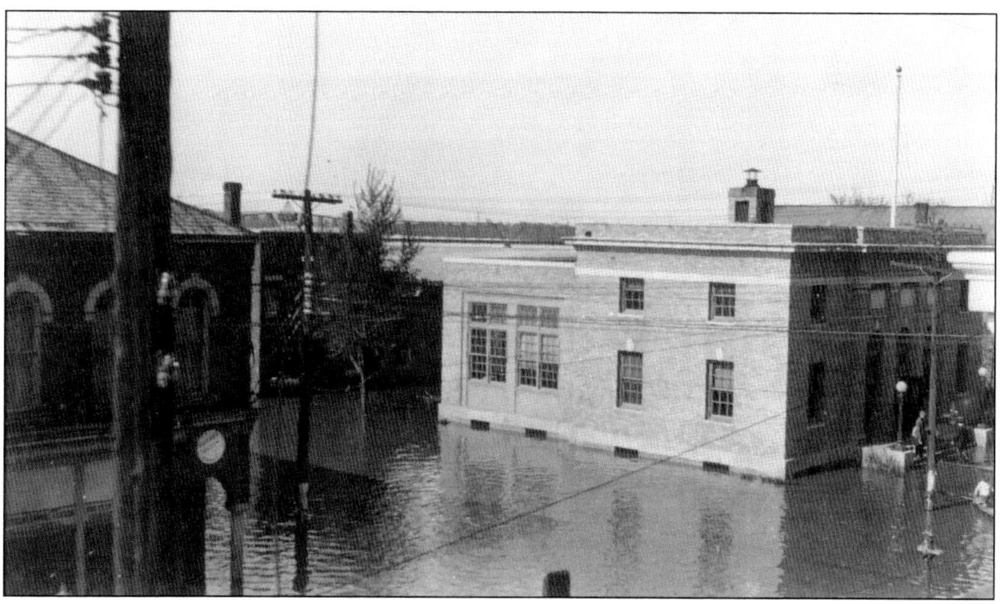

The main building pictured is the US Post Office surrounded by water in the 1922 flood.

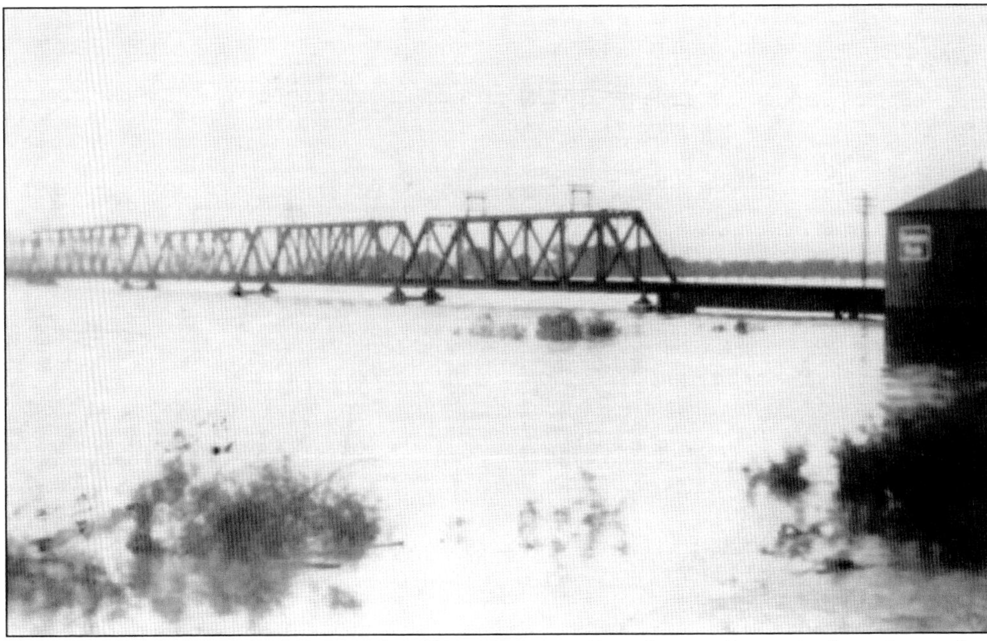

This is the first bridge built across the Illinois River at Beardstown. It was built with wood in 1888 and was a toll bridge that only lasted for 10 years. In 1898, it was replaced with a new steel bridge at a cost of $26,911.60—paid for in tolls. The steel bridge was replaced in 1955 with a free bridge, which is currently still in use.

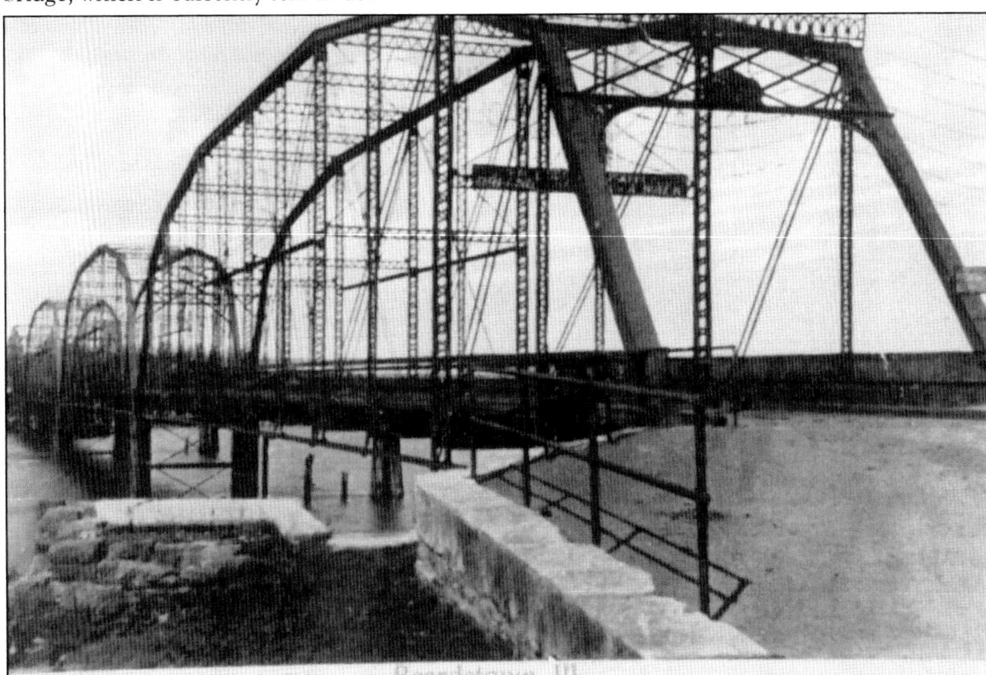

The second bridge across the Illinois River at Beardstown was also a toll bridge. This picture was taken around 1918.

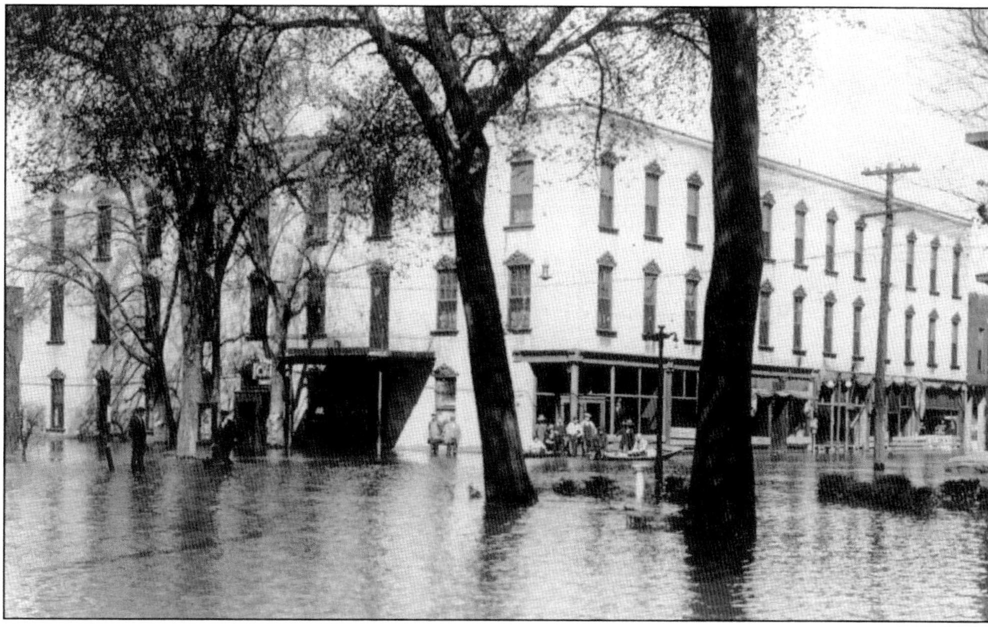

The Park Hotel, located at Second and Washington Streets, is pictured during the 1922 flood.

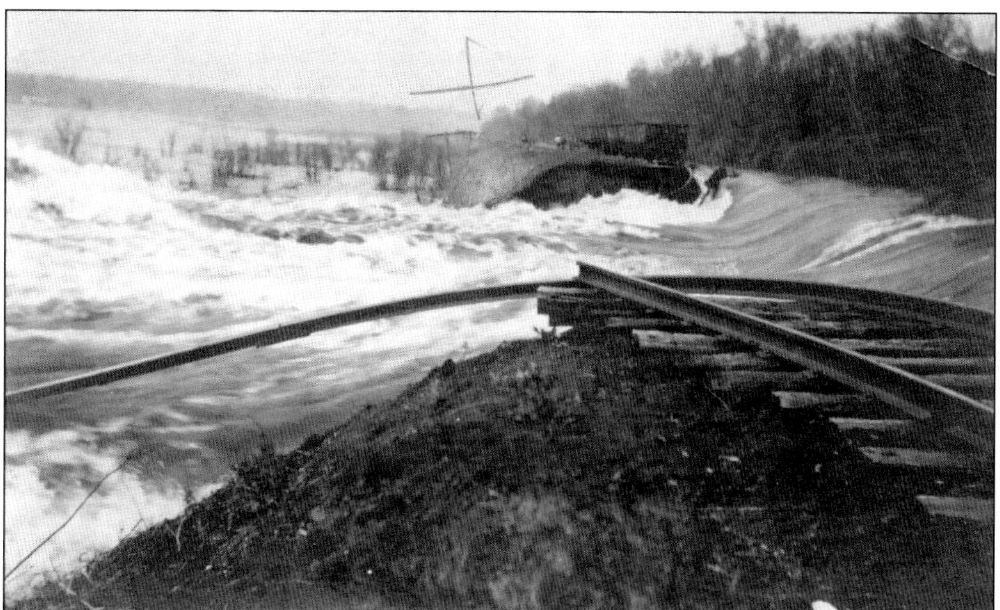

The levee between Beardstown and Frederick broke during the 1943 flood. A railroad car was filled with rock and pushed into the break in hopes it would fill the hole. The railcar was washed away, later hitting and destroying the Walters' family home.

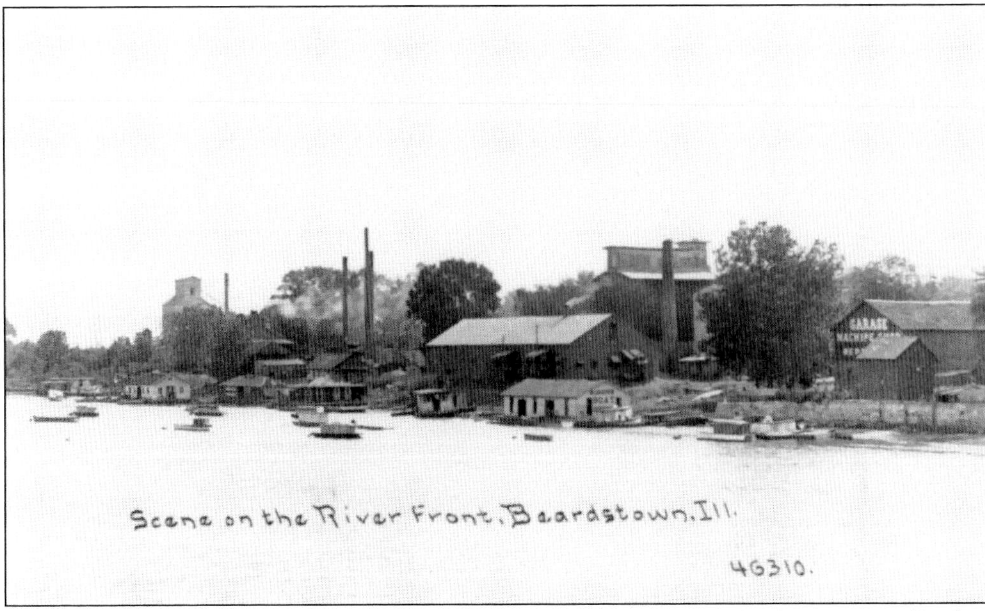

The building in the center of the photograph was used to store wheat for the Home Mills Flour Mill, located directly behind the shed. The mill burned down in 1917. The building on the right was the Charles Hood garage and machine shop. On the far left is the Schultz and Baujan flour mill.

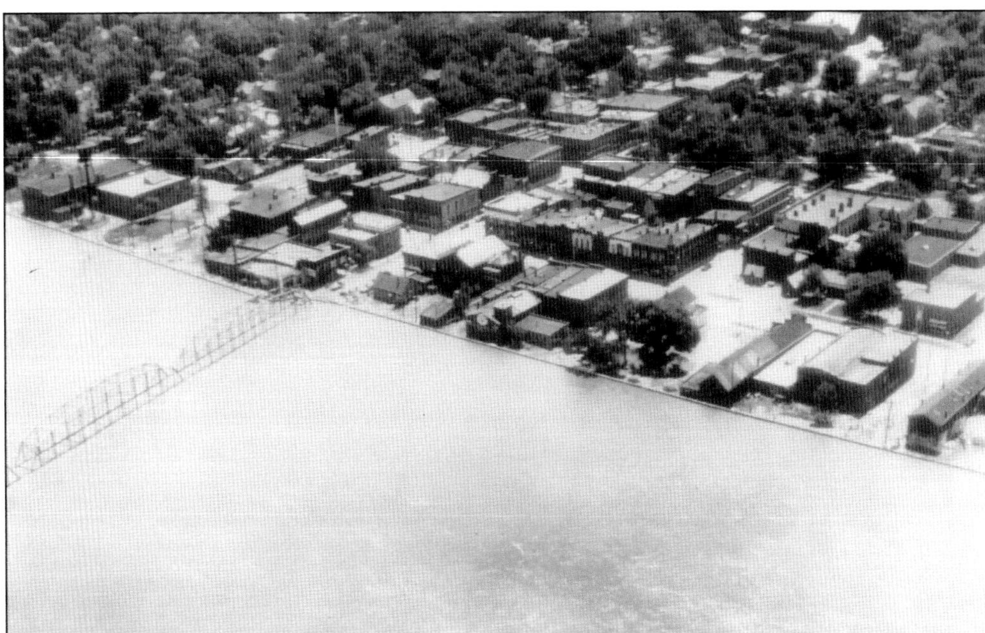

This aerial photograph shows how high the water was near the bridge in 1943. Plywood, plastic, sandbags, and a lot of hard work kept the water out of town.

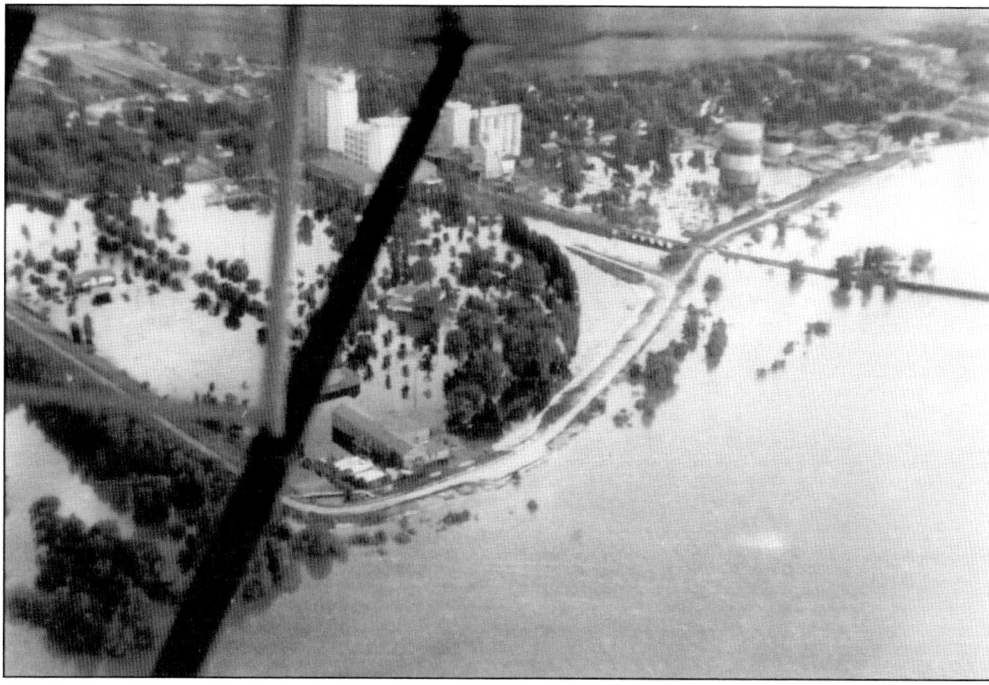

This aerial view of Beardstown was taken above Mascouten Bay in 1943. The Schultz and Baujan flour mill is in the back, with Schmoldt Park and the John Glenn Ice House on the corner of the levee. The Beardstown Marina is at lower left.

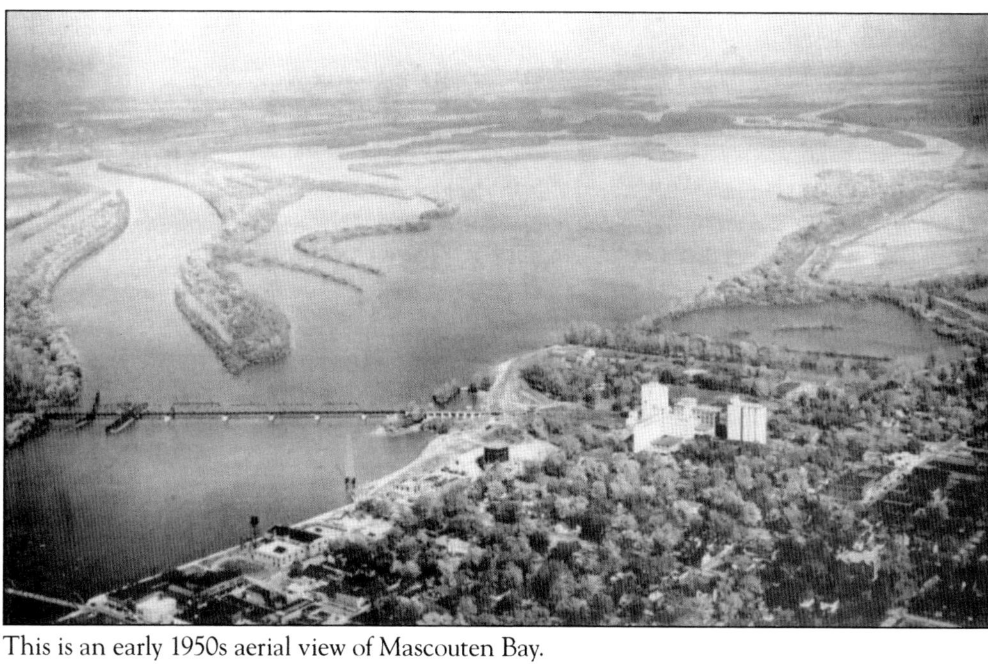

This is an early 1950s aerial view of Mascouten Bay.

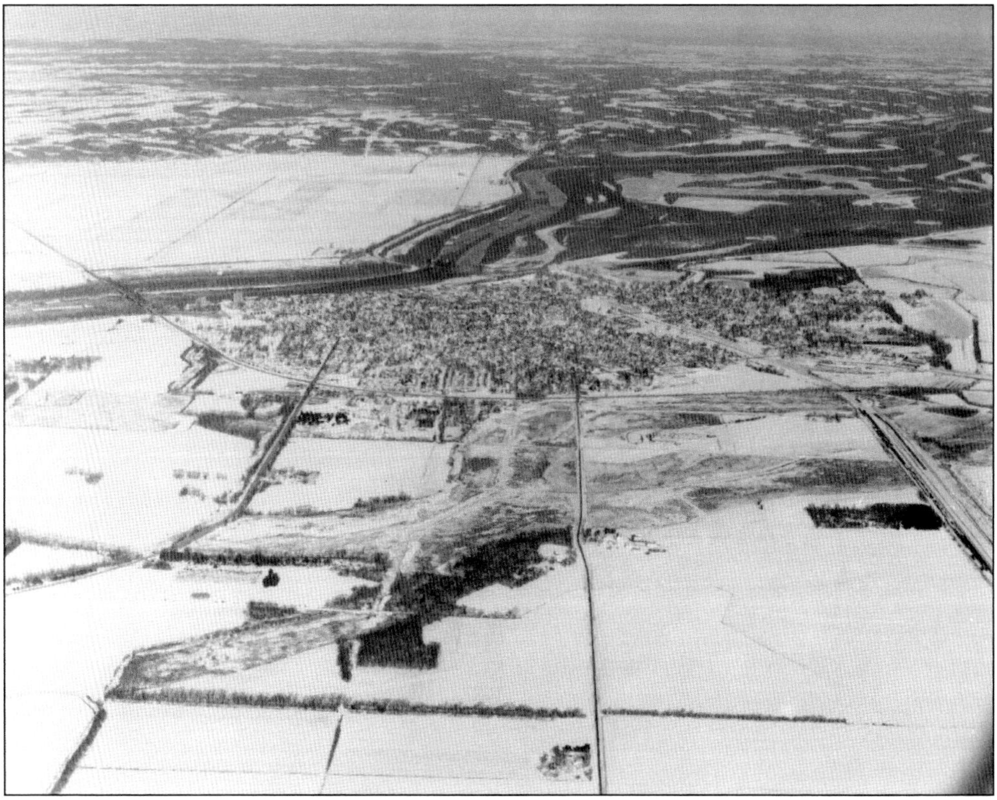

This c. 1970 aerial view of Beardstown was taken by Glenn Herzberger in the winter. Notice the difference in the river, backwater lakes, and Mascouten Bay.

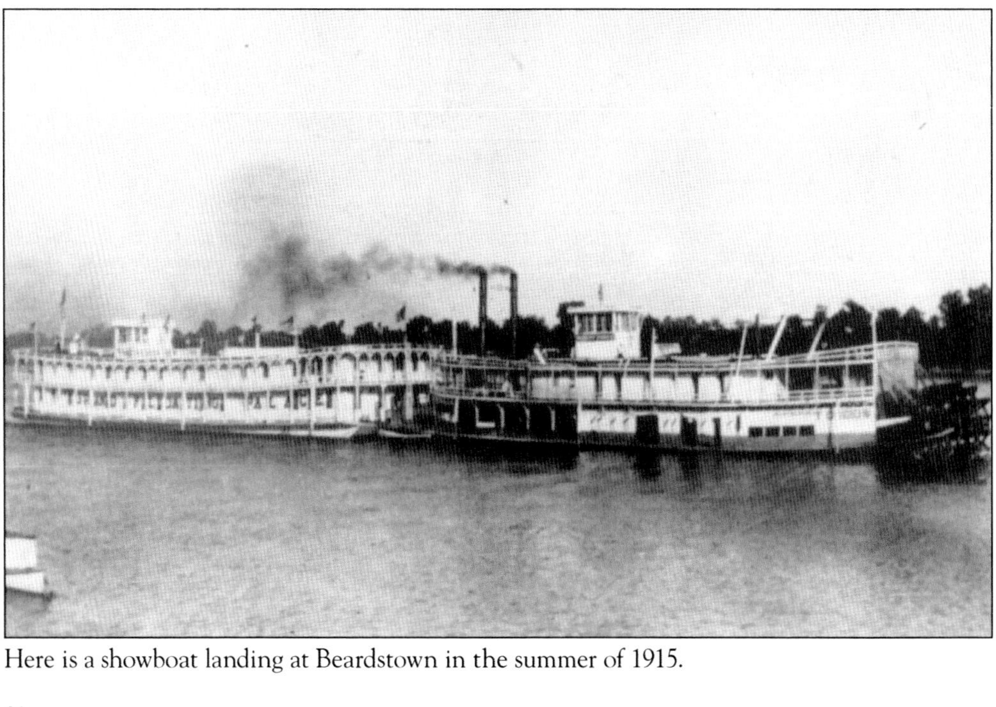

Here is a showboat landing at Beardstown in the summer of 1915.

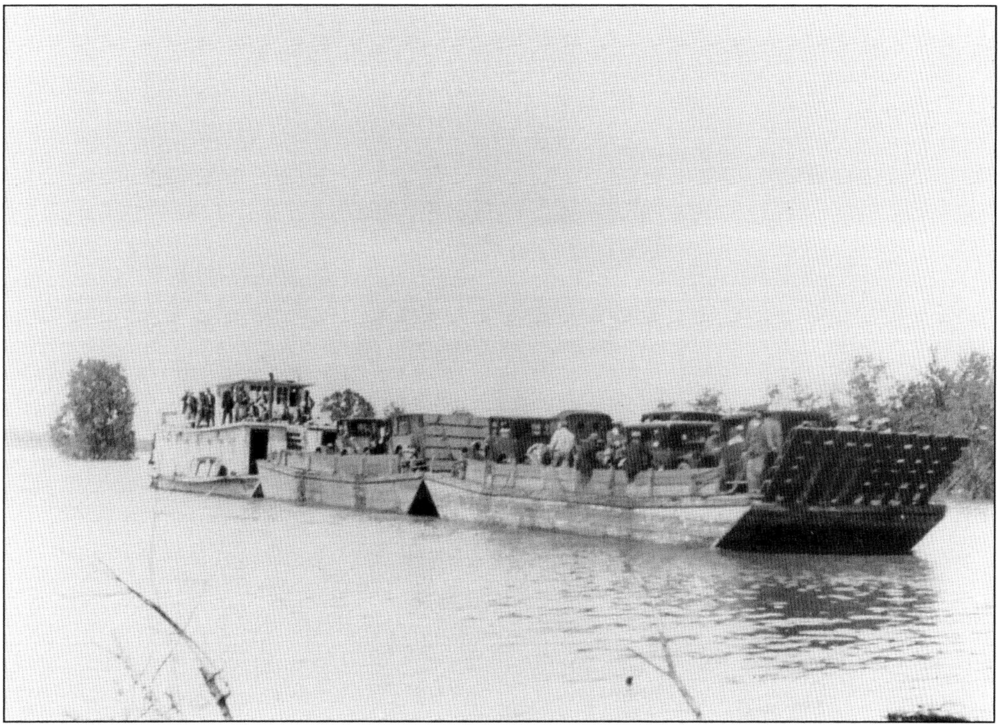

During the high water of 1926, this ferry was put into service. The water was too high for the bridge to be used. This photograph was taken in 1926.

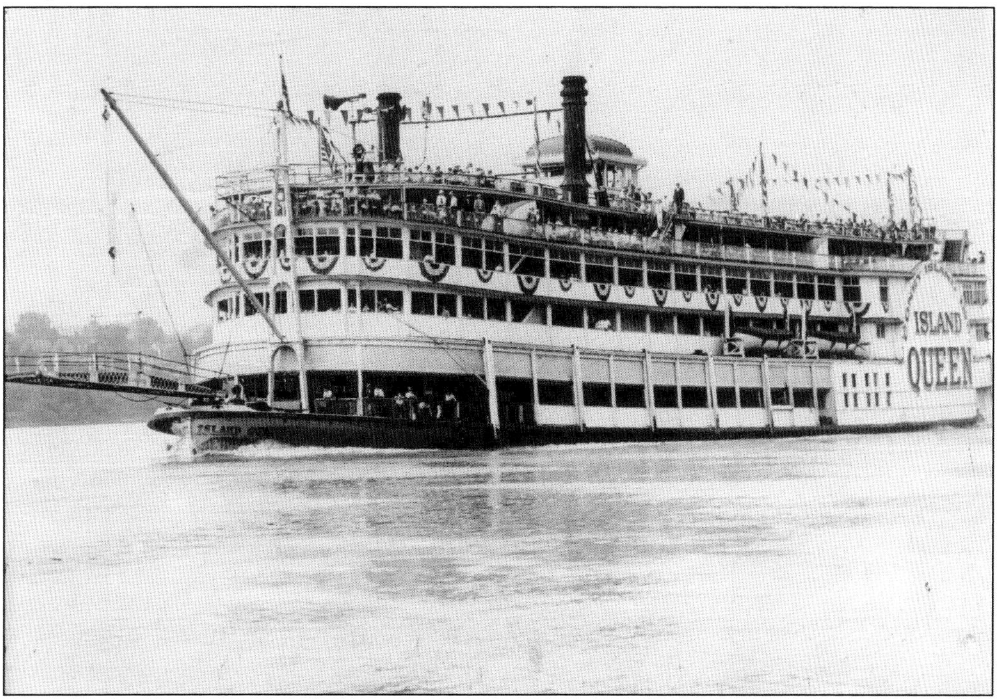

The *Island Queen* was a popular excursion side-wheeler built in 1925. It could carry 4,100 passengers. On September 11, 1947, its fuel tank exploded, and the boat sank at Pittsburgh, Pennsylvania.

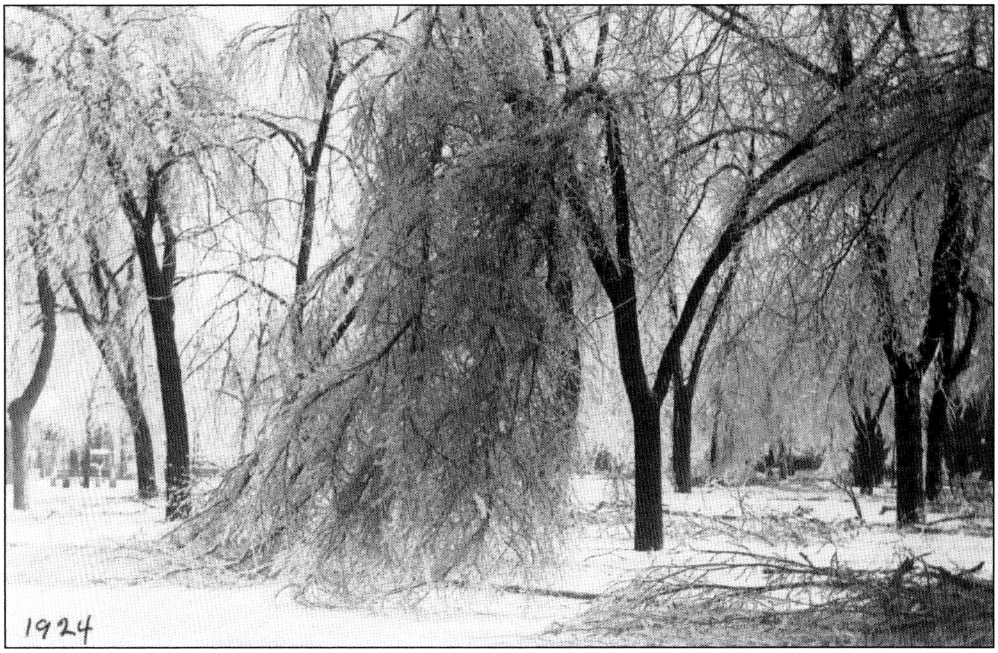

Flooding was not the only problem in Beardstown. An ice and sleet storm hit town on December 18, 1924. This postcard shows the city square.

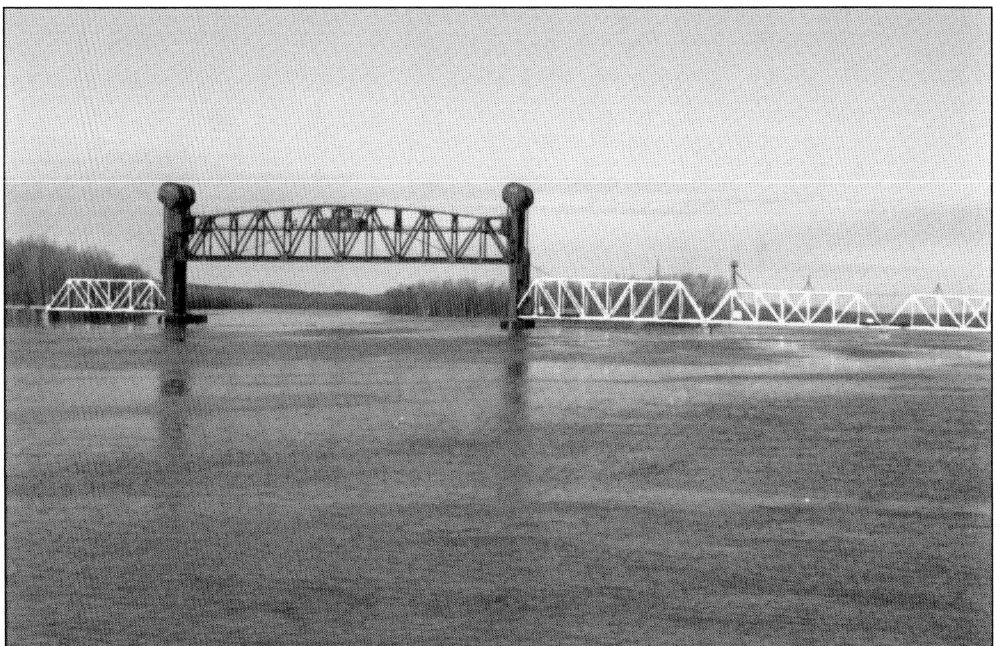

This photograph was taken in the 1970s. The new lift span railroad bridge is shown with the water level at 25 feet 4 inches.

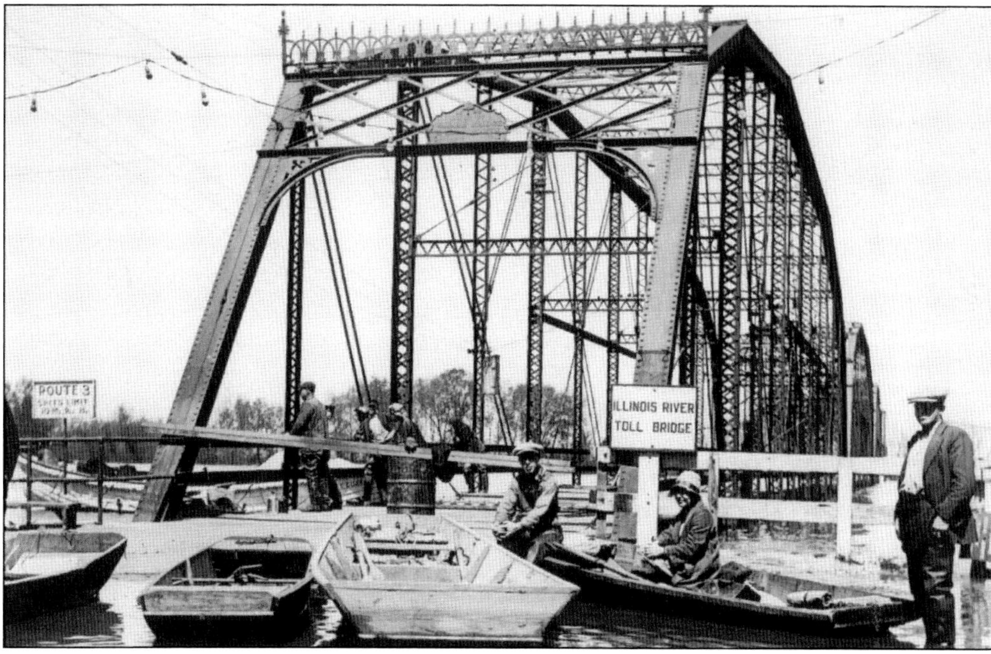

The Beardstown Toll Bridge is pictured during the 1922 flood, when the water was too high for automobile traffic and too low for boat traffic to cross the bridge.

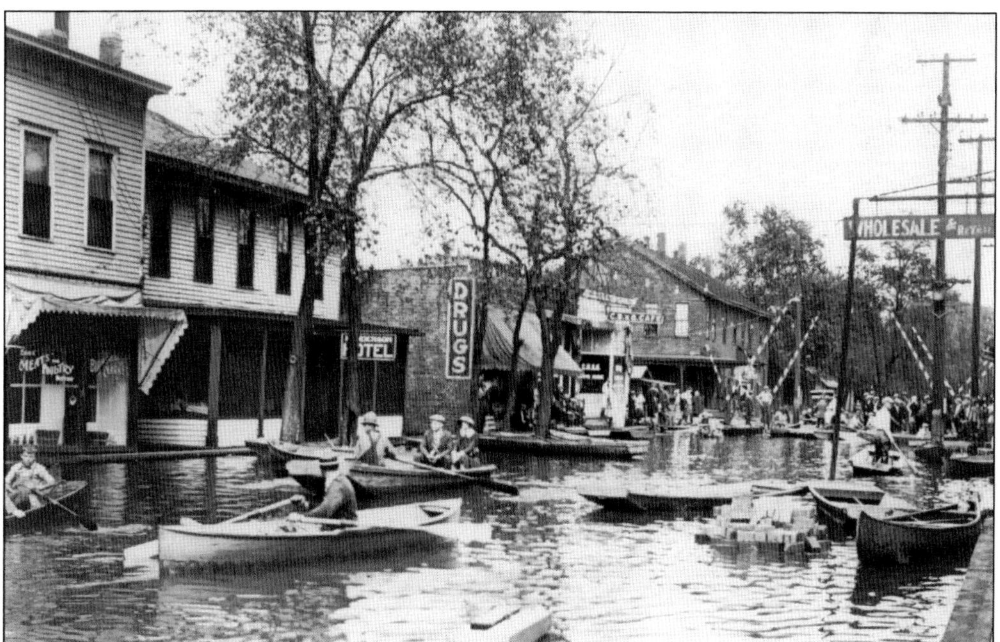

East Fourth Street is shown here during the 1922 flood. From left to right are the Meyer Meat Market, the College Hotel, Benson Drug Store, the CB&Q Café, and the CB&Q Depot.

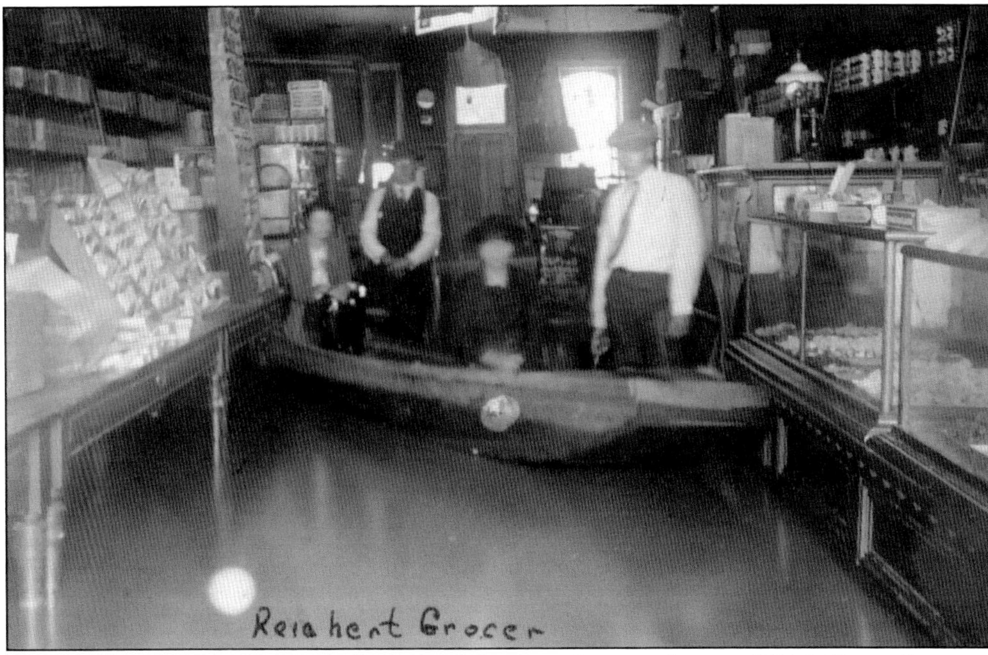

The 1922 floodwaters flowed inside the Fred Riechert Grocery Store at 1121 Jefferson Street.

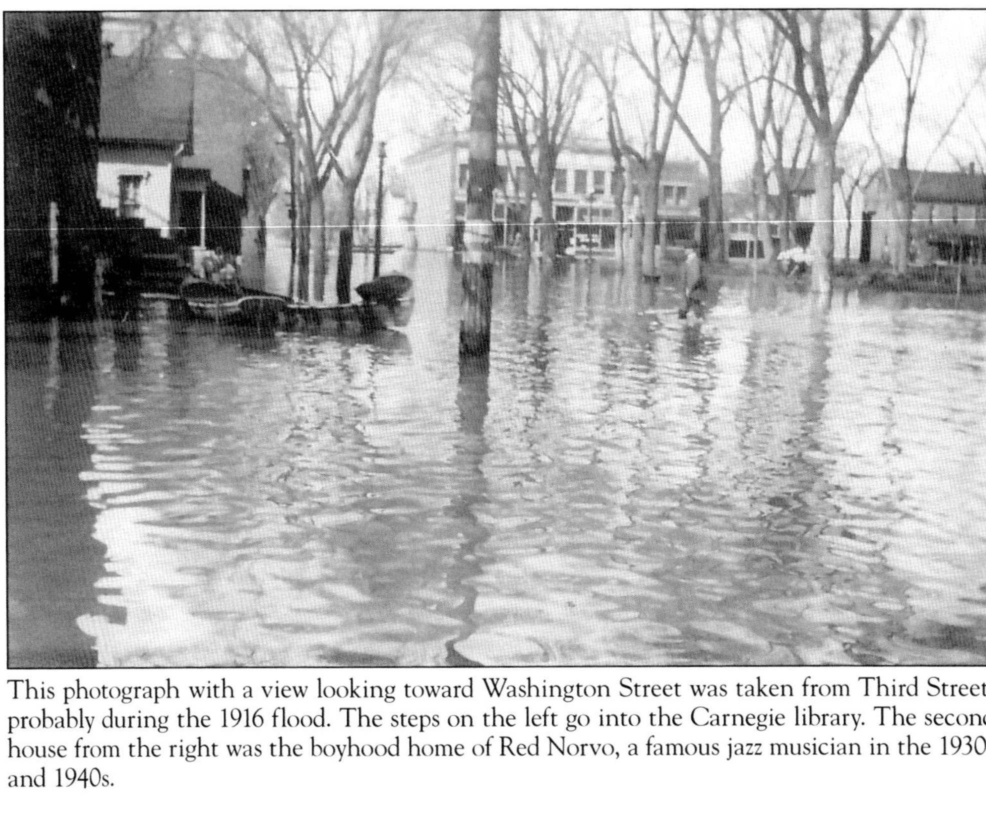

This photograph with a view looking toward Washington Street was taken from Third Street, probably during the 1916 flood. The steps on the left go into the Carnegie library. The second house from the right was the boyhood home of Red Norvo, a famous jazz musician in the 1930s and 1940s.

In 1899, this sternwheeler packet boat docked at the end of Jefferson or Monroe Street in Beardstown.

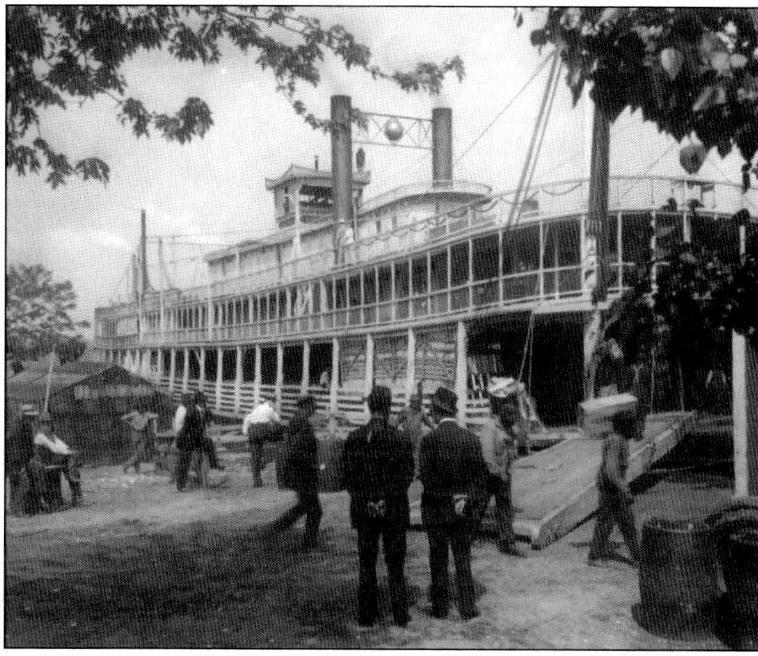

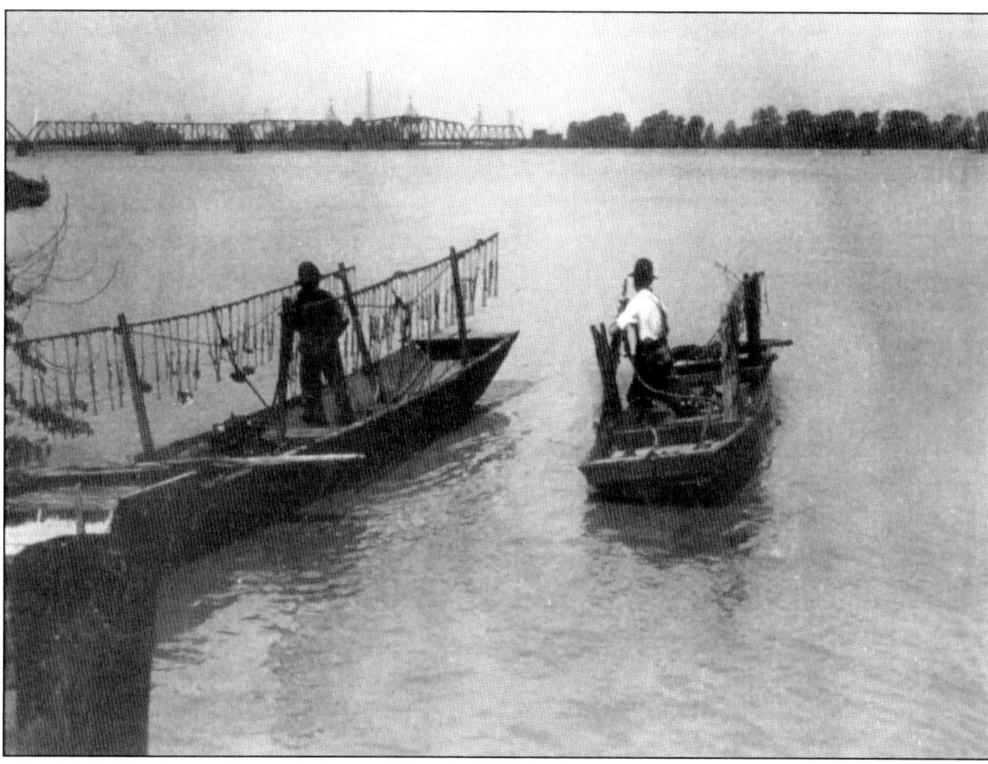

These men are engaged in mussel-shelling in Mascouten Bay above the railroad bridge in 1899.

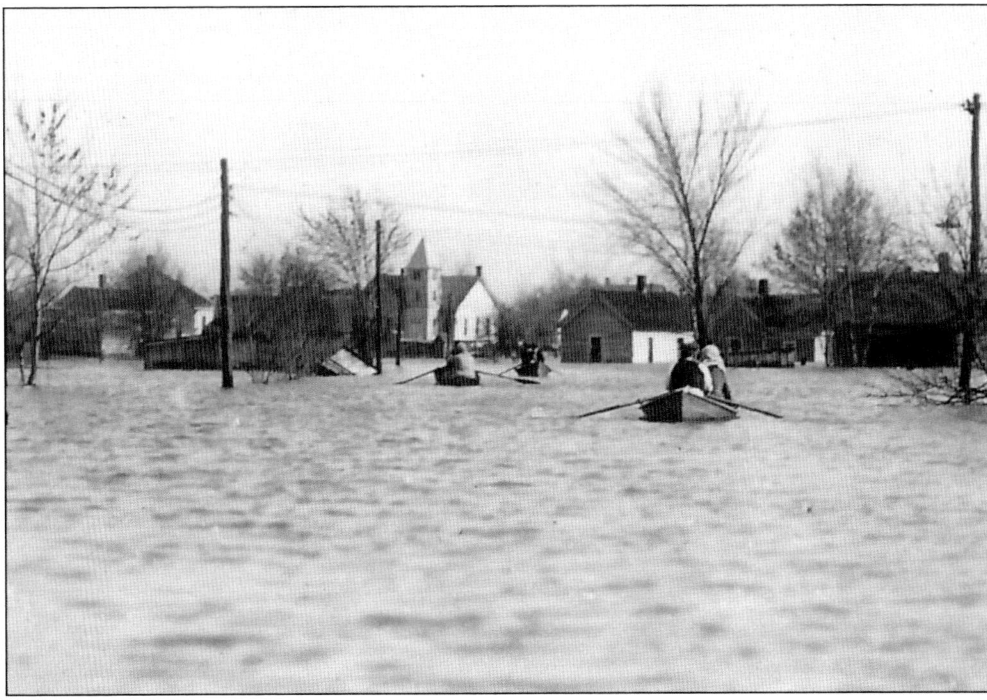

This photograph is one of the few the author has found of the First Southern Baptist Church on Grand Avenue. This image, with a view looking south from the Beard School Mound, was taken during the 1916 flood.

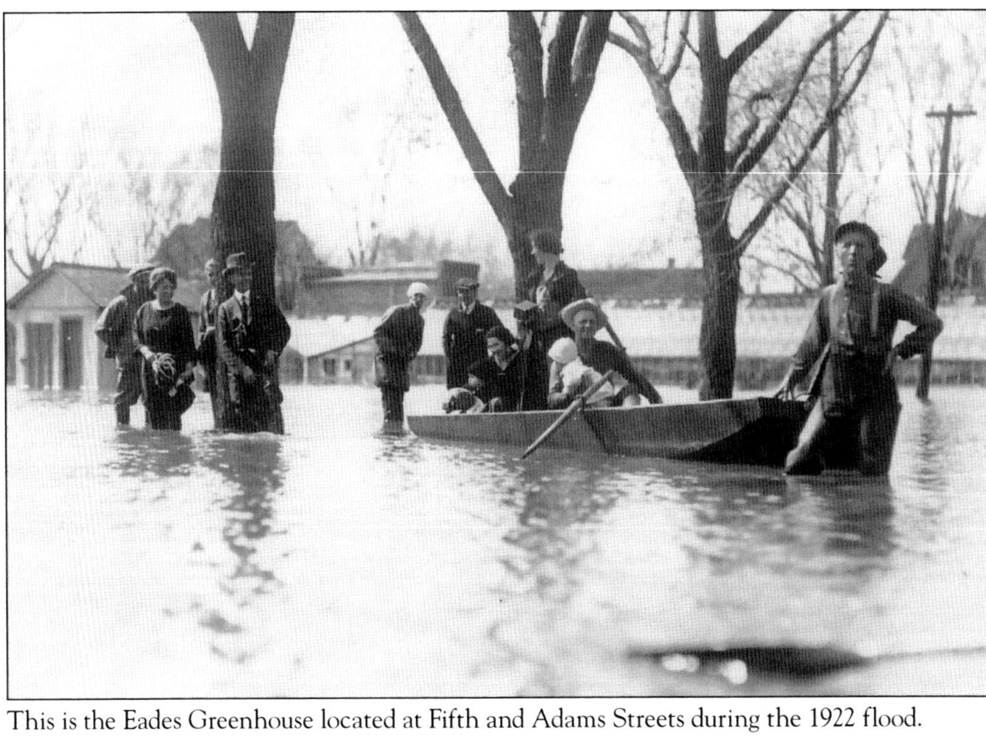

This is the Eades Greenhouse located at Fifth and Adams Streets during the 1922 flood.

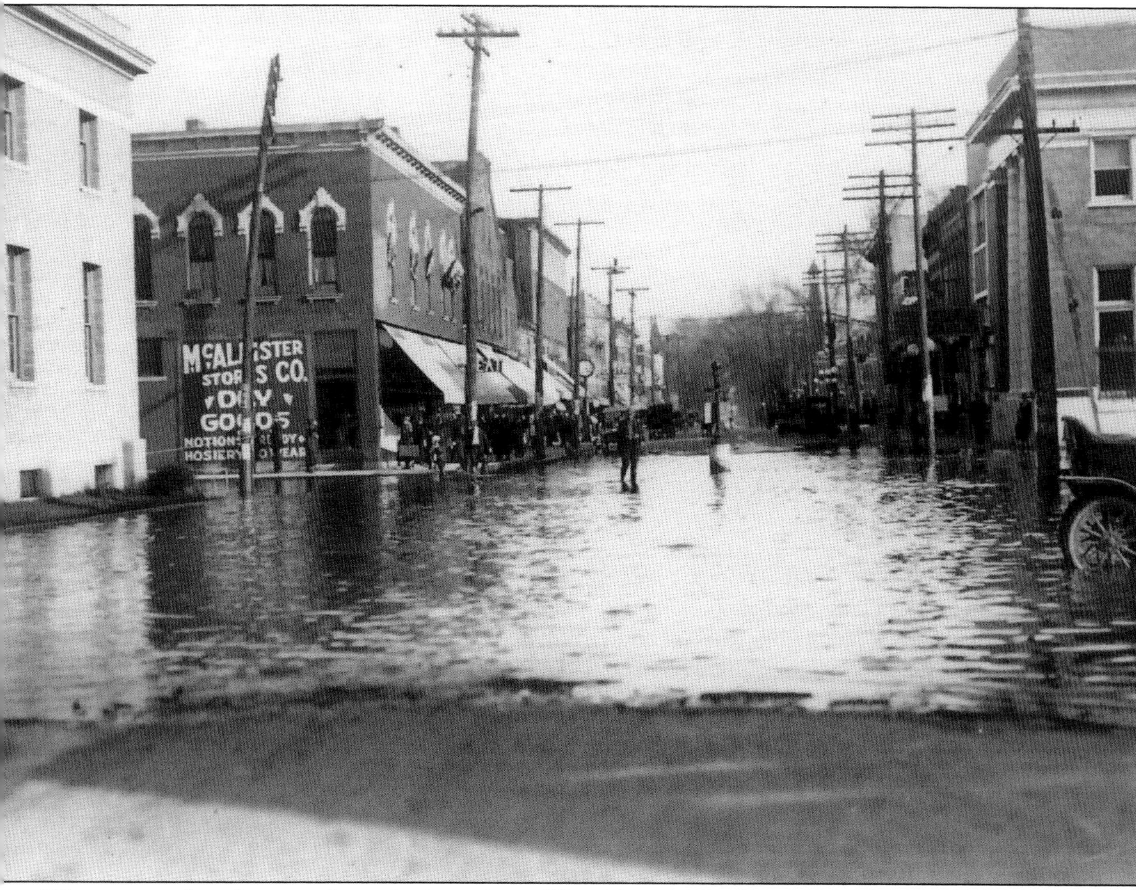

The view in this photographer is looking down West Main Street from State Street. Notice the McAllister Stores sign; this is where the old First National Bank stood.

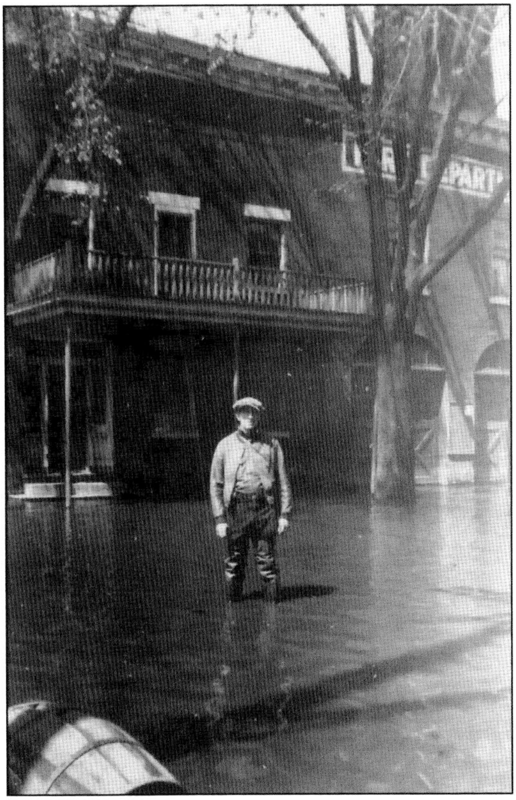

This man is standing in front of the back side of the Old City Hall in Beardstown. In 1922, the fire department, city hall, courtroom, and the jail were all in the same building.

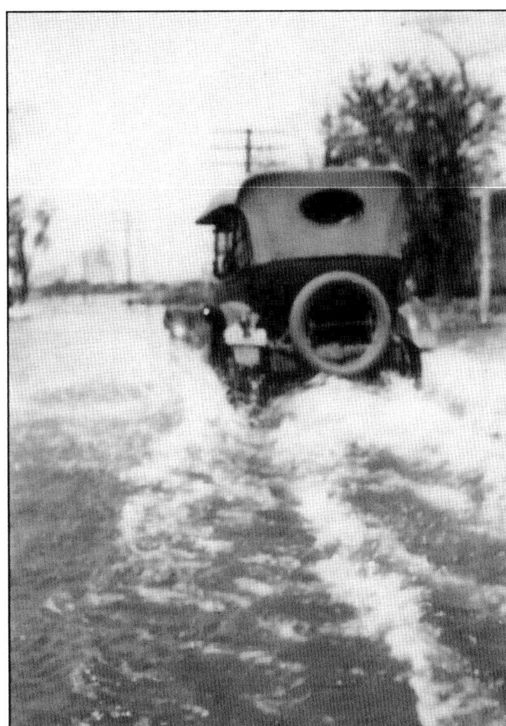

When the water was up, sometimes people just had to drive through it!

Two

CITIZENS OF BEARDSTOWN

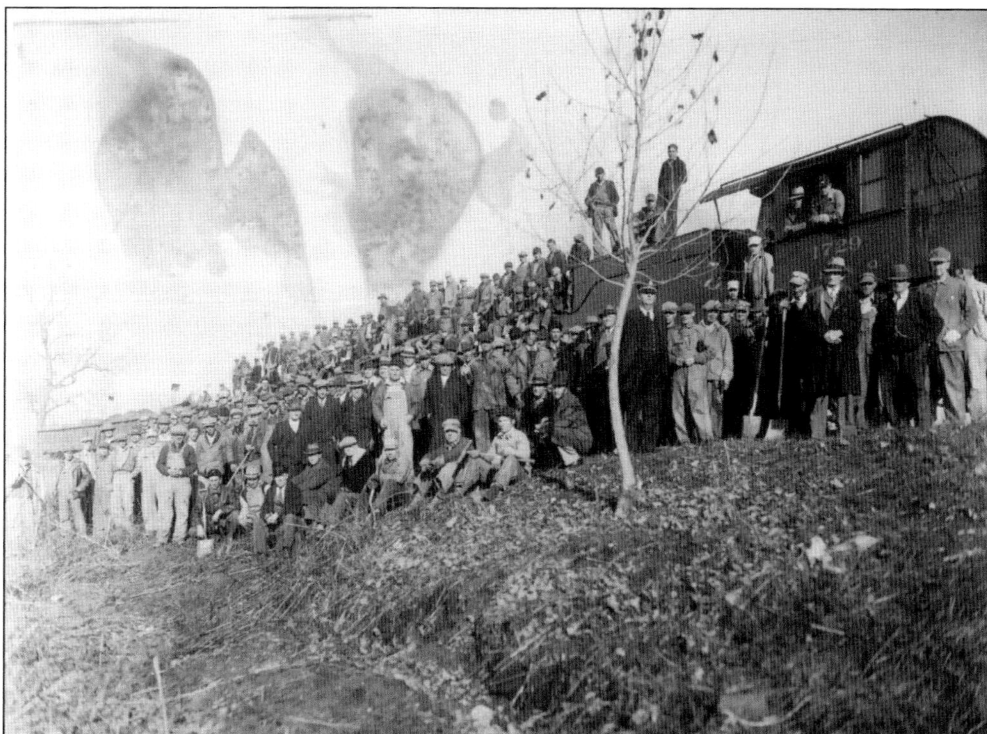

The Works Progress Administration (WPA) was responsible for the manpower that built Schmoldt Recreation Park in 1935. The working men were required to clean up the trash and unload the sand trucks by hand. The federal government wanted to keep them employed for as long as possible.

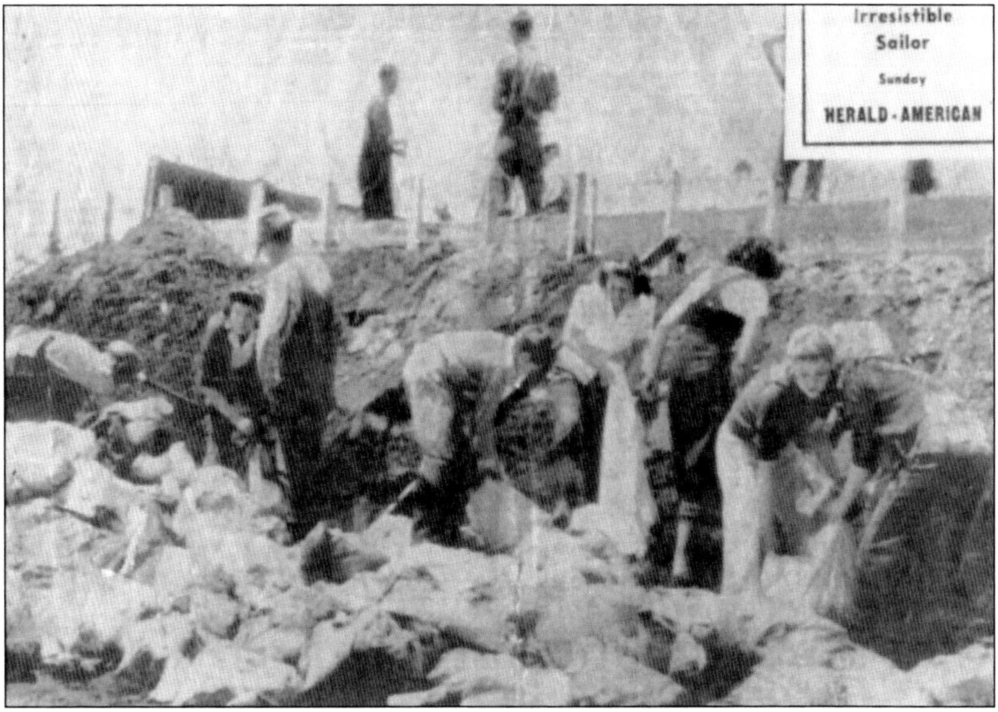

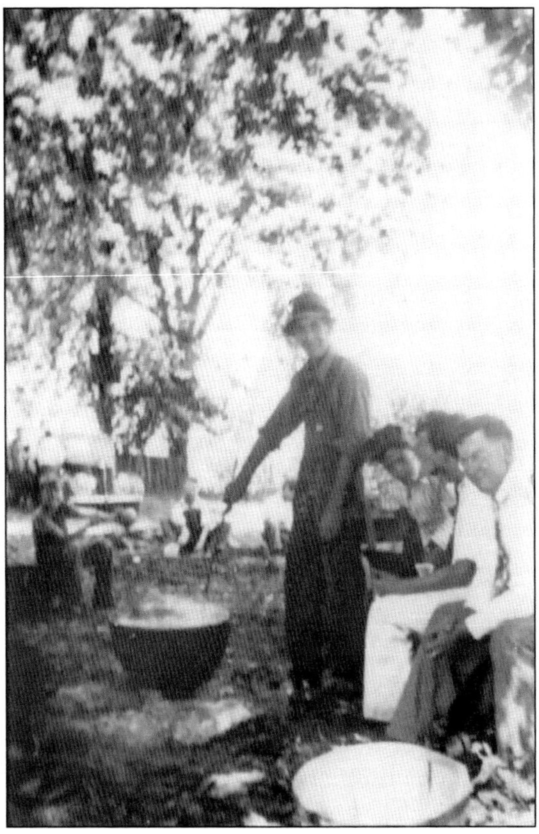

This group of high school girls is shown filling sandbags in 1943. Their efforts were not undertaken in vain—even though the town was evacuated, the levees held.

Fred Rohn is shown cooking burgoo for the Rohn Family Picnic.

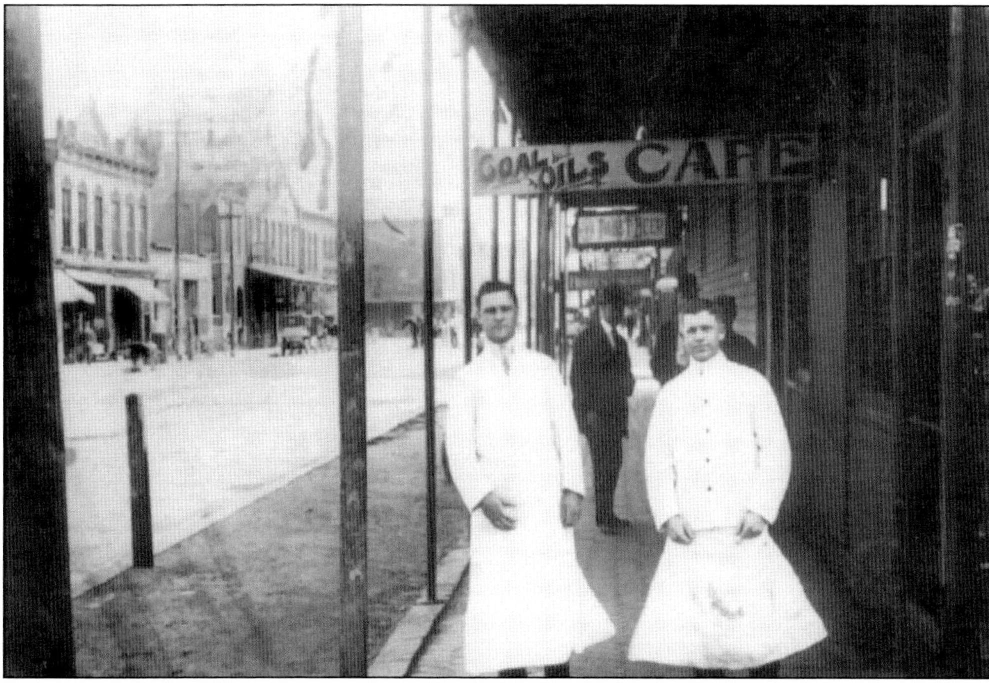

These two gentlemen were workers at the Coal Oils Café located at West Main and Washington Streets. The building behind the Coal Oils Café is the Main Street Tap.

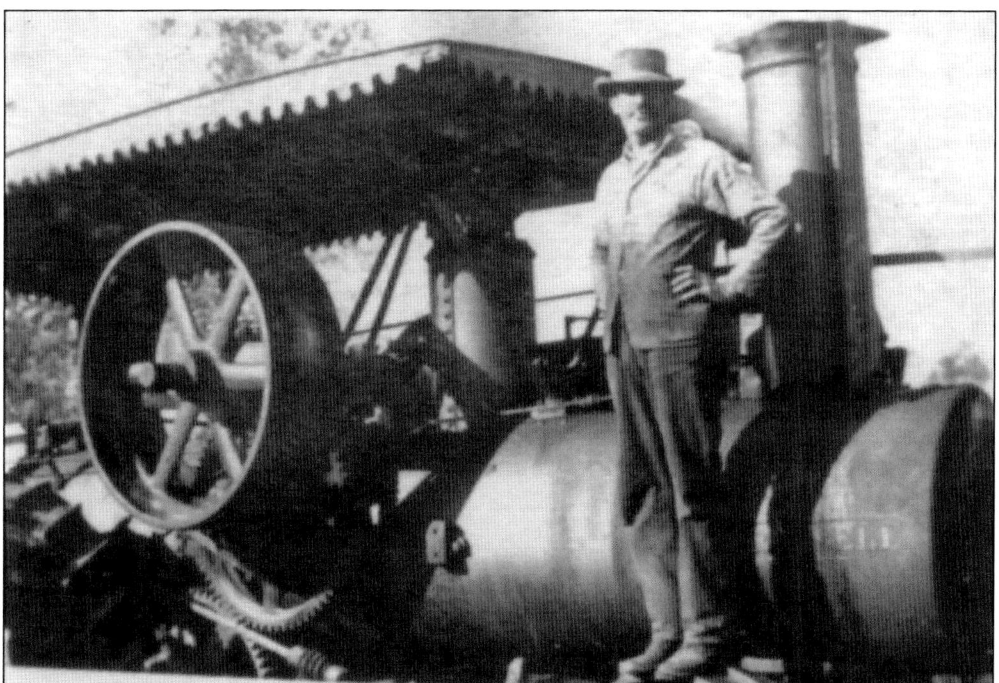

This gentleman operated the steam engine while building the levee across the river in 1929.

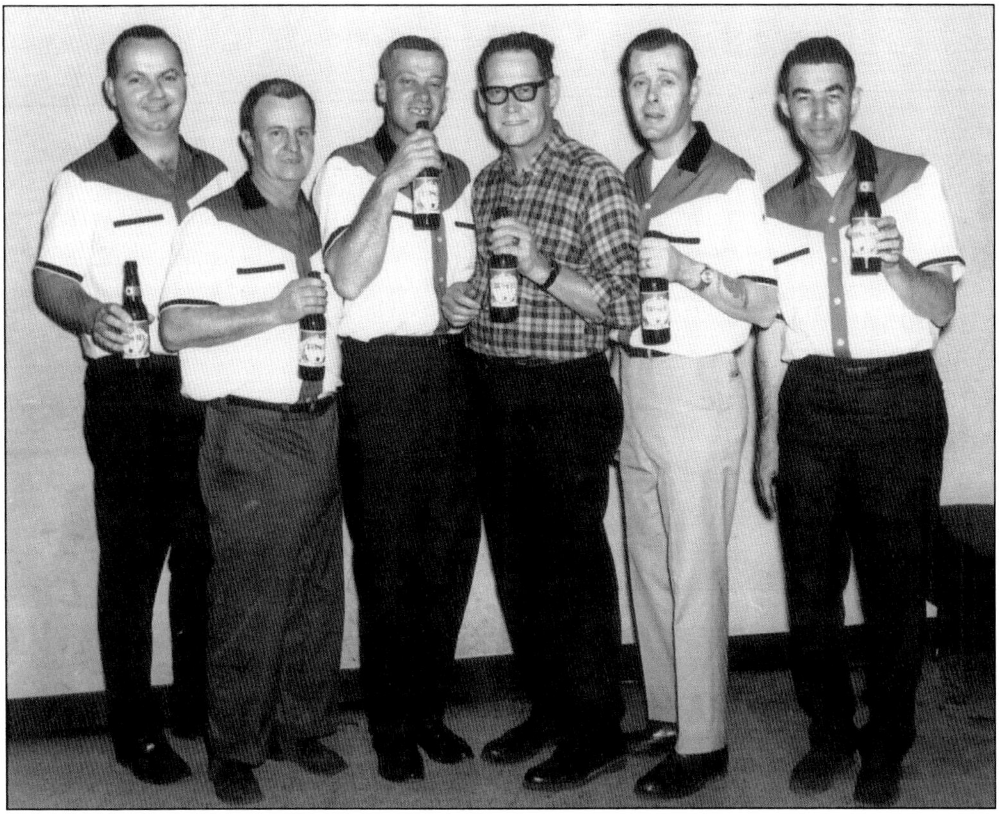

This bowling team won the bowling tournament for the Glendale Tavern. The team members are Corky Kinstle, Earl Loughary, Bob Bolton, Mitch LaMaster, and sponsors Tom Bolhortst and Charlie Petri.

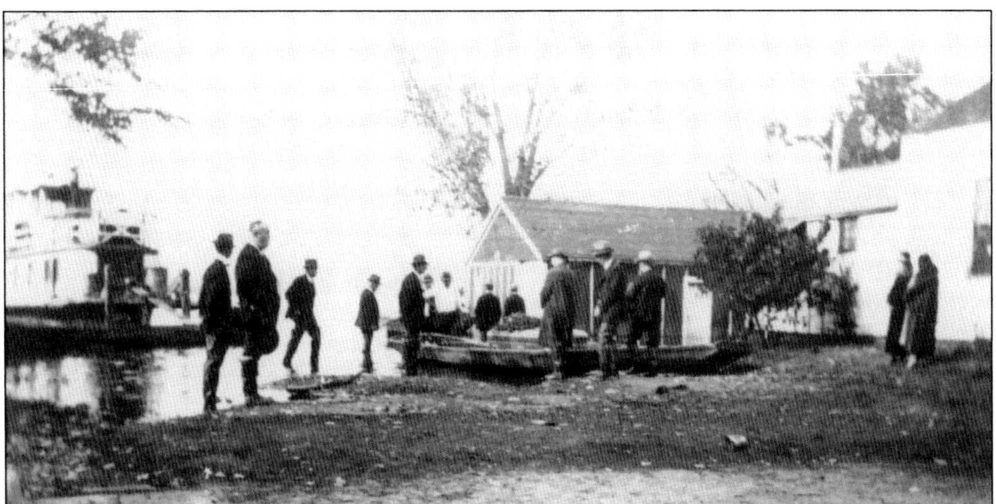

Shown here is the funeral procession for Annie Murphy, who was to be buried in Capt. Henry Hullet's Cemetery in Brown County, near La Grange. The river was high, so they took her by boat to the La Grange Locks. This picture was taken in the 1920s at the end of Jackson Street on the river.

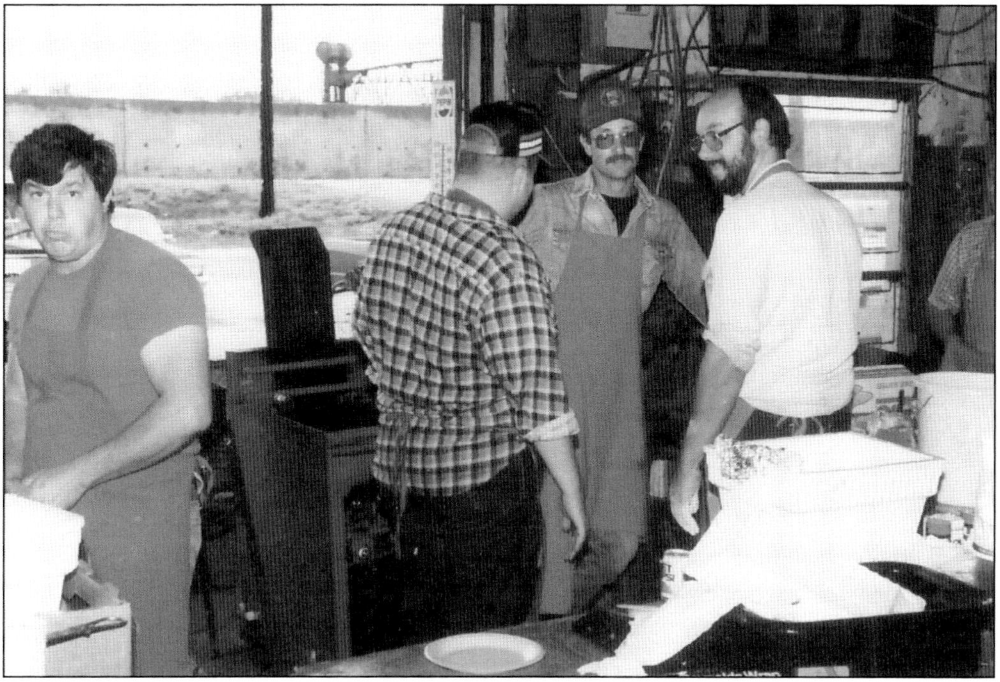

The fish fryers pictured at R and S Auto Supply are, from left to right, Bob Ross, Dude Brasel. Bill Robertson, and the world-famous Bruce Fisher.

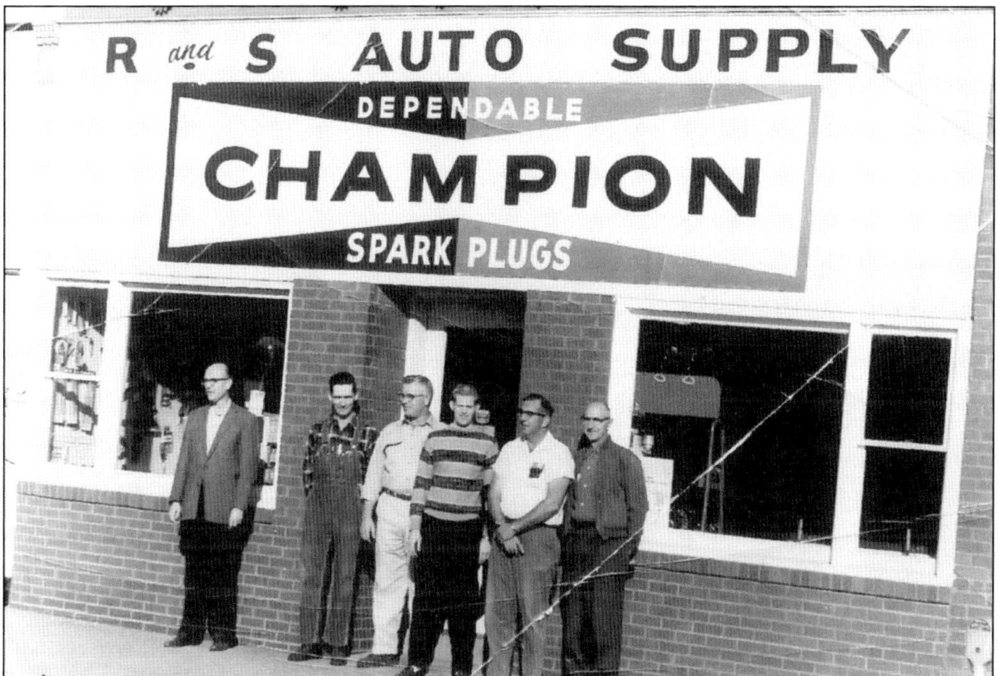

R and S Auto Supply was located on East Main Street. Pictured here are, from left to right, owner Harold Schnake and employees Dale Kruse, Ronald Spencer, David Spoon, Blake Rahn, and Bill Mueller.

The Carver

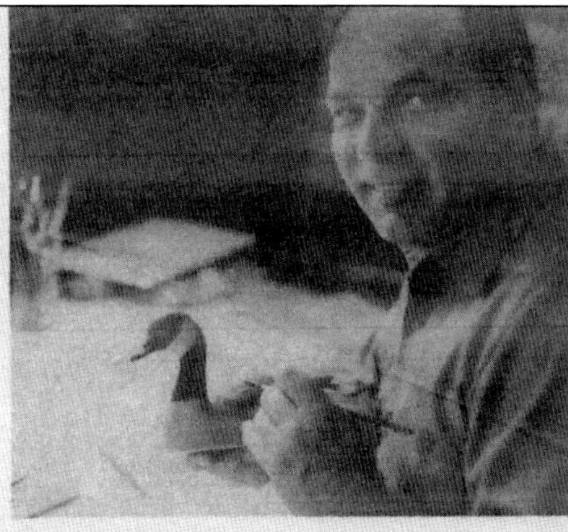

Born in Beardstown, Illinois, near the Sangamon Bottoms along the Illinois River, Tom Newell, a self-taught artist with no formal art training grew up in an area with some of the best waterfowling in the world. And where there are ducks there are decoy carvers.

Perhaps being surrounded by these influences as a youngster is why the desire to carve surfaced later, after moving to Southern California and then to Gig Harbor, Washington.

Ten years of carving for competition in national decoy shows from coast to coast has produced nearly 200 carving show awards. The demand by several galleries for Newell originals has limited the competition exhibiting in the last few years and most carving is now restricted to miniatures and life size carvings for galleries.

These clippings tell the story of Beardstown native Tom Newell, a self-taught artist and award-winning carver of decoys. The photographs in these clippings were likely taken around 1970.

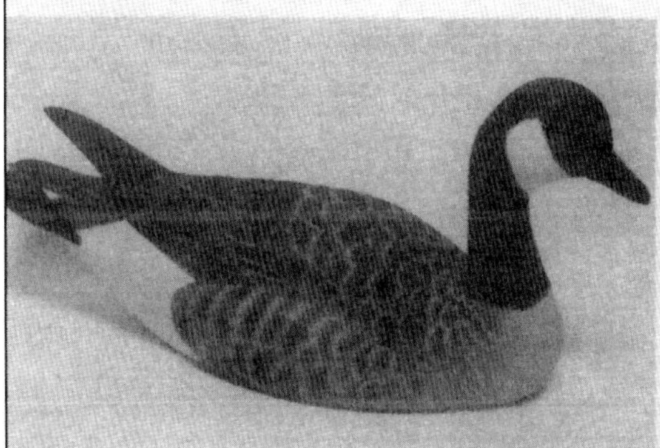

The Carvings

The patterns for the lifelike waterfowl decoys created by Tom Newell are made by the artist from field sketches and photographs.

All carvings are done one at a time, by hand, using knives made of straight razors and small gouges. Some textures are produced by the use of small grinding stones. The carvings are all individually handpainted with acrylic paints using study skins of the real bird to come as close as possible to the correct coloring and feather pattern.

Alaskan yellow cedar is used in most cases for the miniatures while the larger life-sized decorative decoys are carved from basswood.

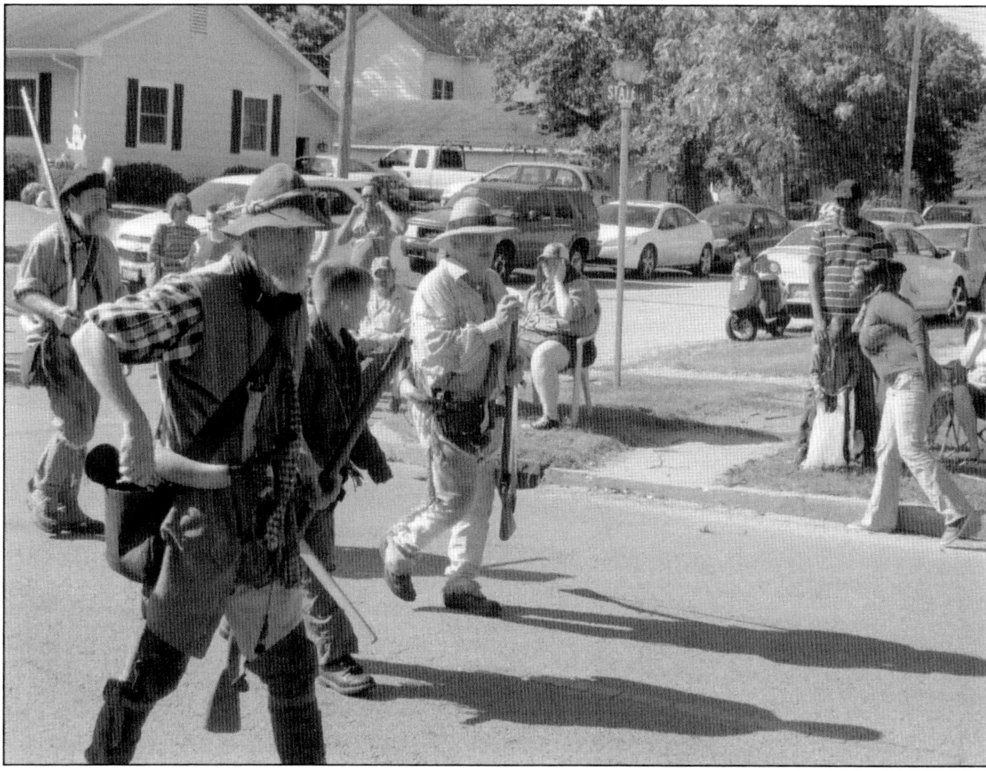

The Mascouten Bay Longrifles are shown marching in a Beardstown Fall Festival Parade. Pictured are, from left to right, Ed Bacon, Harvey Anglum, and Squire (Harold) Tyson.

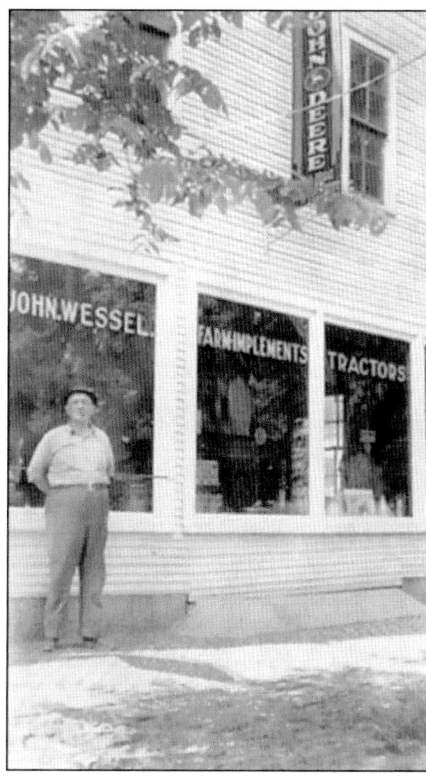

The John Wessel Farm Implements business was located at 311 West Seventh Street, Wessel is pictured here in 1943.

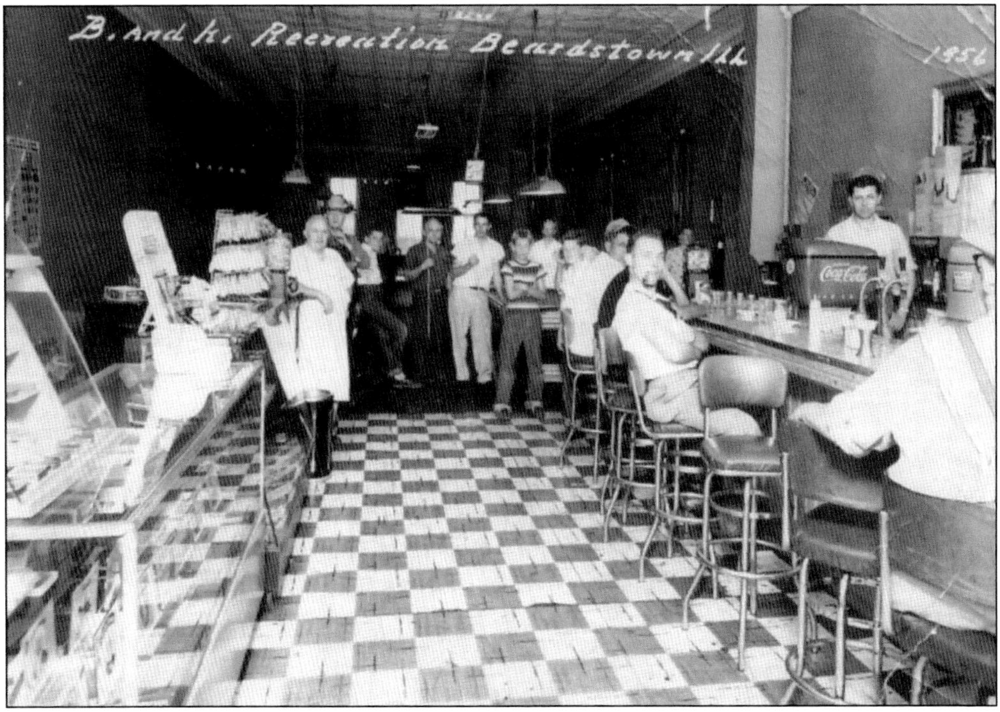

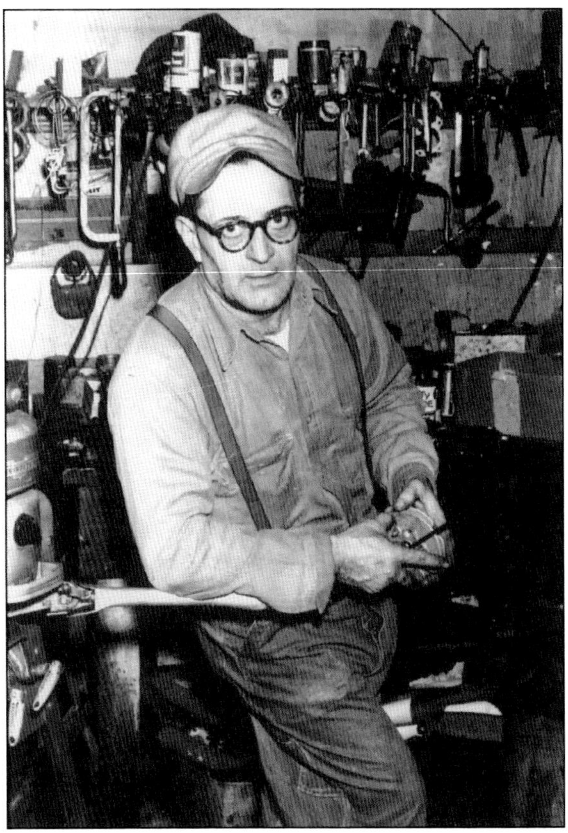

B and K Pool Hall was located at 218 Washington Street. Pictured here are, from left to right, Betty Boggs, Fiddy Hines, Muggs Summey, Ramon Tandy, Larry Stephens, Larry Weller, unidentified, Bub Logsdon, Bob Swan, and Barney Williams (behind the bar).

Clarence Boice (pictured) ran a repair shop for anything that would run. That shop was located at 115 West Main Street in 1948.

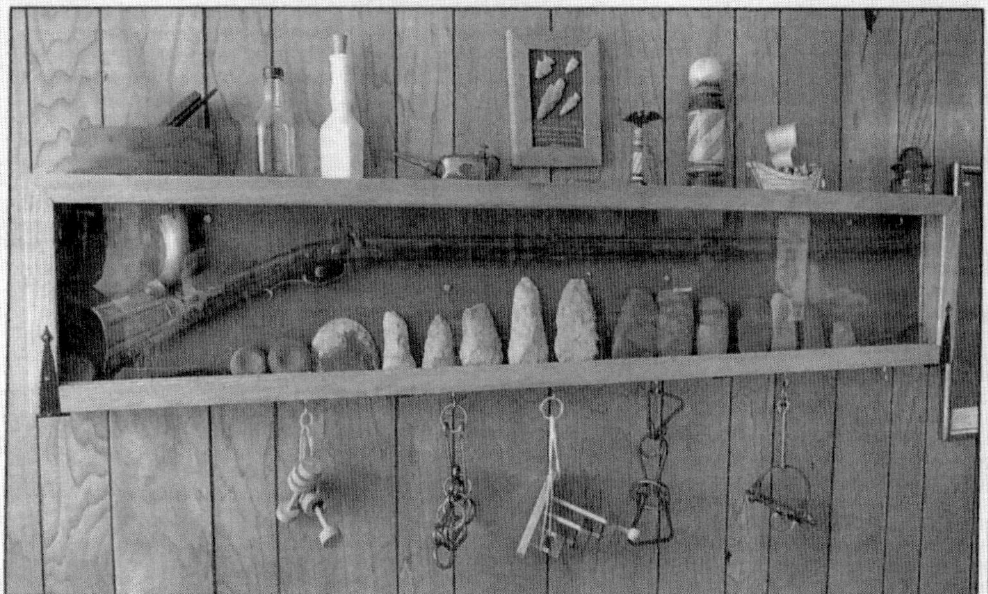

Bill Hagen

Harold Tyson, Beardstown barber and antiquities collector, has collected Native American artifacts, above, and studied the Beardstown area's Native American history since boyhood. Tyson is shown below with a set of Indian blades and projectile points.

Author Harold Tyson, owner of Tyson's Barber Shop, spent much of his life collecting Native American artifacts, including those from tribes that resided near the Beardstown area. He is pictured here along with some of the items from his collection.

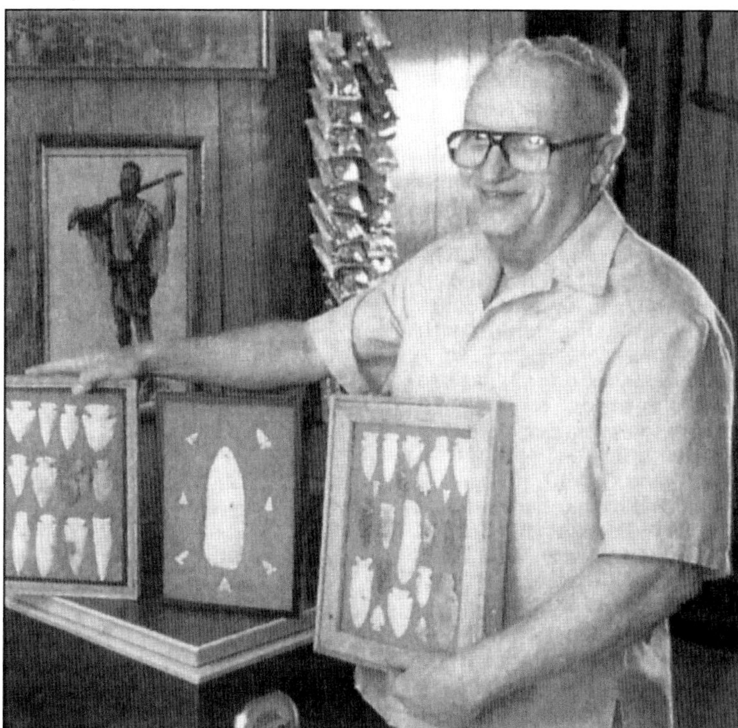

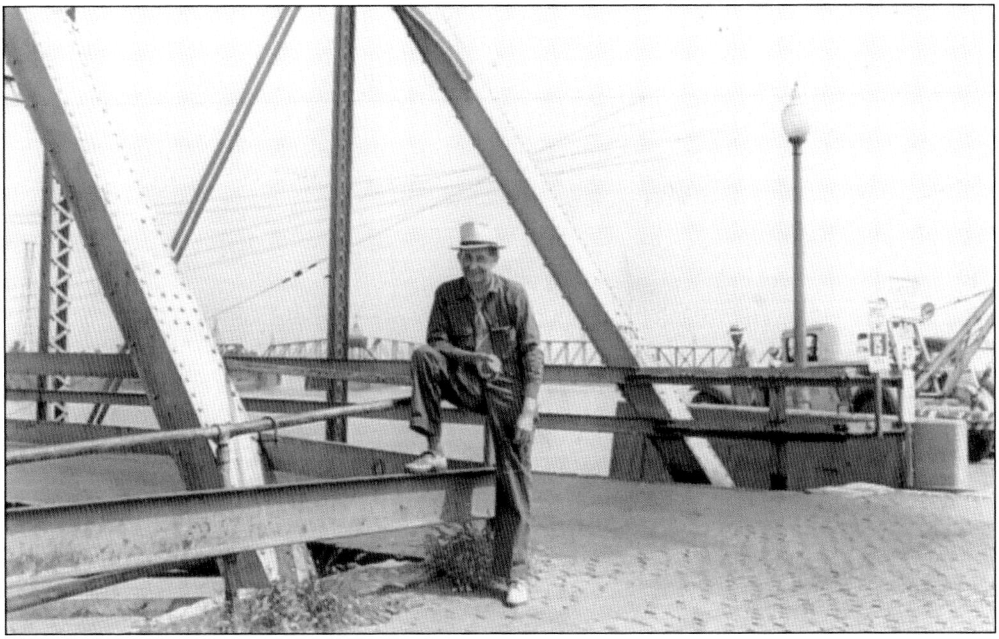

Chinie Colvin is shown resting at the Beardstown end of the toll bridge in 1950.

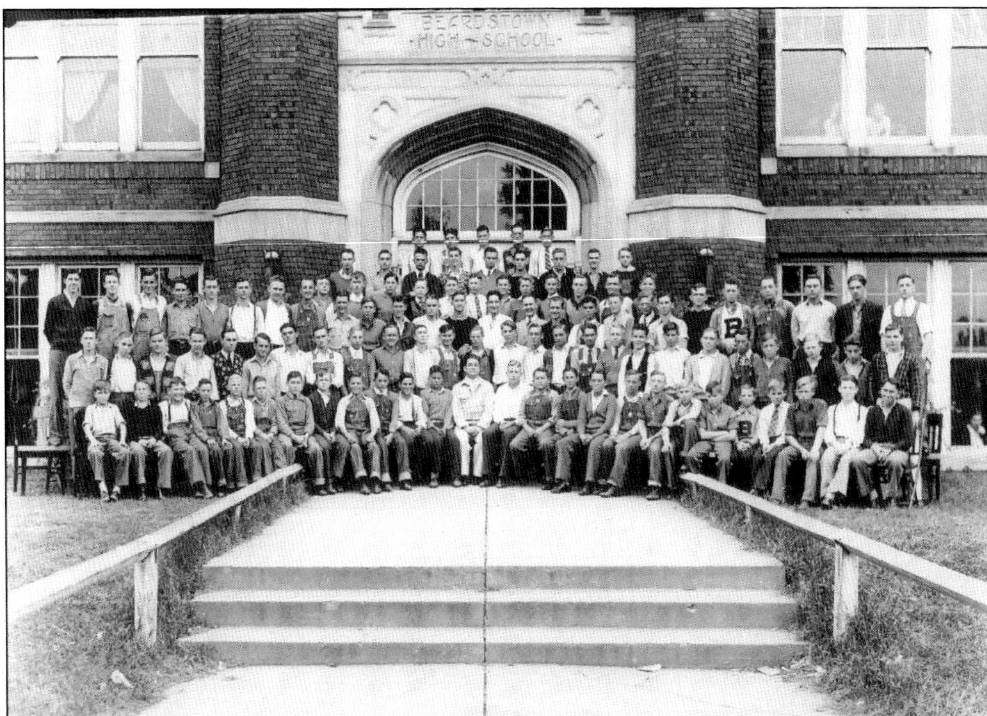

B. W. Smith (front row, center) is pictured with his Future Farmers of America club at Beardstown High School around 1940.

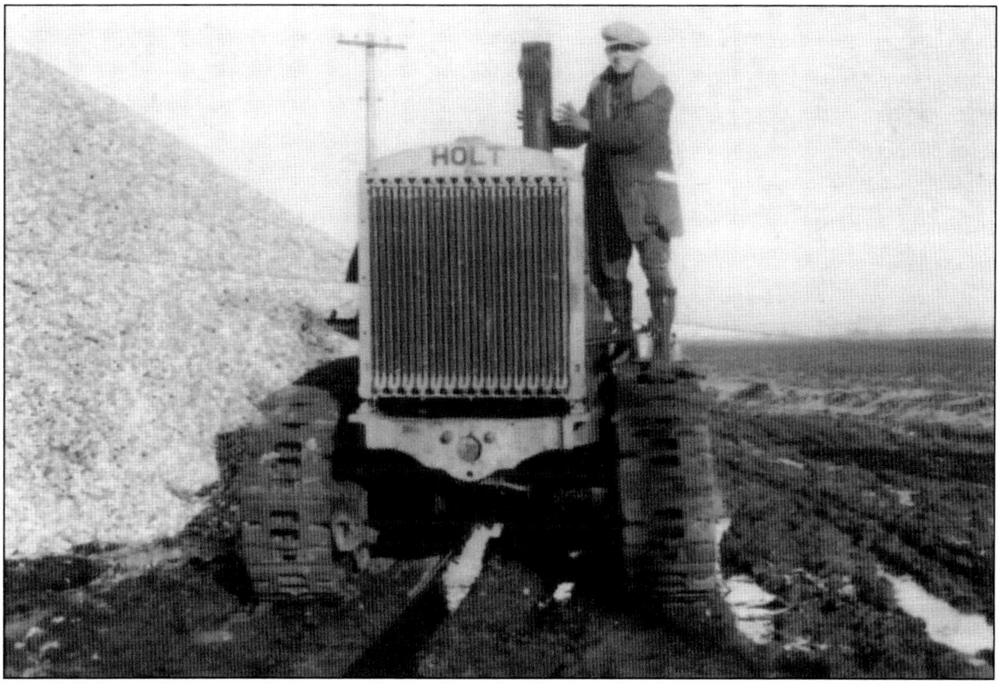

An early-1900s Holt tractor and its operator stand next to a gravel pile across the river.

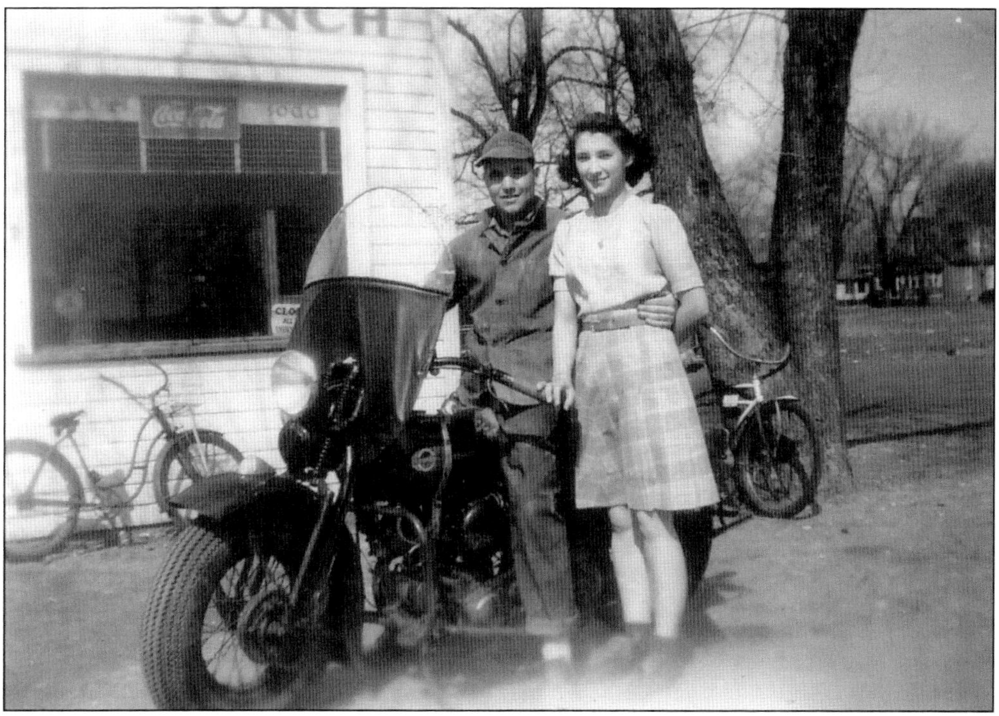

A daredevil, his girlfriend, and his motorcycle pose in front of the Campus Inn at State and Fifteenth Street across from the high school. Both are unidentified.

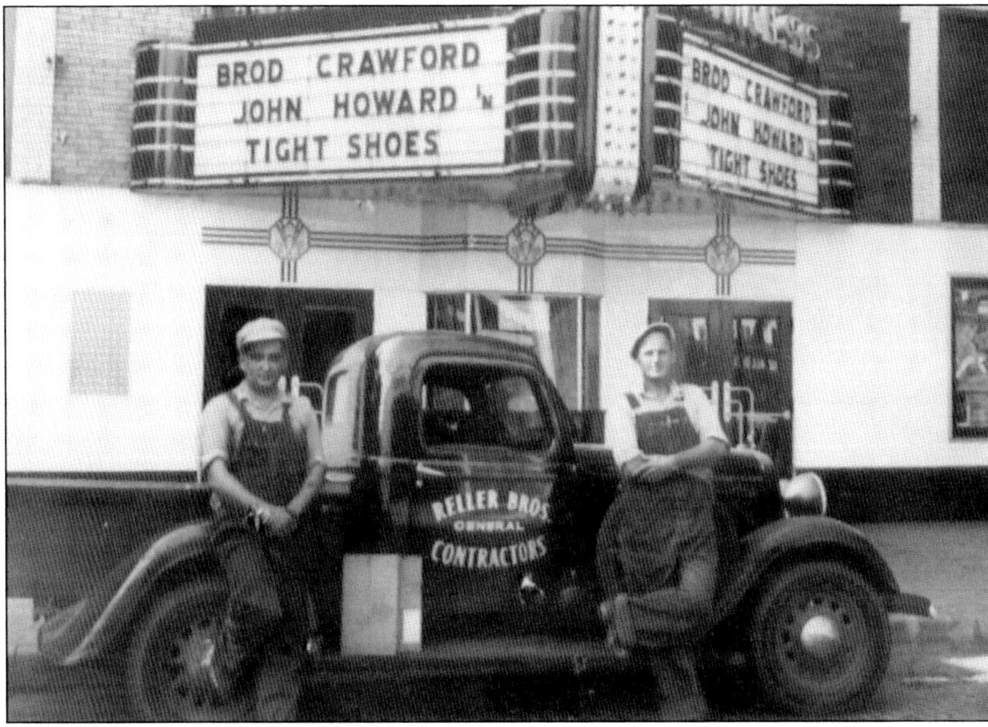

The Princess Theater is pictured here in 1941. On the left is Paul Woods, owner of the Princess, and on the right is Elmer Reller.

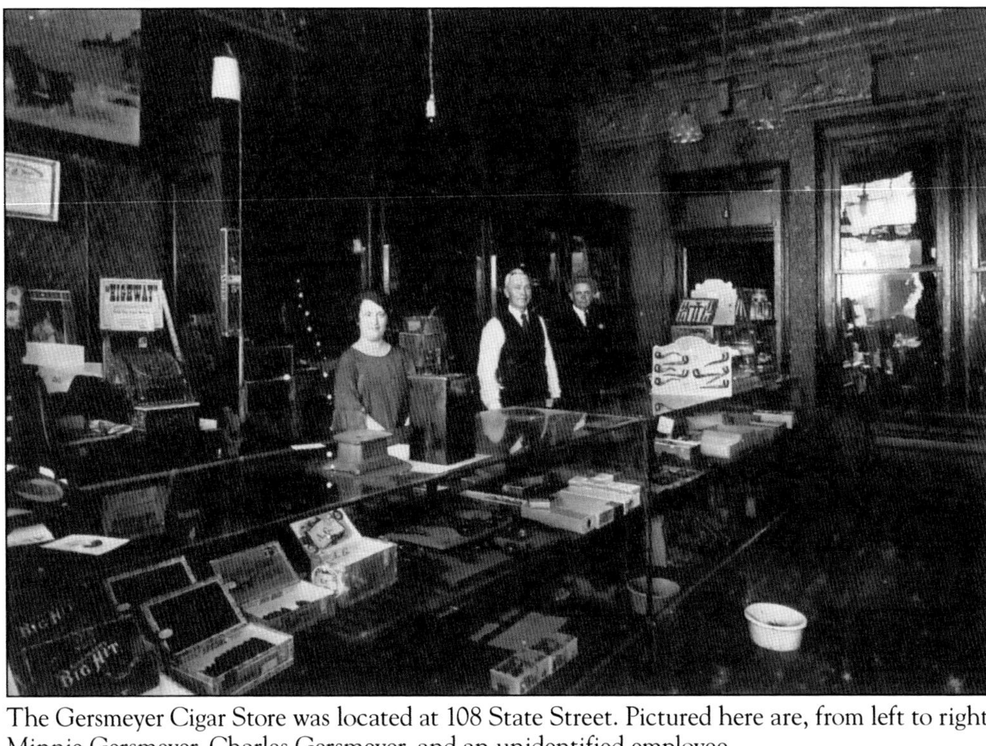

The Gersmeyer Cigar Store was located at 108 State Street. Pictured here are, from left to right, Minnie Gersmeyer, Charles Gersmeyer, and an unidentified employee.

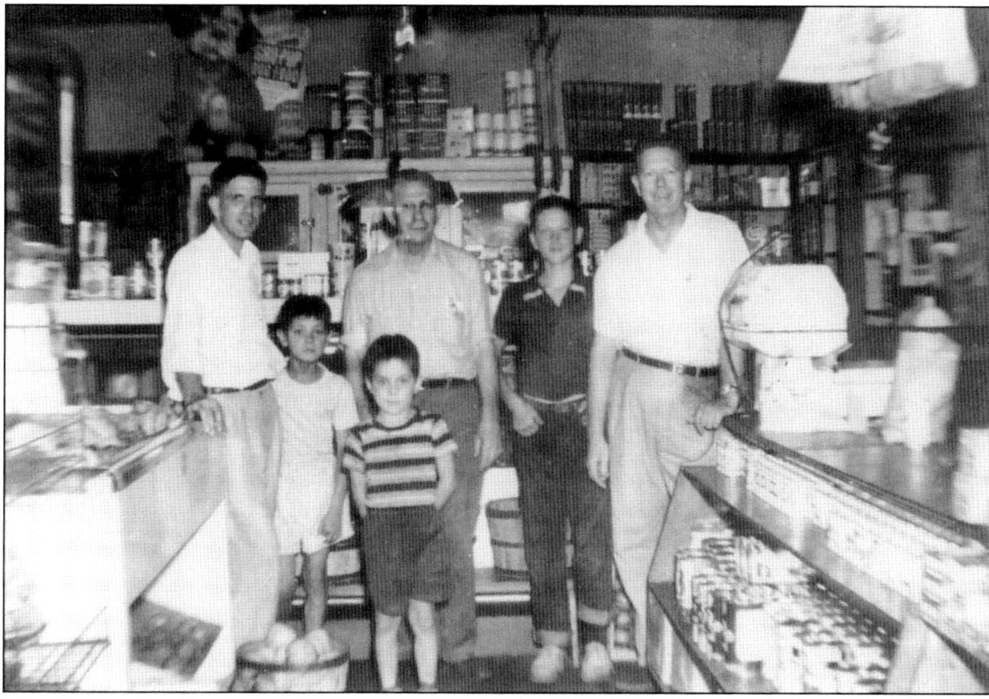

The George Coy Grocery store was located at 1320 Adams Street. Pictured are, from left to right, Don Barker and sons Tom and Lynn, Wiggles Coy, Mike Barker, and George Coy.

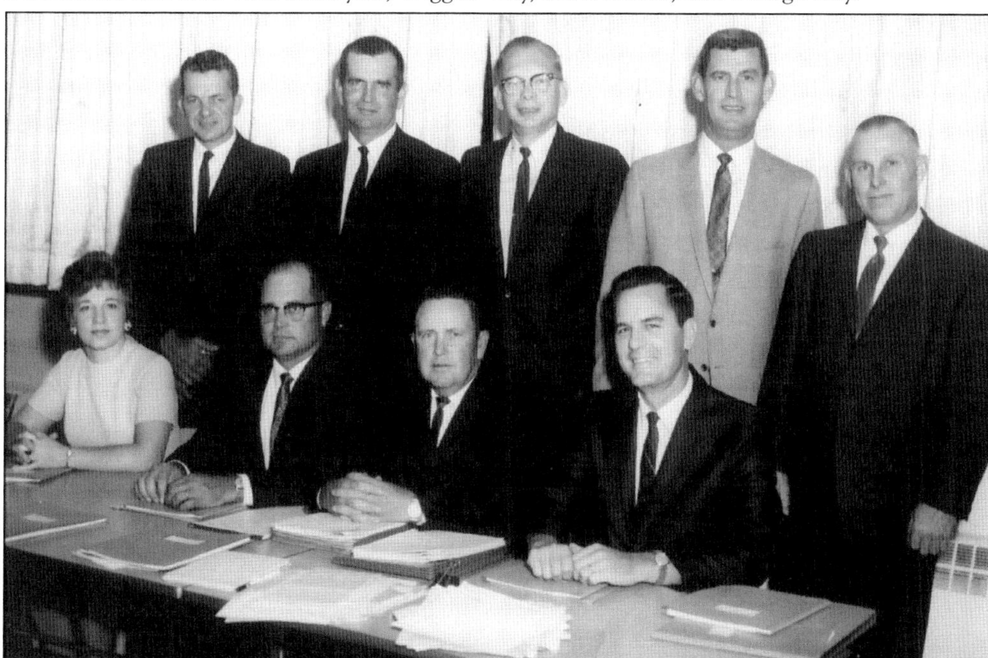

This is the 1977 Beardstown Community School District 15 school board. Pictured are, from left to right, (seated) Ann Brewer (secretary), Harold Kuhlman, Andy Taylor, and Herbert Darnell (superintendent); (standing) Bud Stock, Homer Rohn, Bob Huss, Bob Gillenwater, and Bill Fischer.

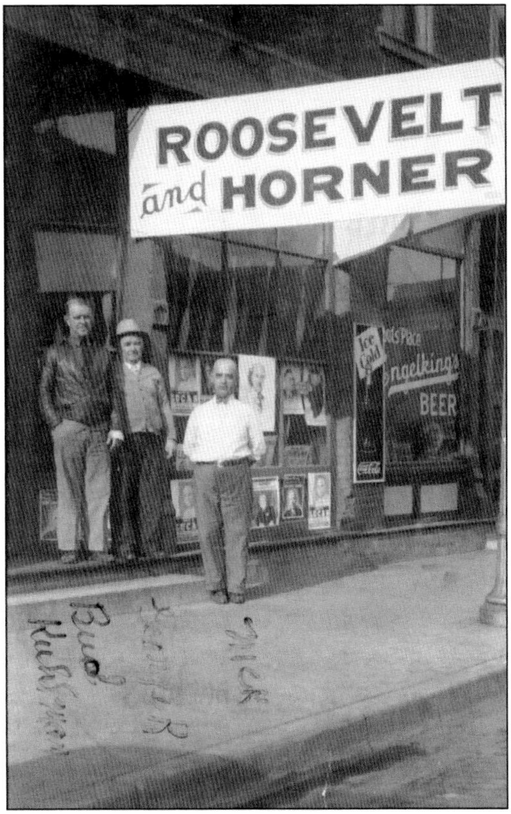

These three Democrats are standing in front of the American Sugar Bowl at 120 Washington Street. Pictured are Bud Kuhlman (left), George R. Lekas (center, brother-in-law of Nick), and owner Nick Leocis.

This is the Beardstown Police Department in 1987. From left to right are Smooch Davis, Bob Lael, unidentified, Jerry Kiser, Pete Wilcox, and Manny Arenz.

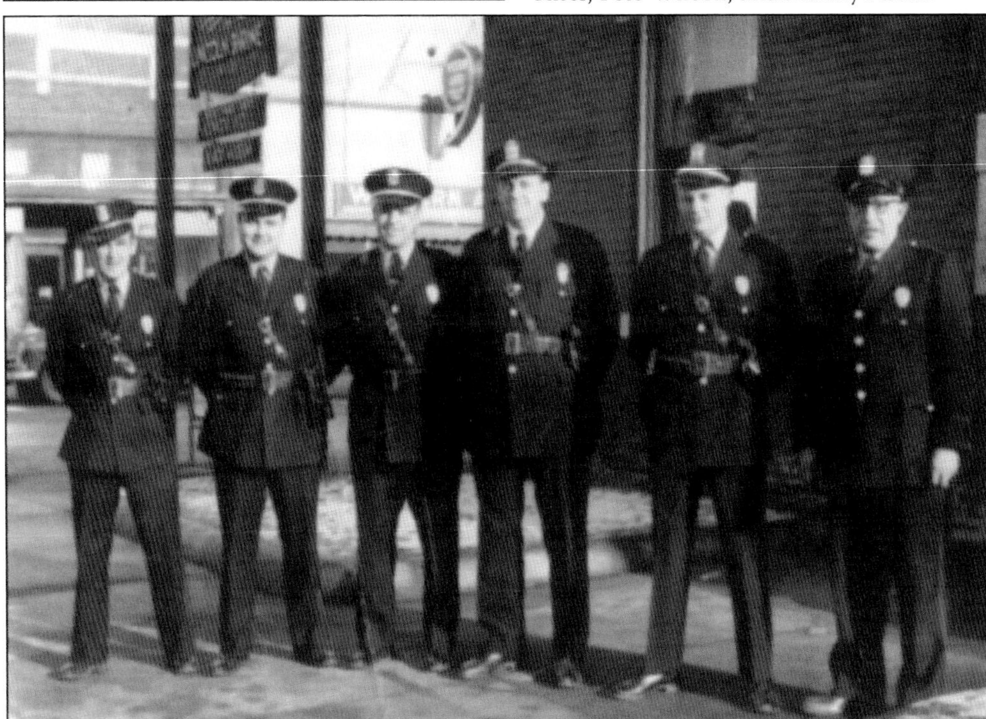

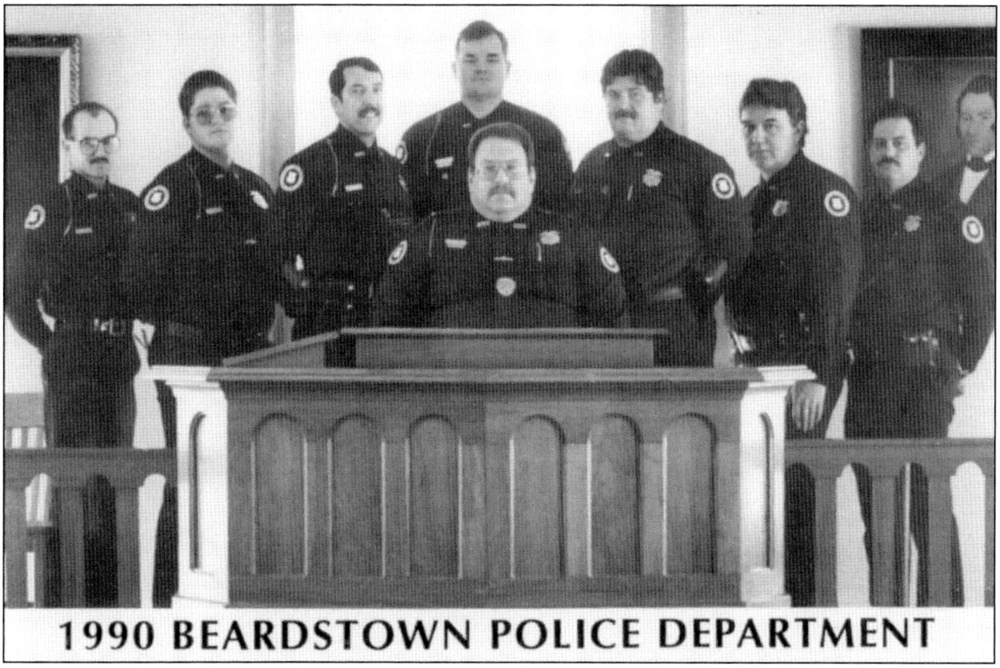

The Beardstown Police Department is pictured here in 1990: (seated) Chief Bob Flood; (standing) from left to right, Steven Patterson, Mike Cockerill, Brian Deloche, Rick Kays, Terry Phillips, Jim French, and John Swan.

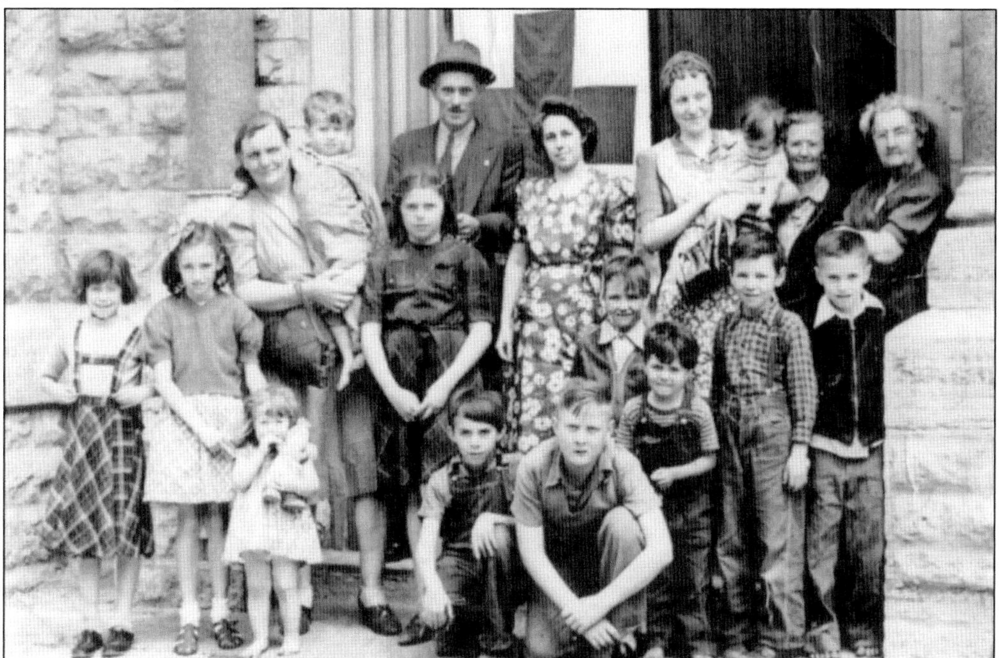

The Ed Smith family was displaced from their home during the dry flood of 1943. The family stayed at the First Methodist Church in Springfield until the waters receded. The young boy in the front with the striped shirt is Burr Smith.

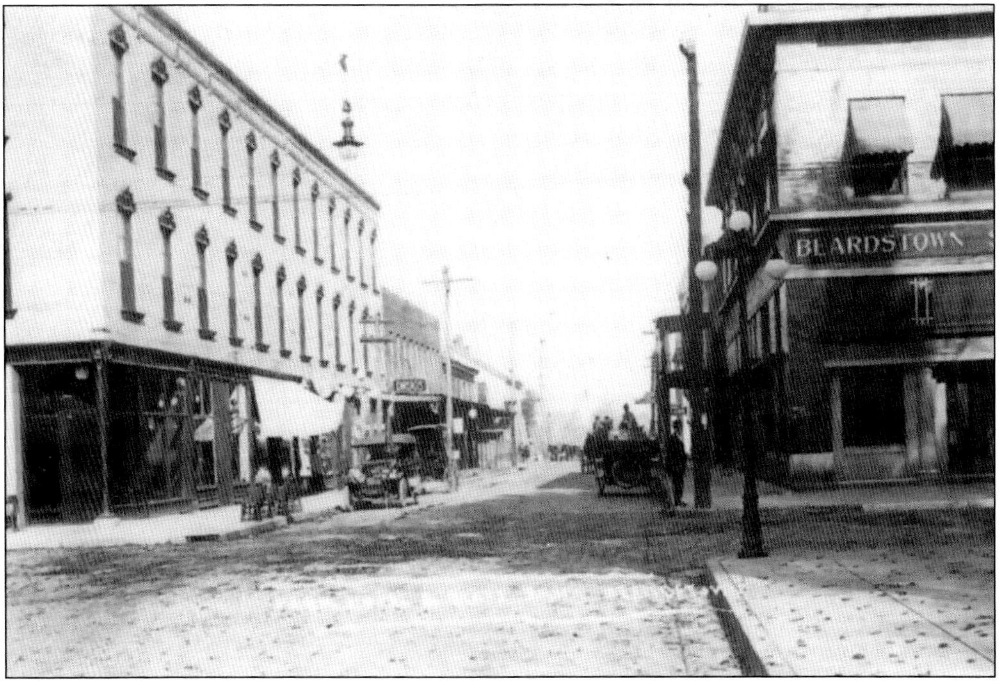

This early-1900s view is looking across the intersection of Second and Washington Streets toward the river. The Park Hotel is on the left, and the Beardstown State Bank is on the right.

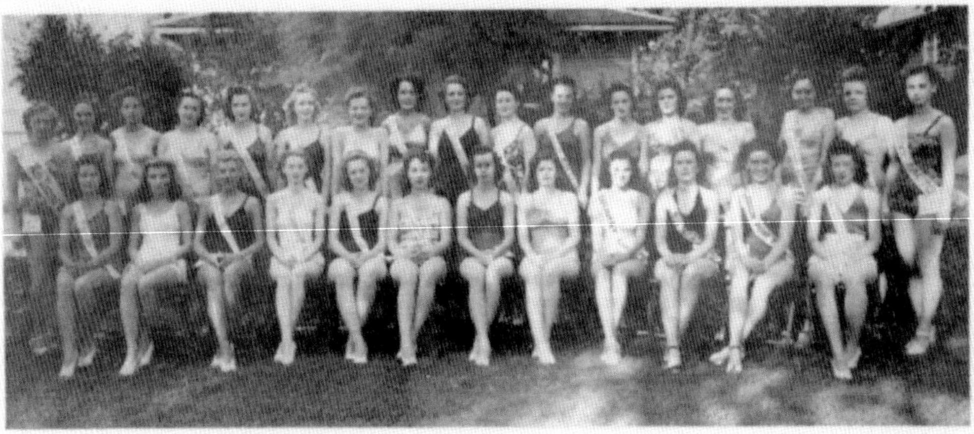

Bathing Beauty Contestants

came from 22 towns for our 4TH ANNUAL event. Over 12,000 people enjoyed it. Station WMBD of Peoria broadcast the contest.

Since 1935 We Have Inaugurated:

The ANNUAL BOAT RACES—Bringing our largest crowds.

The ANNUAL HALLOWEEN PARTY—Cutting Vandalism

This photograph of "Bathing Beauty Contestants" was taken around 1939.

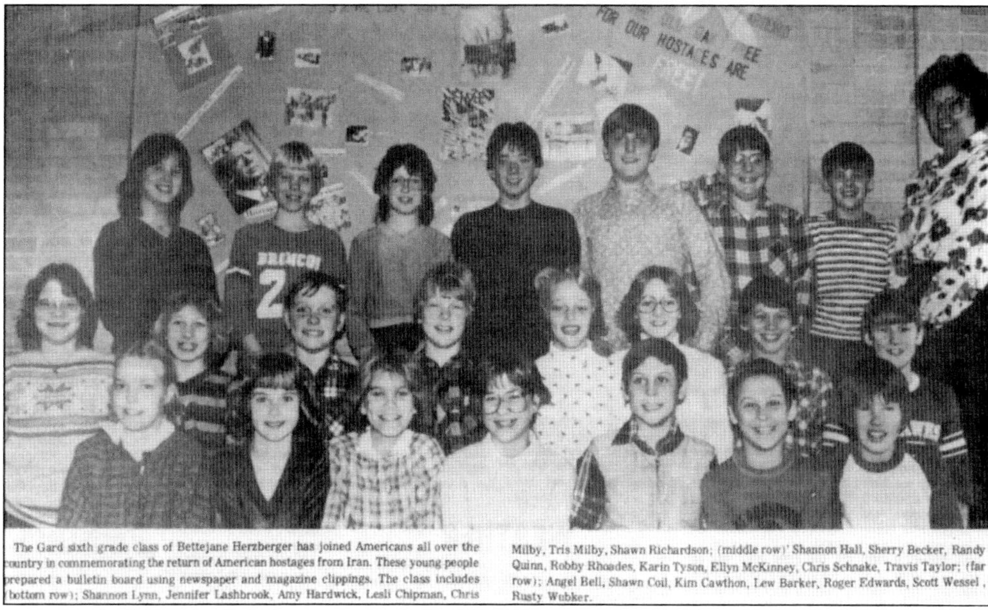

The Gard sixth grade class of Bettejane Herzberger has joined Americans all over the country in commemorating the return of American hostages from Iran. These young people prepared a bulletin board using newspaper and magazine clippings. The class includes (bottom row): Shannon Lynn, Jennifer Lashbrook, Amy Hardwick, Lesli Chipman, Chris Milby, Tris Milby, Shawn Richardson; (middle row)' Shannon Hall, Sherry Becker, Randy Quinn, Robby Rhoades, Karin Tyson, Ellyn McKinney, Chris Schnake, Travis Taylor; (far row); Angel Bell, Shawn Coil, Kim Cawthon, Lew Barker, Roger Edwards, Scott Wessel, Rusty Wubker.

This 1981 image shows the sixth-grade students at Gard School with their teacher, Bettejane Herzberger (third row, standing at far right), in front of a bulletin board they made to commemorate the return of American hostages from Iran.

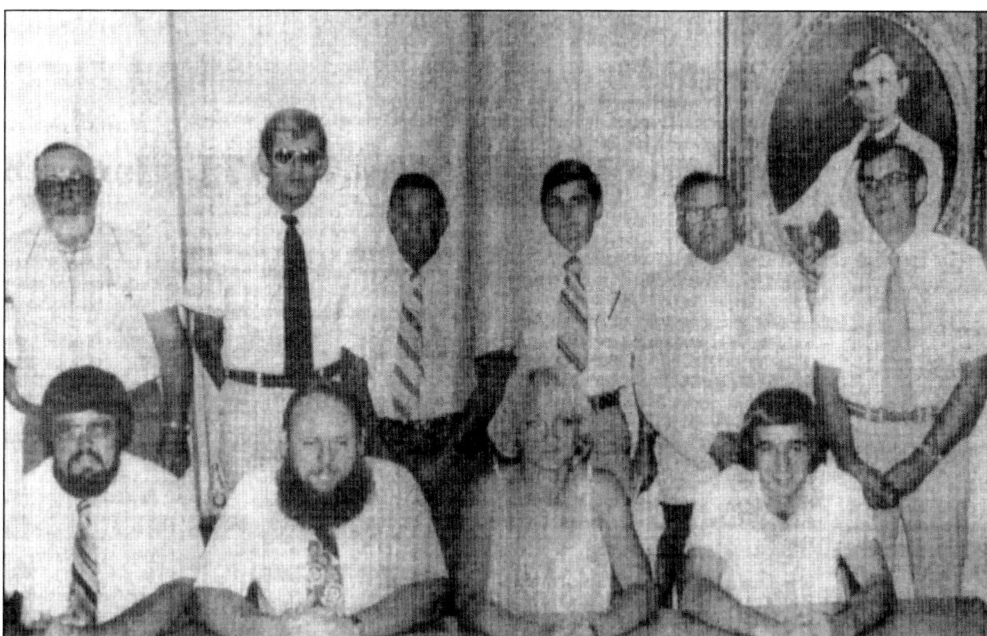

The Beardstown City Council is pictured here in 1979. Shown are, from left to right, (seated) Dan Wessel, Thomas Brewer, Judith McCombs, and Robert Walters; (standing) Emerson Moss, Robert Gillenwater, Edwin F. Brockschmidt, Thomas Lashbrook, Ted Curtin, and Bert Lerch.

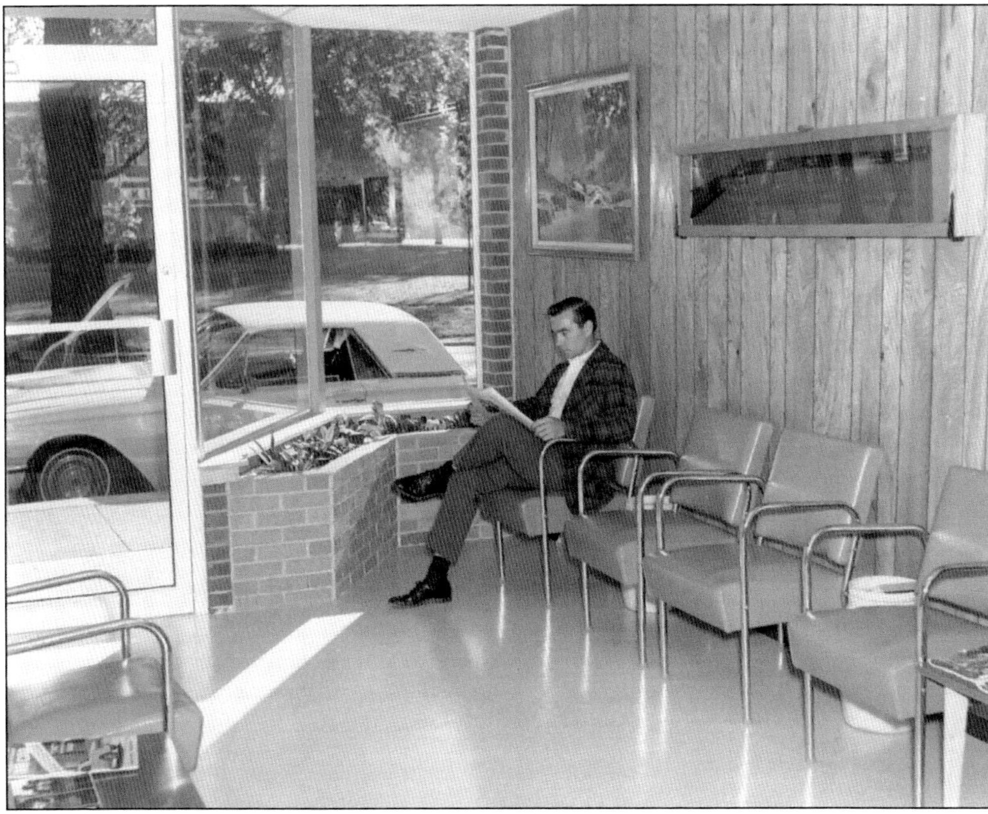

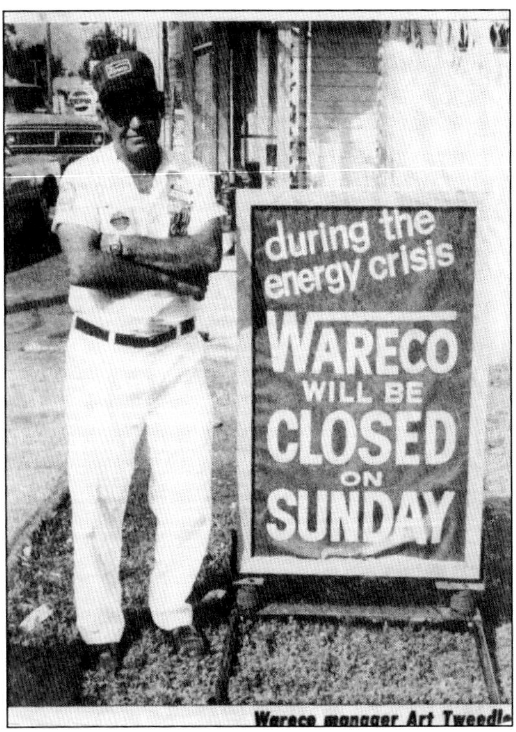

Oscar Mathews is shown waiting for a haircut at Tyson's Barber Shop in 1965.

Art Tweedle was the manager of the Wareco gas station at 517 East Fourth Street.

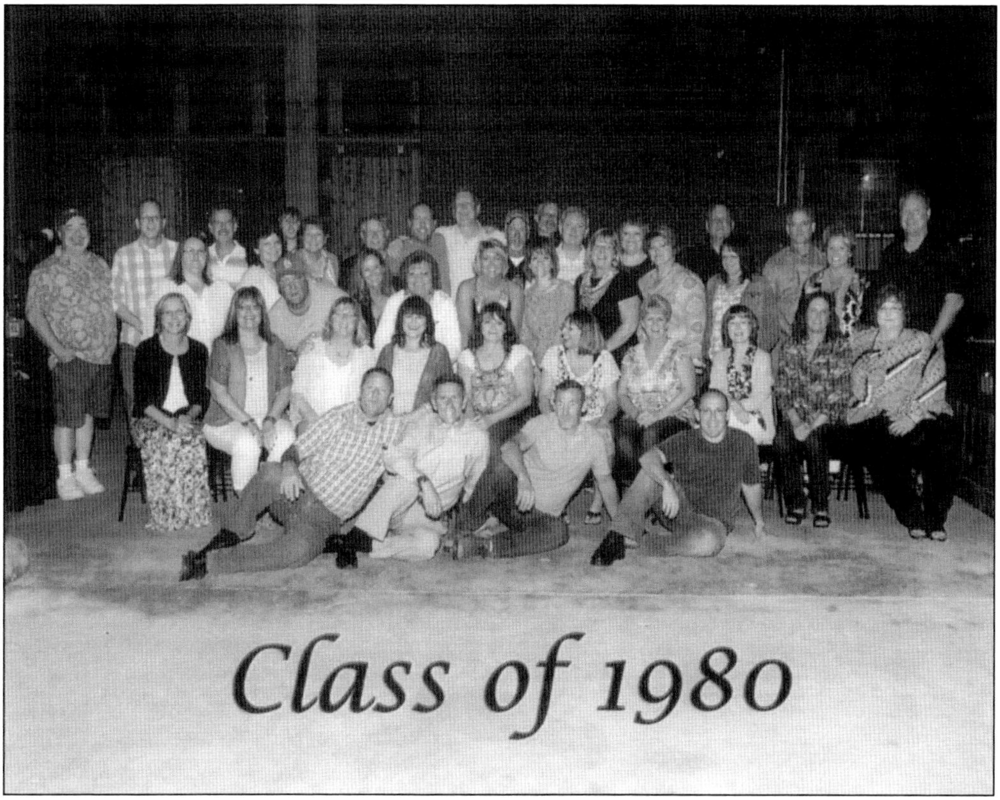

Members of the Beardstown High School class of 1980 posed for this picture at their 25-year reunion in 2005.

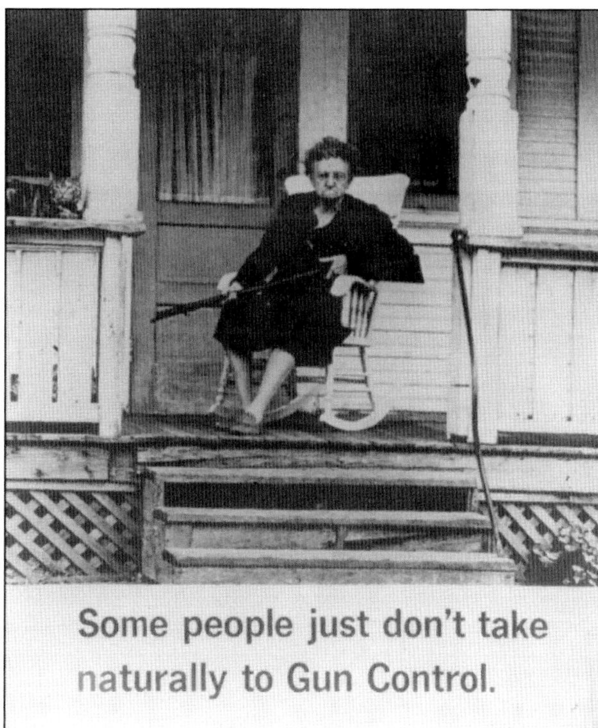

This woman resented the city wanting to take down a tree in her yard. The tree still stands.

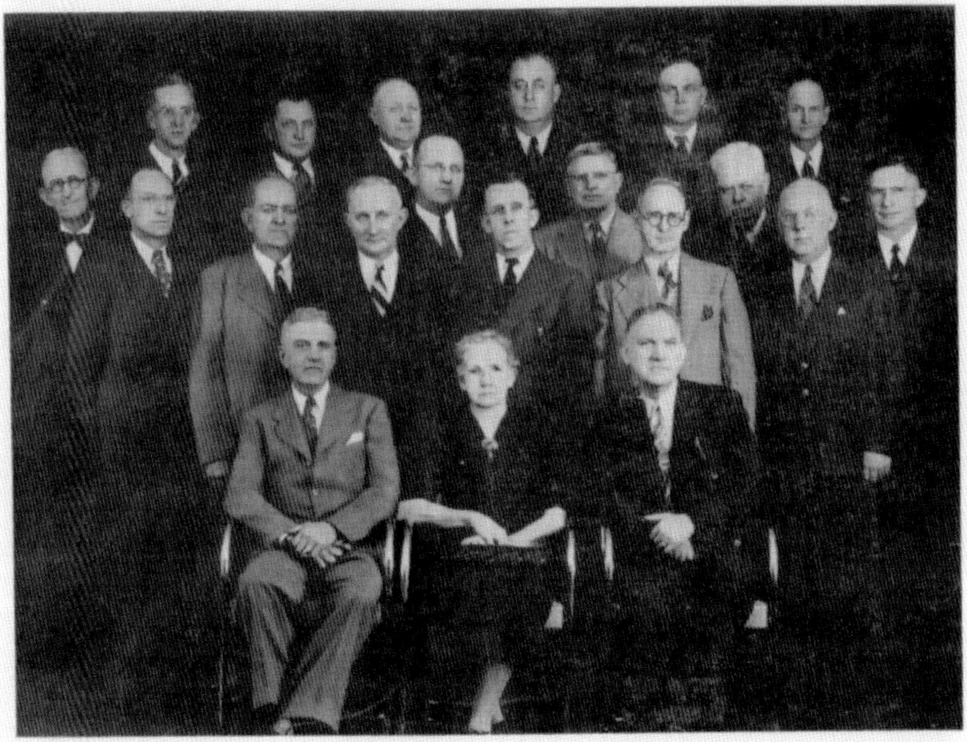

City Officers As They Appear in Picture on Opposite Page

Seated: Mayor Fred I. Cline, 1935-41; Margaret Swan, City Treasurer, 1937-41, first woman ever to be elected to a city office; Robert B. Maslin, City Clerk, 1909-41, who has been re-elected to that office more times than any other city clerk in the state.

Second row: Alderman 2nd Ward, Eldo Thomas, 1935-41; Alderman 2nd Ward, Chas. E. Phelps, 1927-43; Alderman Carl Harre, 5th Ward, 1926-35, 4th Ward 1935-43; Alderman 4th Ward, W. G. McKenzie, 1921-41; Alderman 5th Ward, Robert Shupe, 1933-41; City Attorney L. M. McClure.

Third row: Alderman 1st Ward, Reuel R. Rahn, 1935-41; Alderman 3rd Ward, George E. Ring, 1937-41; Alderman 3rd Ward, William E. Fischer, 1939-43; Alderman 5th Ward, Harry Buck, 1937-43; City Electrician and Supt. of Water Works, Fred G. Heintze.

Back row, standing, left to right: Alderman 1st ward, Turner R. Antrobus, 1935-39; Alderman 1st ward, Wm. Applegate, 1939-43; Supt. of Streets, Fred H. Schumacher; Chief of Police, Harold Webster; Head Bridge Tender, Carl Pilger; Fire Chief, W. D. Colvin.

These are the city officers of 1943. Pictured are, from left to right, (first row) Fred I. Cline, Margaret Swan, and Robert B. Maslin; (second row) Eldo Thomas, Chas. E. Phelps, Carl Harre, W.G. McKenzie, Robert Shupe, and L.M. McClure; (third row) Reuel R. Rahn, George E. Ring, William E. Fischer, Harry Buck, and Fred G. Heintze; (fourth row) Turner R. Antrobus, William Applegate, Fred H. Schumacher, Harold Webster, Carl Pilger, and W.D. Colvin.

Three

SPORTS

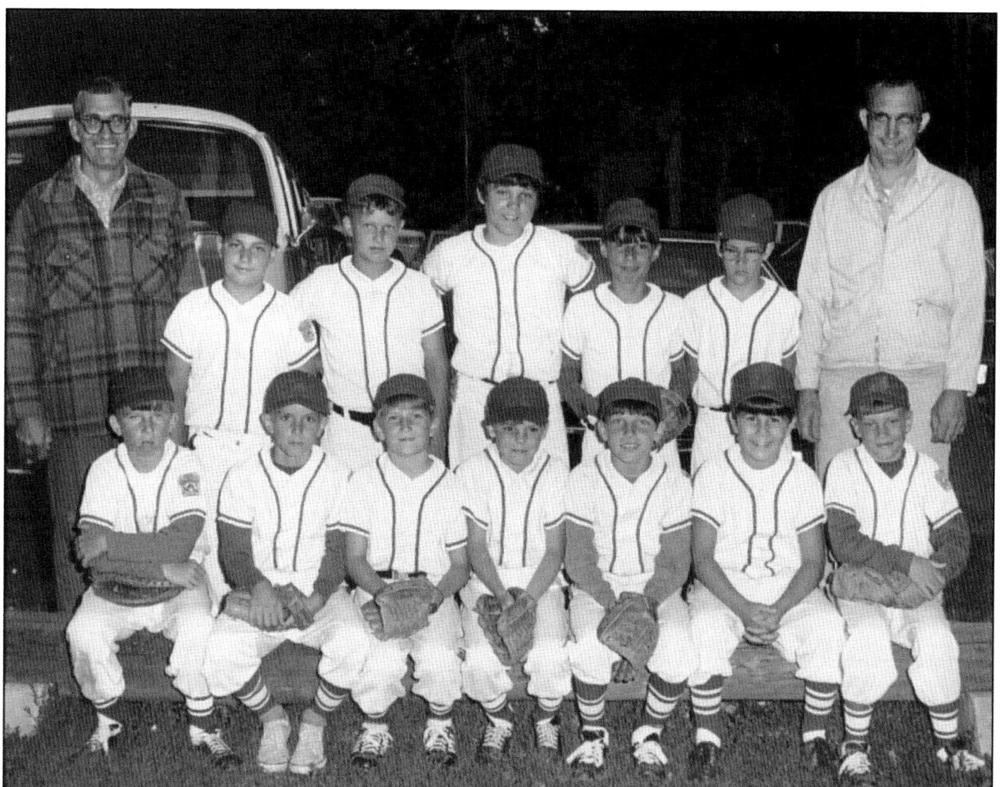

This is a Beardstown Little League team in the early 1970s. Pictured are, from left to right, (first row) C.S. Burget, Marty Coleman, Vince Warden, Kenny Lindley, Kirk Rice, Troy Brockschmidt, and Greg Upchurch; (second row) Bert Lerch (manager), Kevin Lerch, Dan Meyer, Aaron Stock, Ric Dennis, unidentified, and George Belville (coach).

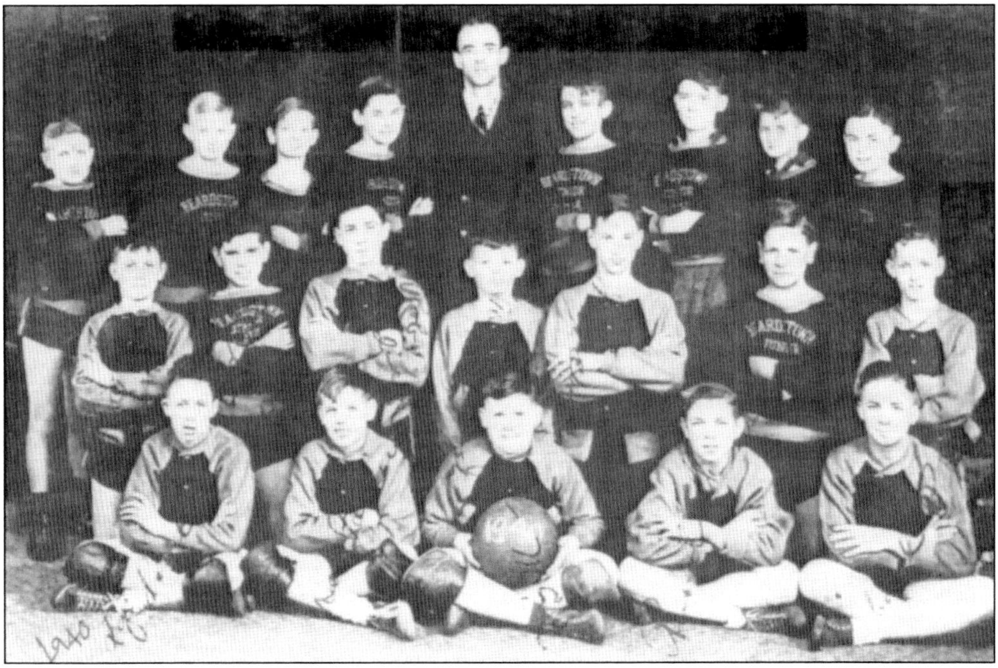

This is the 1940 Beardstown Junior High School basketball team. Pictured are, from left to right, (first row) Lafe Lamb, Don Perine, Joe McCollogh, Russel Shouse, and Richard Patterson; (second row) Bob Reller, Kenneth Foster, Bob Hardwick, Bob Defenbaugh, Jim McClure, Bob Launer, and Jim "Cat" Riggal; (third row) Ansel Taylor, ? Meyer, Dick Taylor, Bob Treadway, Robert Scott (coach), Jerry Alcorn, Sam Hardwick, Bill Mueller, and Robert "Woody" Sudbrink.

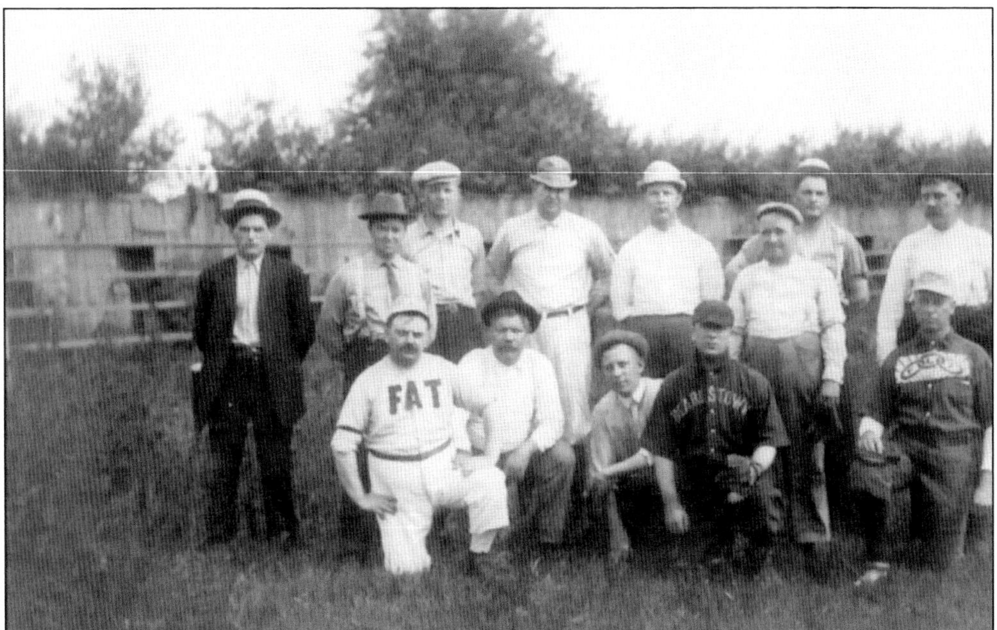

This early baseball team played at the end of Wall Street near where the Belville Garage now stands.

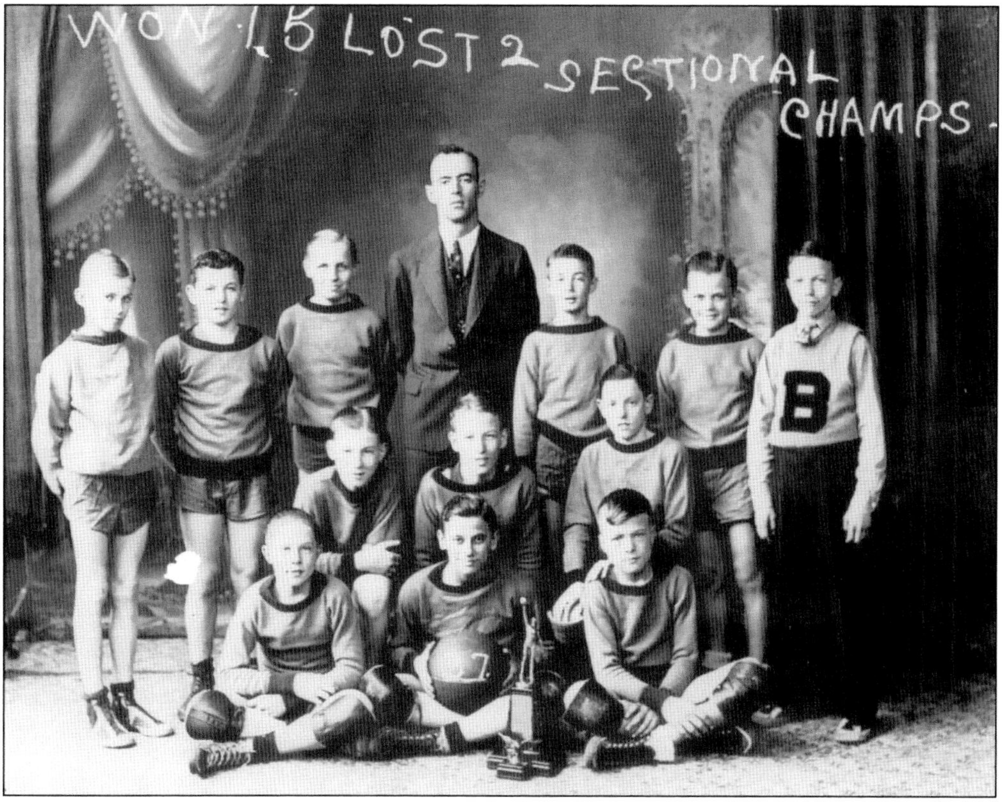

These are the 1937 Beardstown Junior High Sectional champions. Pictured are, from left to right, (first row) Tim Ohara, Bob Phelps, and unidentified; (second row) Bob Seaman, Dick Stephenson, and Mick Steele; (third row) Bob Fischer, John Phelps, Jack Reller, Bob Scott (coach), Charlie Petri, Carl Ed, and Elmore Harbman.

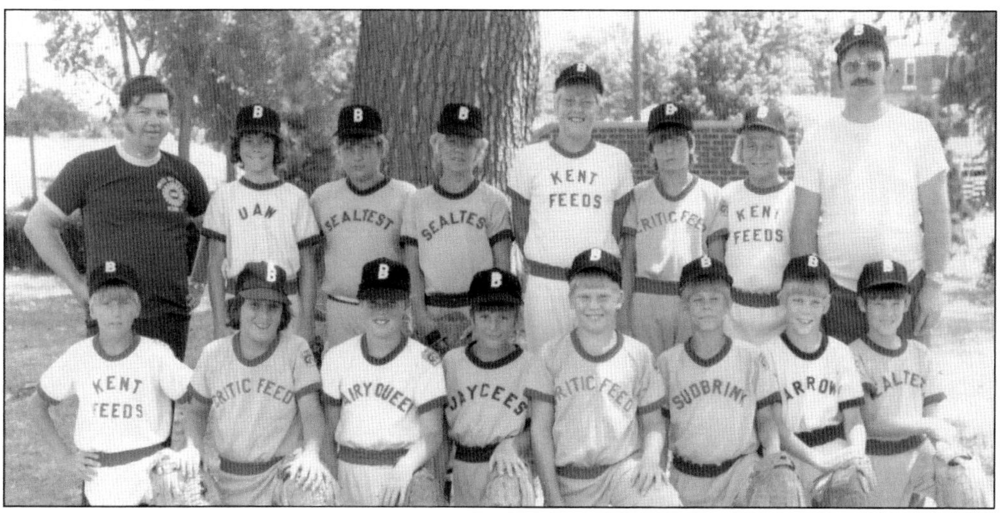

This is a Beardstown Little League All-Star team in the 1970s. Pictured are, from left to right, (first row) Jerry Walker, Matt Fiegl, Joe Robertson, Brian Bettis, Kevin Upchurch, Joe Wherly, John Sheahan, and Dave Krohe; (second row) Dennis Reily (coach), Doug Wilson, John Genseal, Bill Cawthon, Joe Andres, Rod Dennis, Bruce Smith, and George Belville (coach).

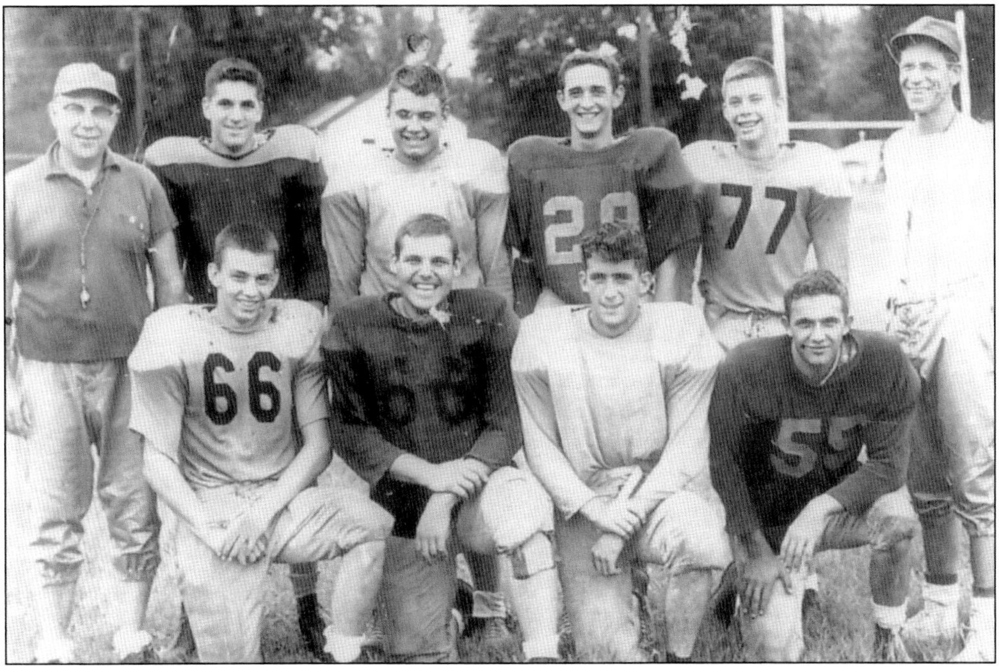

This is a Beardstown High School football team in the 1960s. Pictured are, from left to right, (first row) George Quin, Dick DeSollar, John Warden, and John Logsdon; (second row) Nic Carter (coach), Sam Seward, Mo Genseal, Mike Dyche, Rick Shultz, and Ed Lewis (coach).

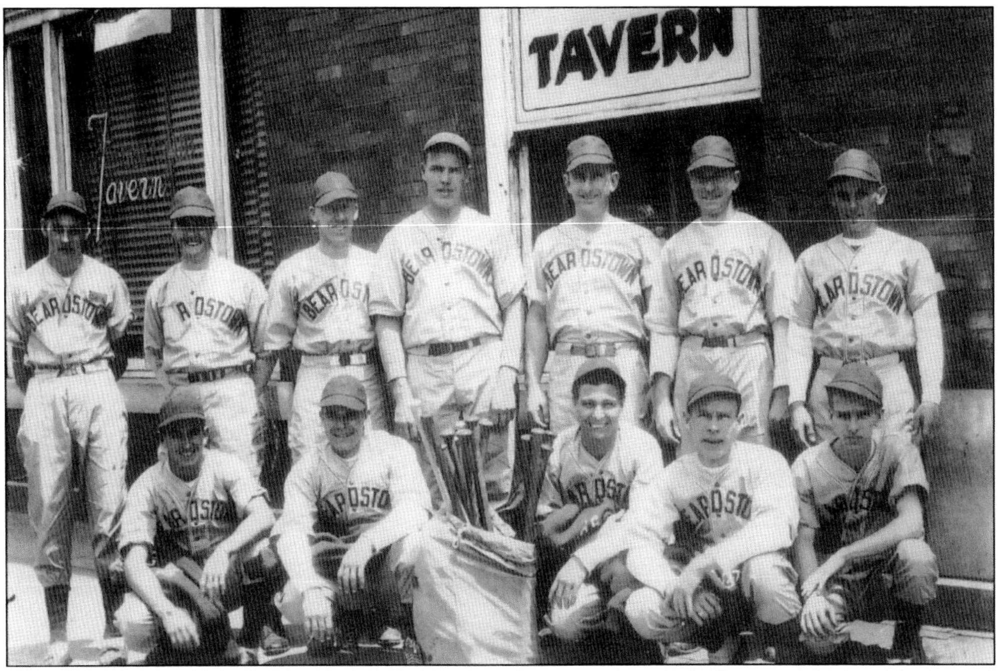

This photograph is of the Rod and Gun Tavern professional baseball team taken in the 1950s. Pictured from left to right are (first row) Stub Briggs, Virgil Perry, (sack of baseball bats), Albert "Randy" Lee, Verlin Perry, and Bumps Riley; (second row) Jim Skiles, Bob Ross, Red Schnepper, Lefty Conner, Chick Redshaw, John Swan, and Bob Phelps.

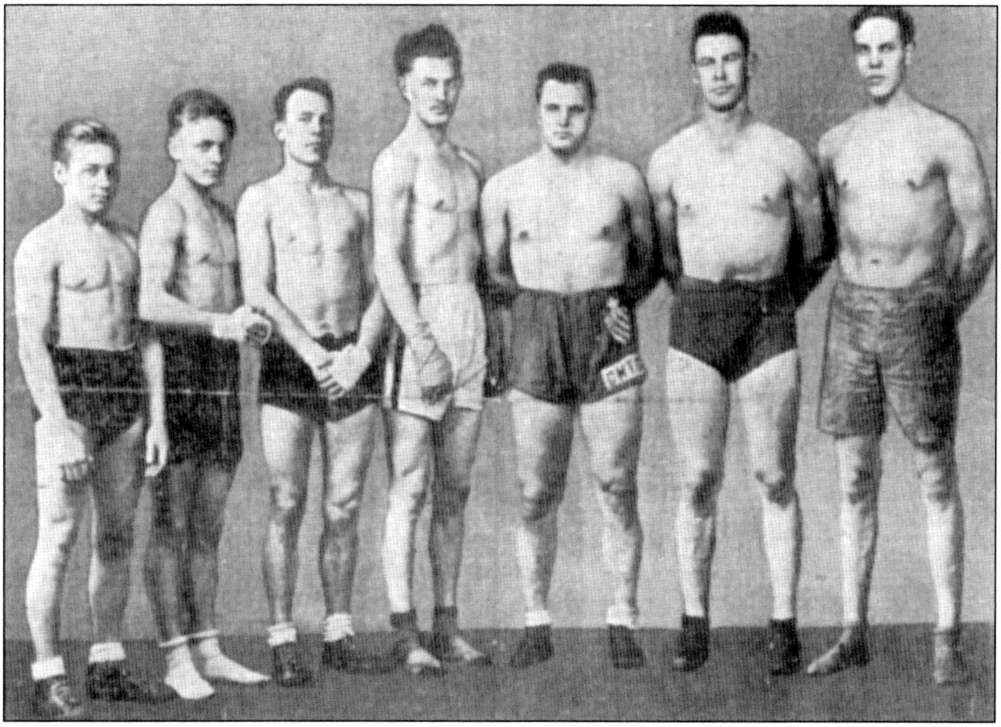

Here are some Beardstown Golden Gloves entrants from the 1950s. Pictured are, from left to right, Don Brewer, John Anderson, Verlin Perry, Clarence "Ki" Hacker, Dalton Stocker, Charles Dewitt, and John Conner.

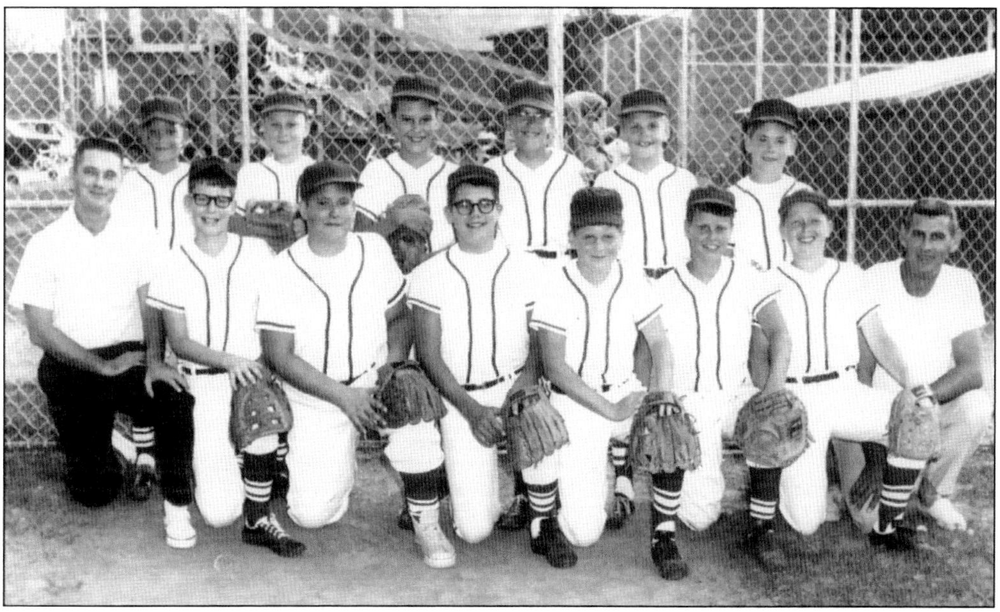

This is a Beardstown baseball team in the early 1970s. Pictured, from left right, are (first row) Tom Baer, Mike Mitchel, Greg David, Lew Korsmeyer, Ken Korsmeyer, and Doug Pilger; (second row) Lew Barker (coach), Joe Hyde, Steve Lovekamp, Scott Gillenwater, Scott Epping, Jim Offerdahl, Terry Mitchel, and Bob Gillenwater (coach).

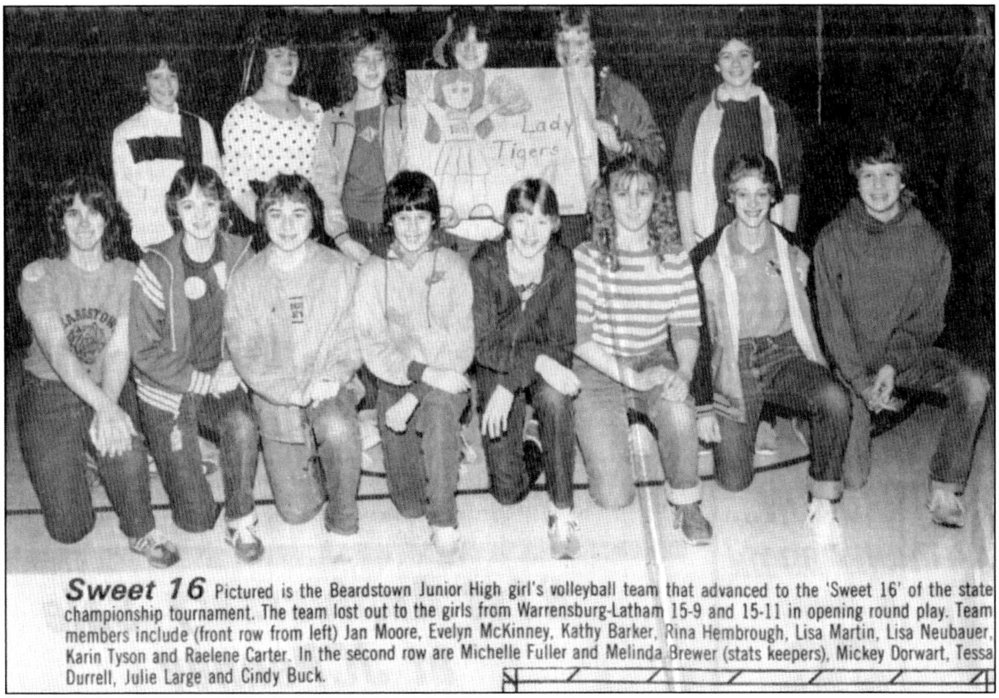

This Beardstown Junior High girls' volleyball team advanced to the "Sweet 16" of the state championship tournament. Pictured here are, from left to right, (first row) Jan Moore, Evelyn McKinney, Kathy Barker, Rina Hembrough, Lisa Martin, Lisa Neubauer, Karin Tyson, and Raelene Carter; (second row) Michelle Fuller, Melinda Brewer, Mickey Dorwart, Tessa Durrell, Julie Large, and Cindy Buck. This photograph was taken in 1983.

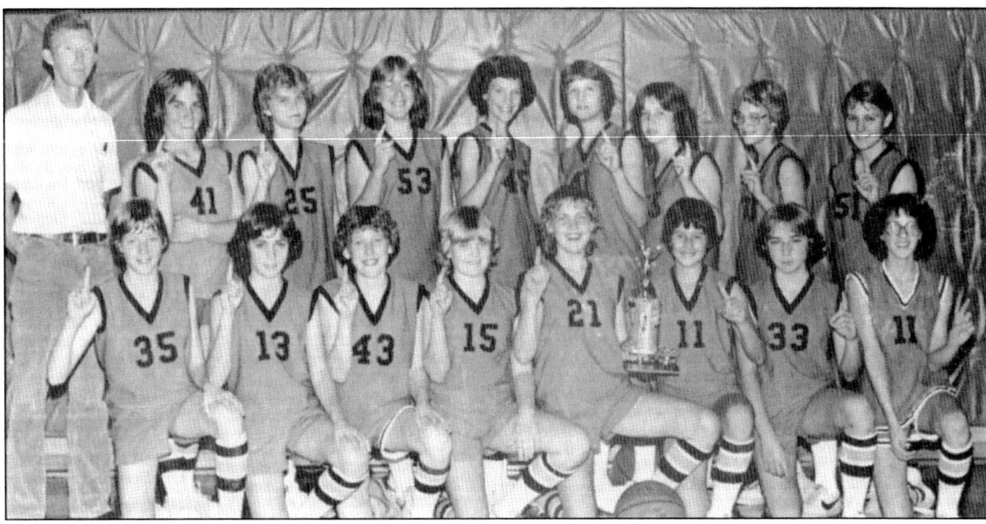

This Beardstown Junior High girls' basketball team became the first to win the "title of the North Grade girl's [*sic*] basketball tournament in Mt. Sterling," according to this newspaper clipping. Pictured here in 1983 are, from left to right, (first row) Lisa Martin, Denise Dyche, Kristy Pilger, Kristy Dick, Becky Maltby, Rina Hembrough, Kathy Barker, and Melissa Gragg; (second row) coach Larry Kight, Renee Jansen, Amy Hardwick, Brenda Self, Randi Crum, Raelene Carter, Angel Bell, Karin Tyson, and Lisa Neubaur.

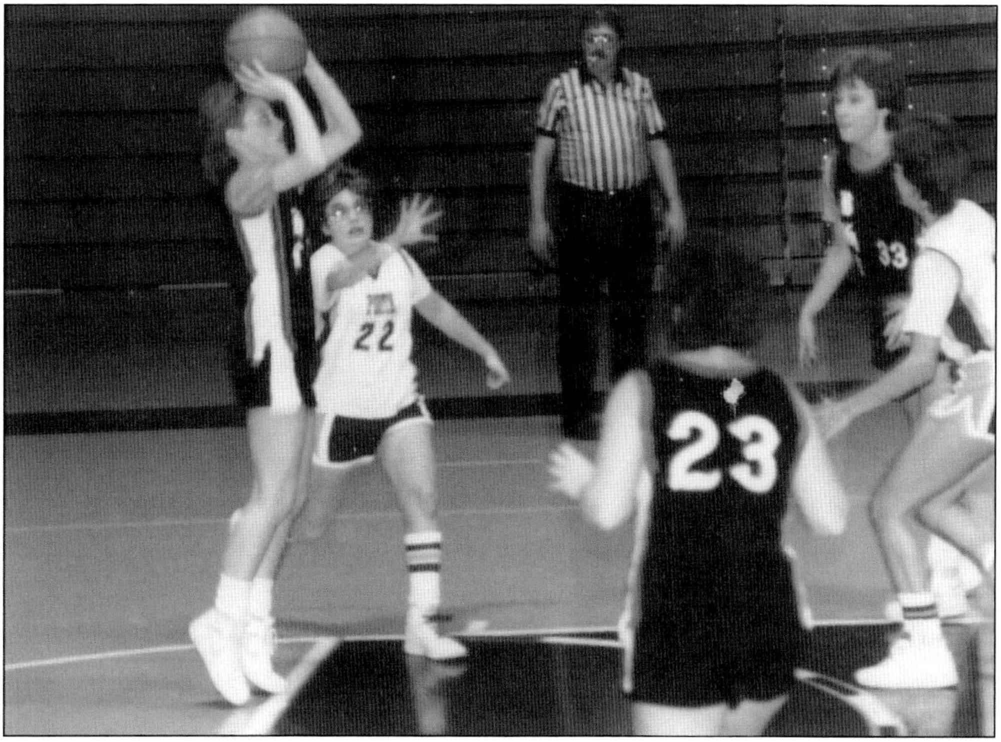

Karin Tyson is shown shooting the winning basket for the Beardstown High School Lady Tigers in 1985.

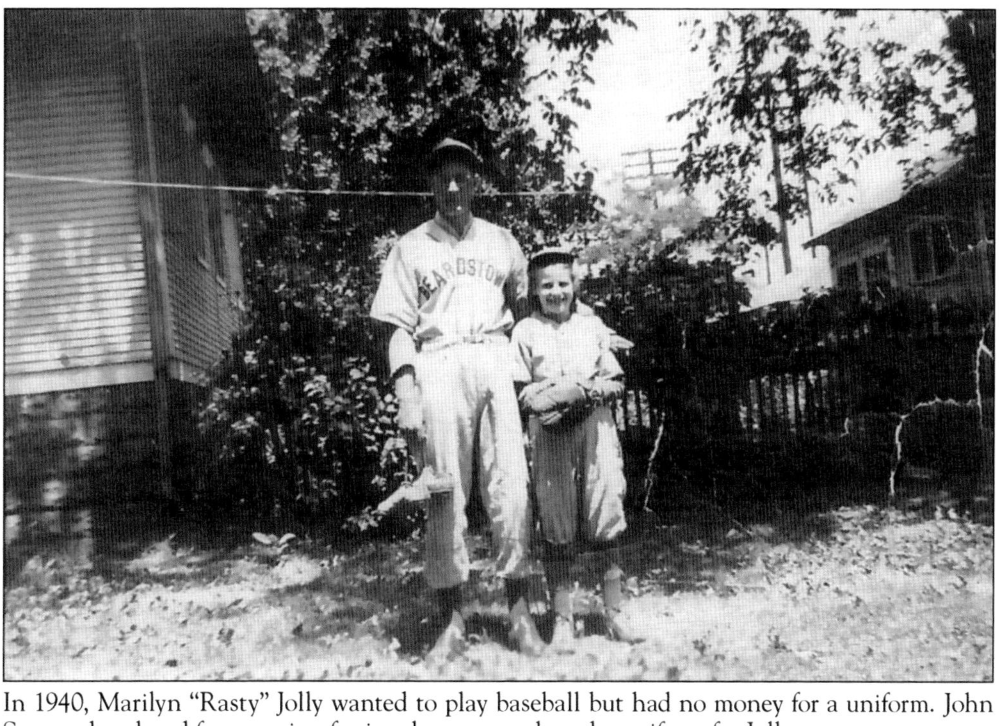

In 1940, Marilyn "Rasty" Jolly wanted to play baseball but had no money for a uniform. John Swan, who played for a semiprofessional team, purchased a uniform for Jolly.

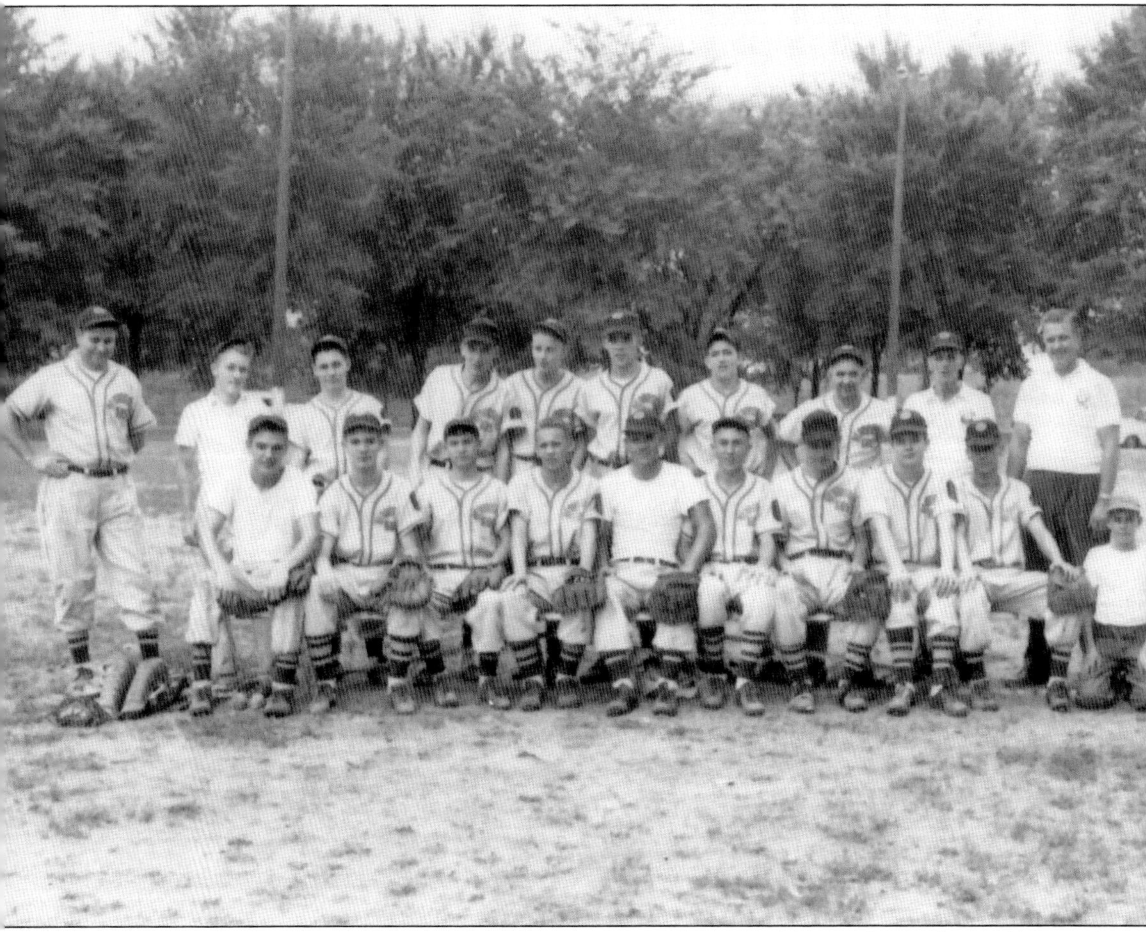

This is a Beardstown baseball team around 1951 or 1953. Pictured from left to right are (first row) Dick Bingham, Jerry Wedeking, Red Lewis, Bill Summey, Bill Ingle, Pete Wessel, Bill Moore, Larry Niemeyer, Mike Summey, and unidentified; (second row) Harold "Fuzzy" Spoon, Greg Sinnock, Larry Moore, Rich Summey, Tom Patterson, Dick Vancil, Don Huston, Marcus Houston, unidentified, and Bert Lerch.

Four

Parades and the Annual Free Fish Fry

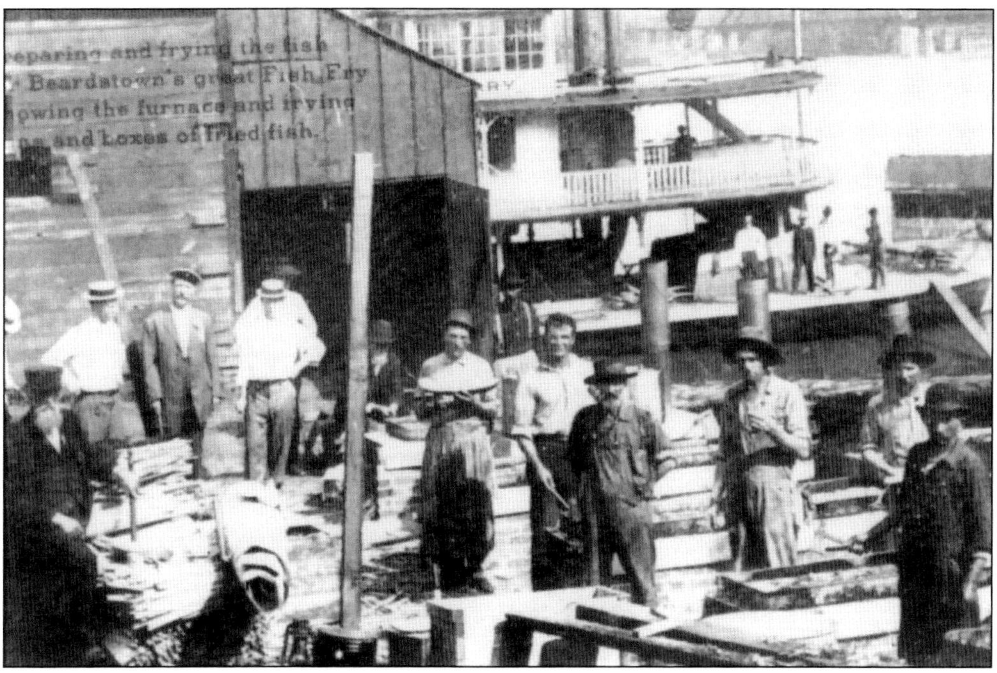

In this photograph taken at the end of Washington Street at the river, people are preparing and frying the fish for the annual Beardstown Free Fish Fry. The man in the black derby is John Swan; he was in charge of catching and frying the fish.

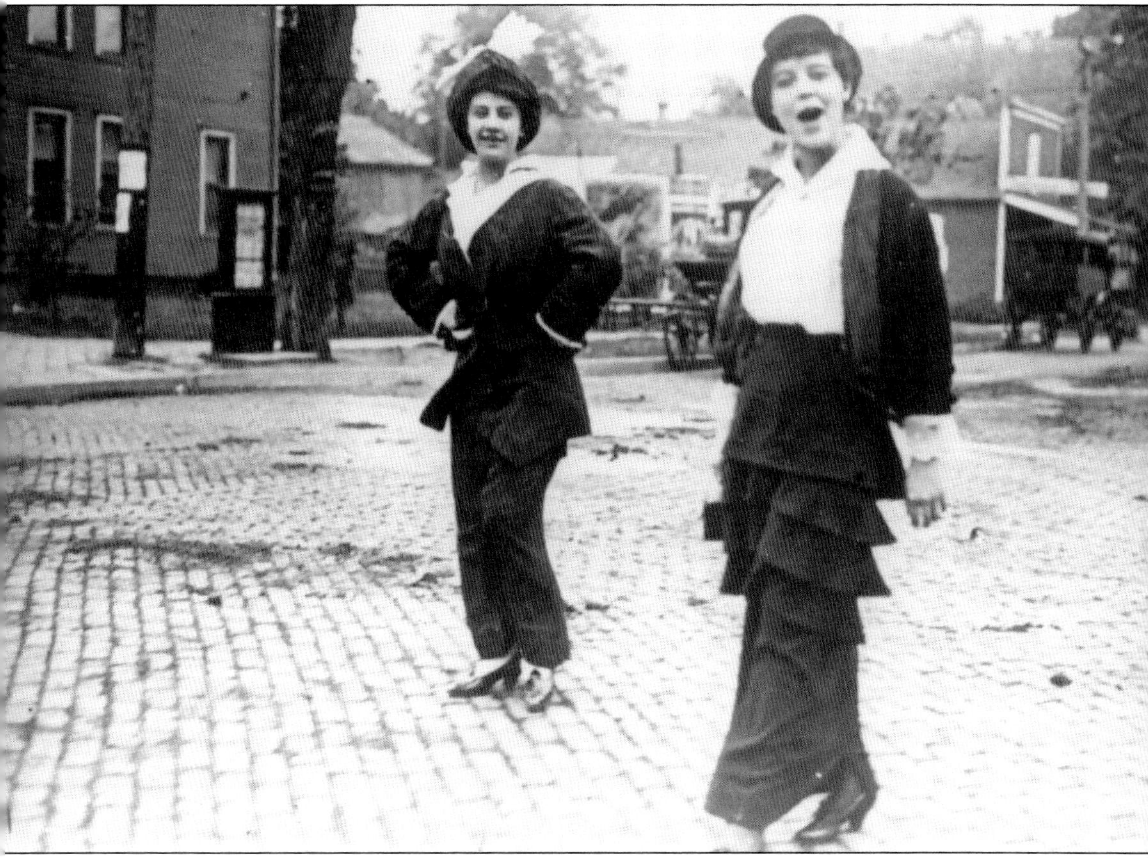

These ladies are part of the 1922 Fourth of July parade. The picture was taken at Second and Washington Streets.

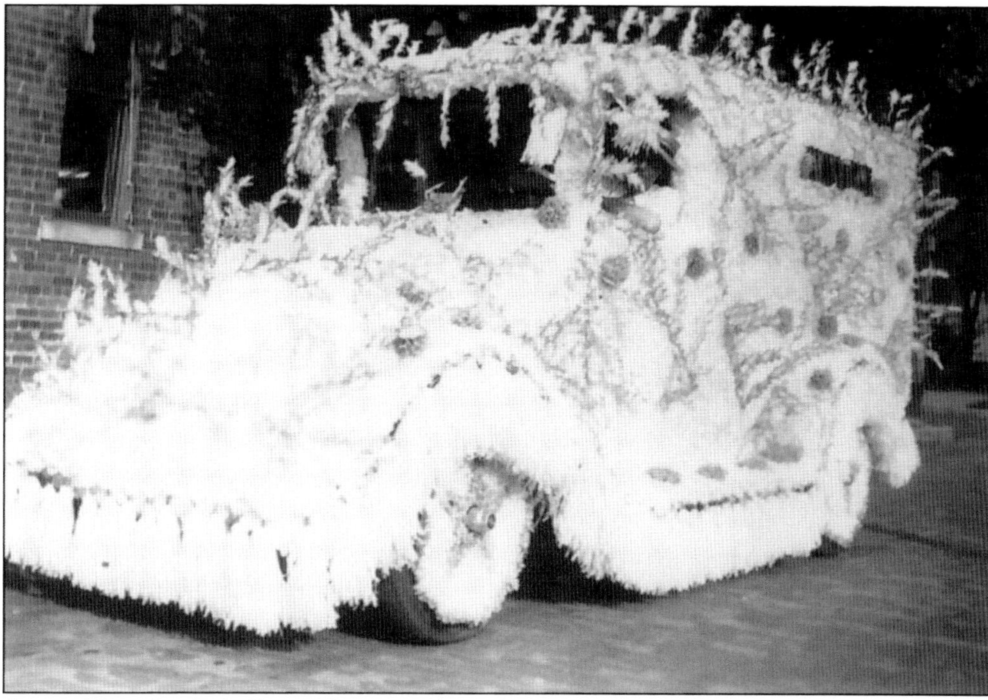

A grand Fourth of July float is shown in the early 1920s in downtown Beardstown.

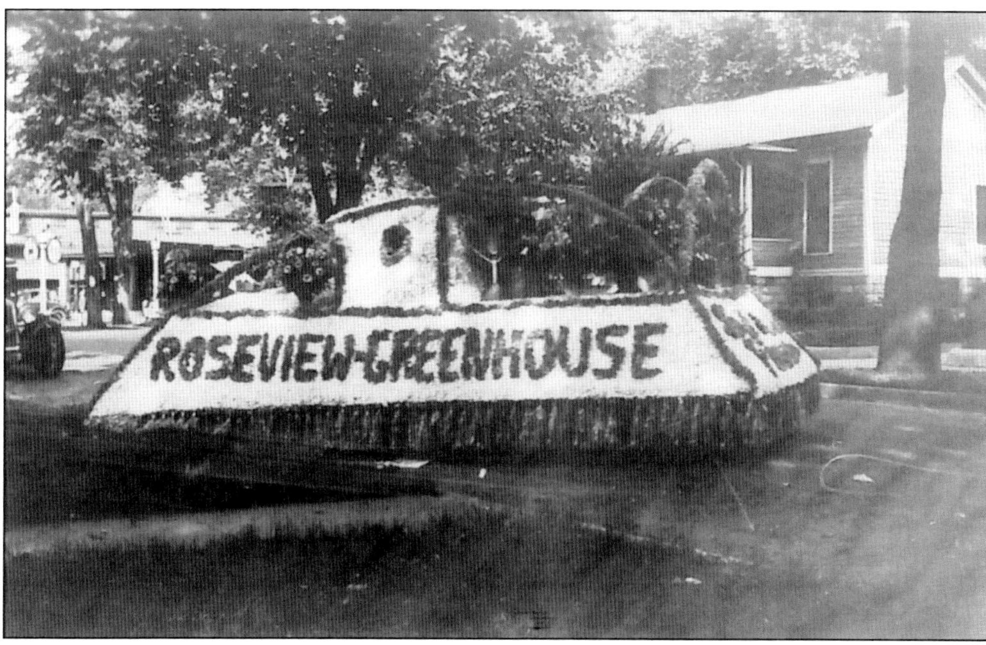

The Roseview Greenhouse float is shown in this photograph taken in 1923. The greenhouse was located at West Fifth and Adams Streets and owned by Carl, Ed, and Arvid Anderson.

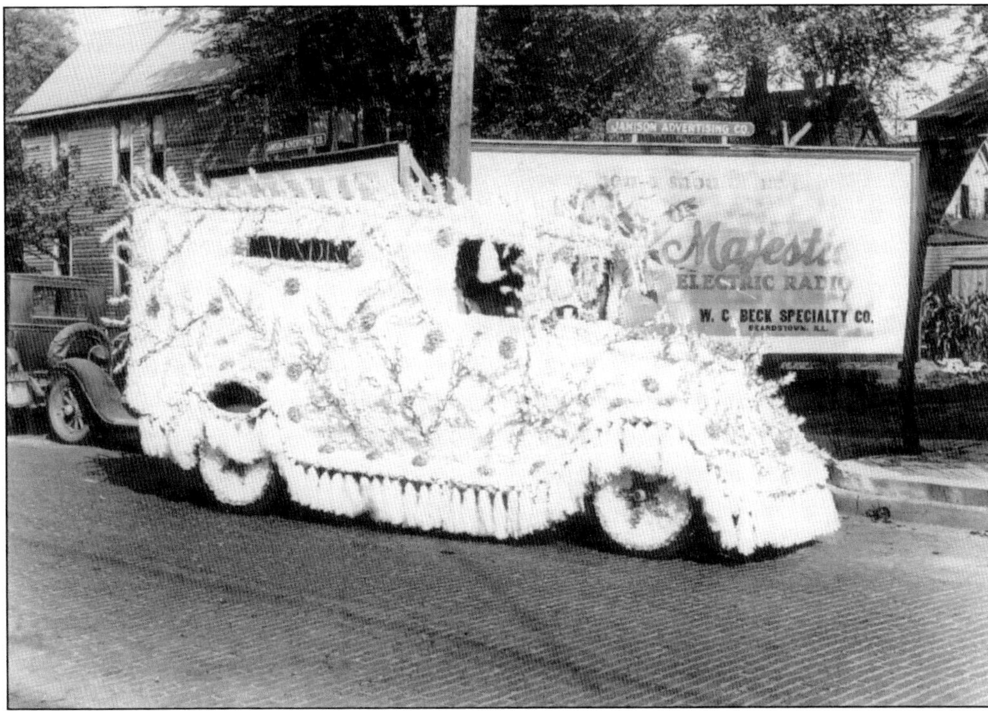

The Beardstown Steam Laundry delivery van was decorated for the Fourth of July parade.

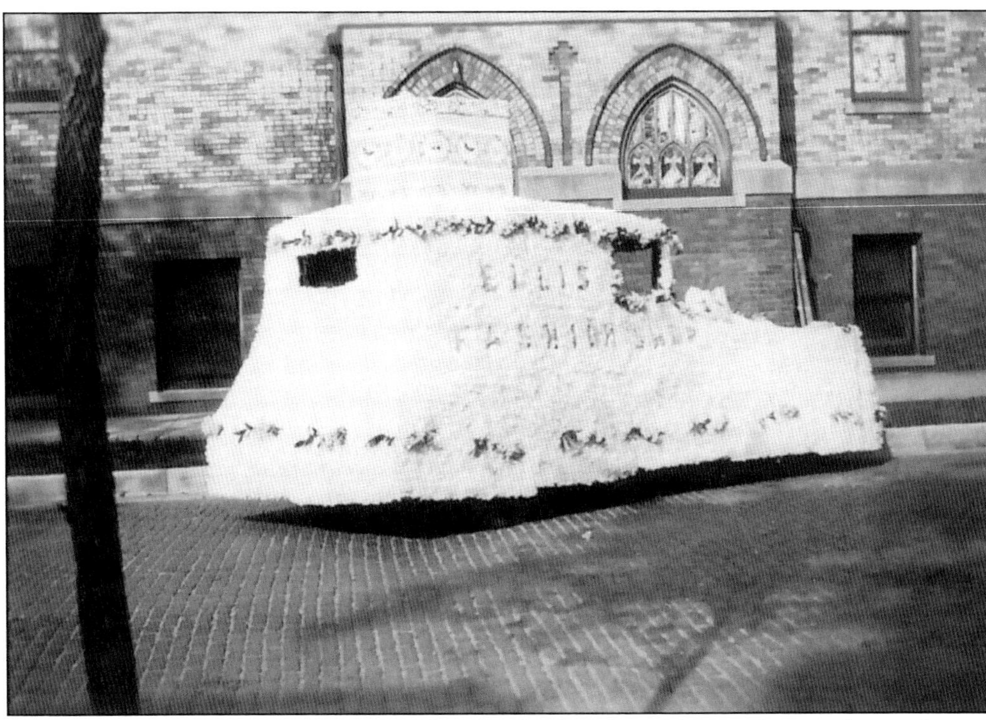

This photograph of Ellis Fashion Shop's float for the Fourth of July parade was taken in front of the Old Congregational Church at Third and Washington Streets.

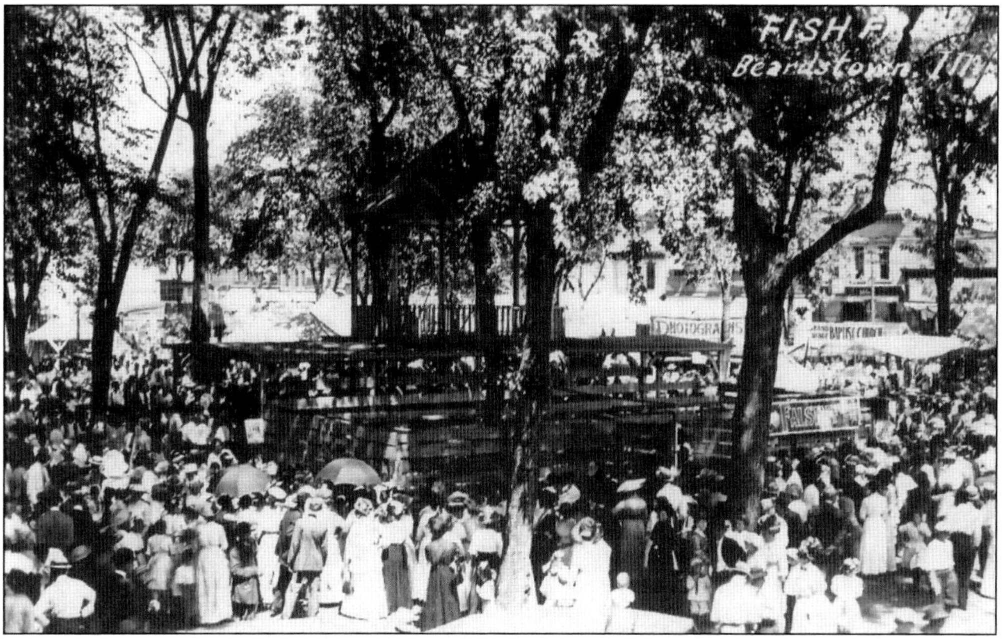

Here, one can see the large crowd gathered for the Beardstown Free Fish Fry in 1900. People had to walk through the long enclosure in the center to get their fish.

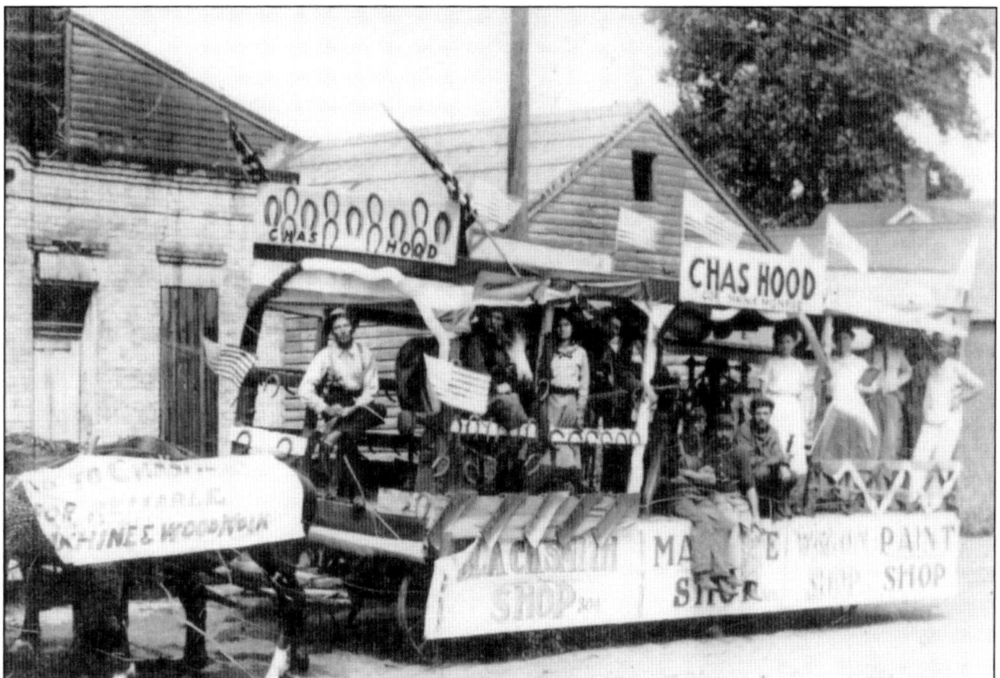

Charles Hood's entry in the Fourth of July parade is pictured here. His blacksmith shop was located on West Main Street where the Beardstown Bowling Alley was later located. The former bowling alley is now home to the Riverview Restaurant.

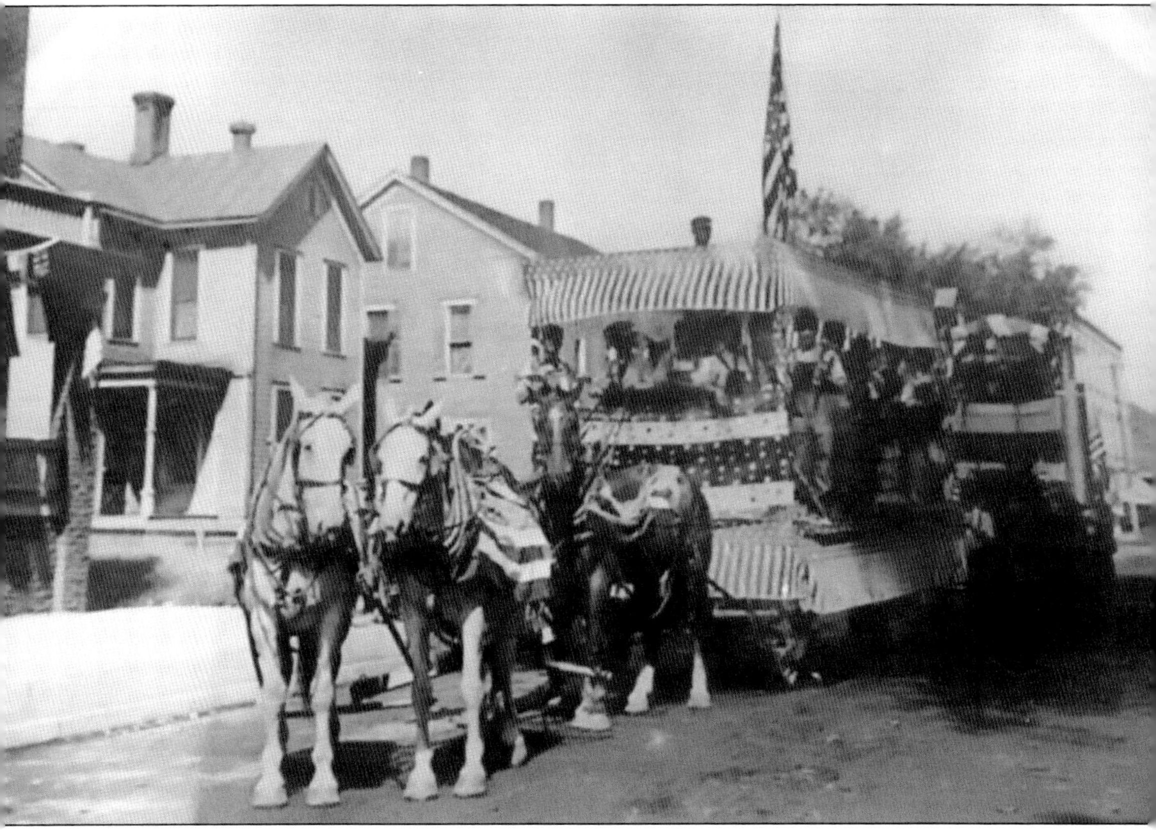

This picture was taken at the Fourth of July parade around 1910. The house at left with the porch is where Tyson's Barber Shop now stands at 212 Washington Street.

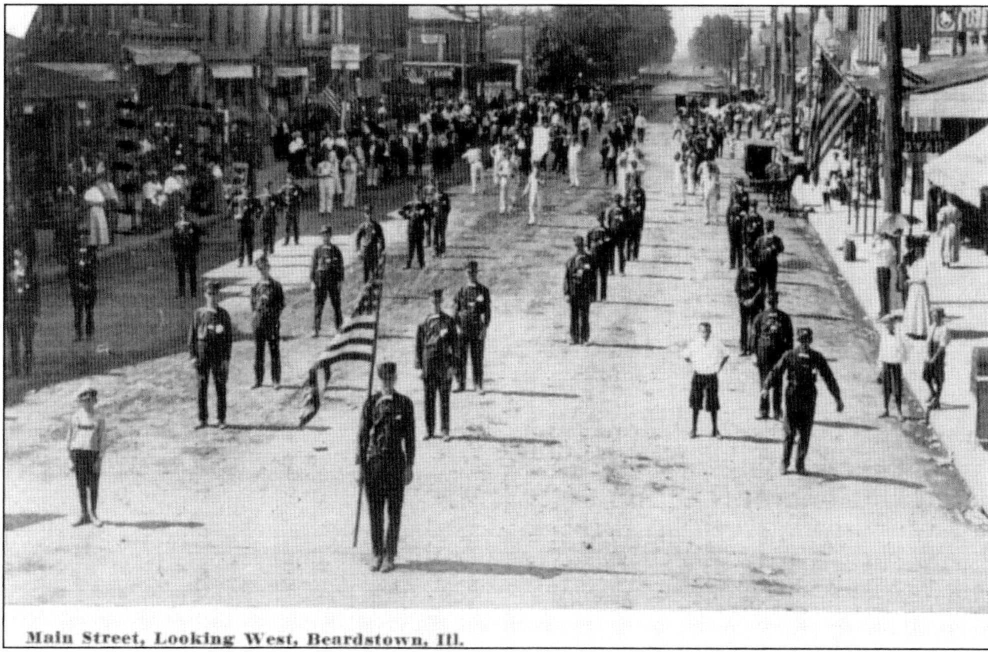

This Fourth of July parade took place in 1915. The parade was on Main Street at Washington.

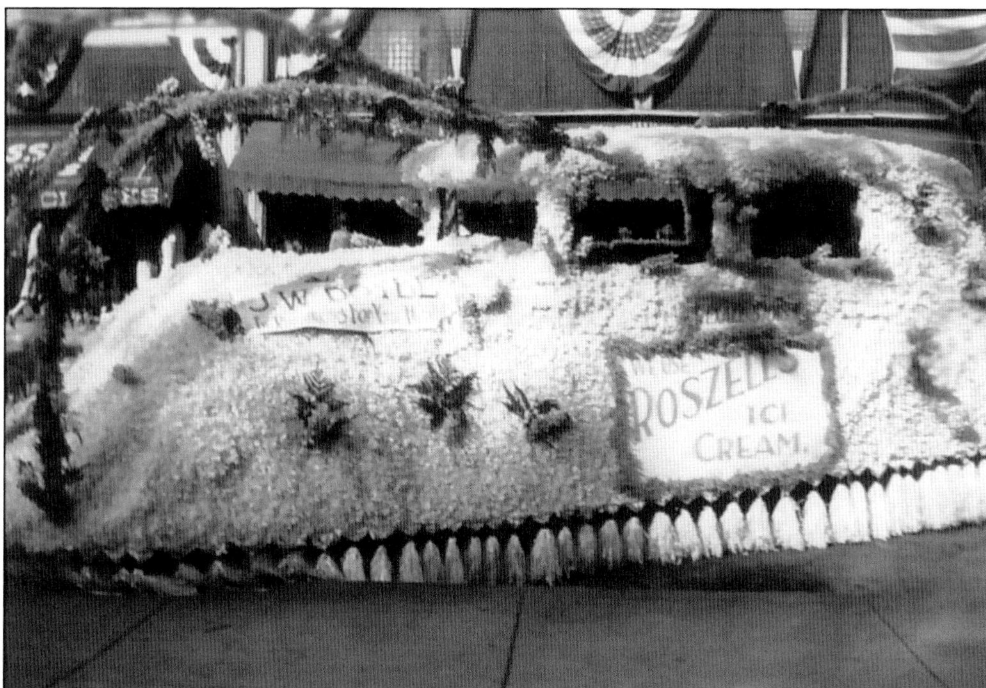

This J.W. Doyle Drug Store float was included in a Fourth of July parade. The store was located at 118 West Washington Street.

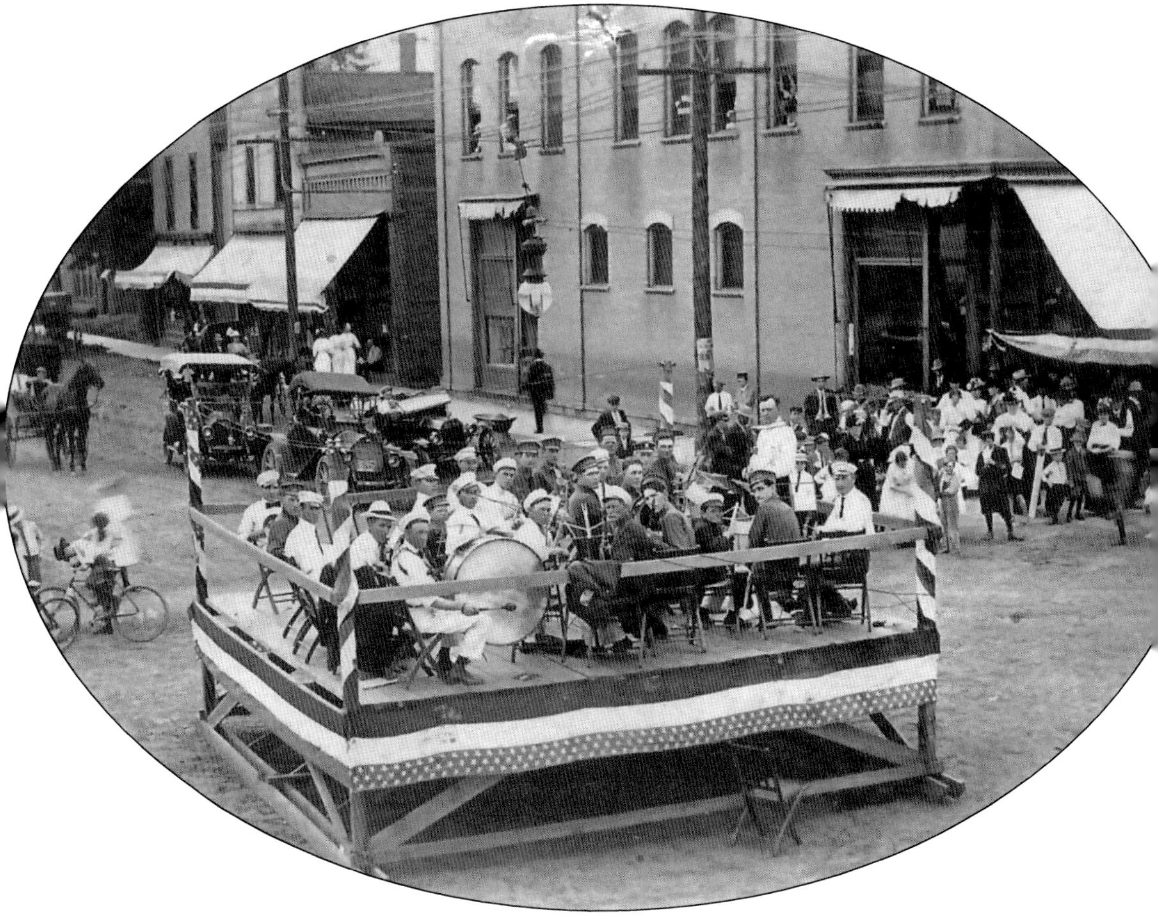

A band is playing for one of the early fish fries around 1900 at Second and State Streets.

Five

Hunting and Fishing

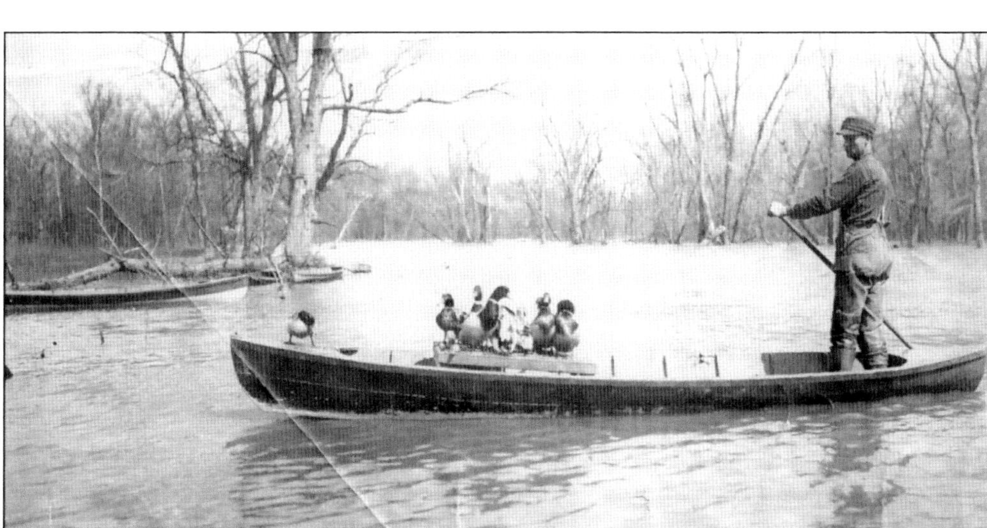

This duck hunter is using live decoys. The ducks have rings around their necks that are attached to a long string.

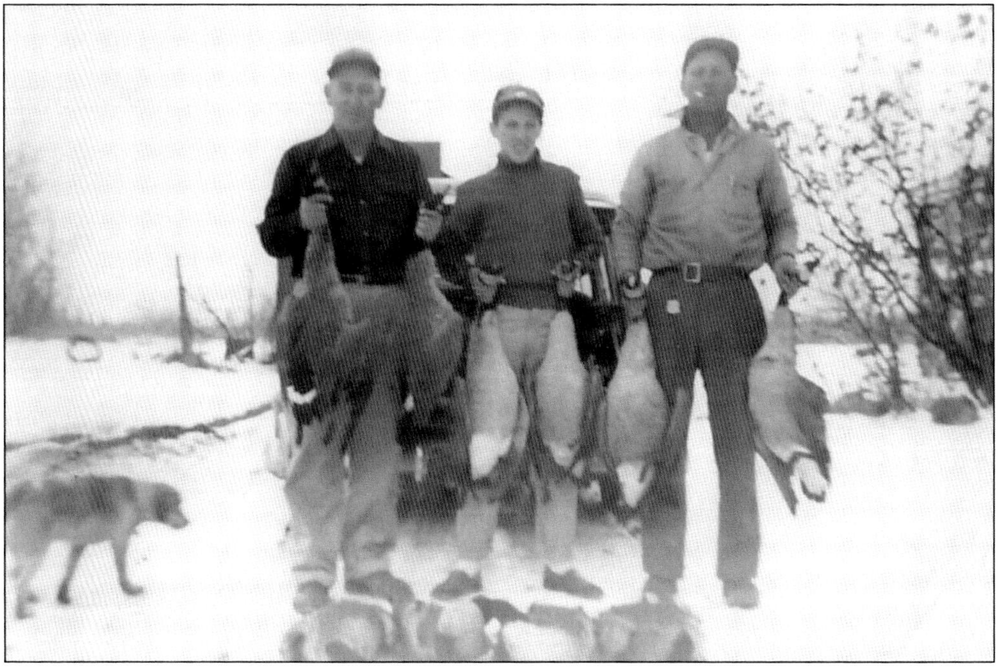

Louie (left), Doug (center), and Muddy Sherril are pictured here with their daily limit of geese. This picture was taken in December 1956.

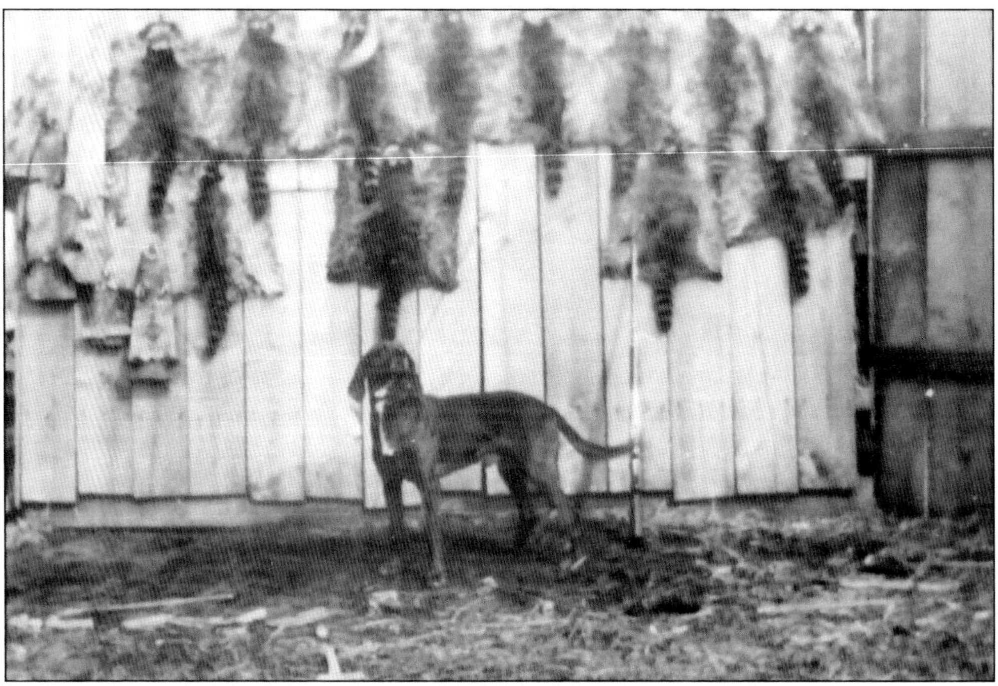

This is Frank Sommers's coon hound, Old Joe. In 1912, Sommers was offered $25 for the dog.

Muddy Sherril is shown with his limit of geese in 1956.

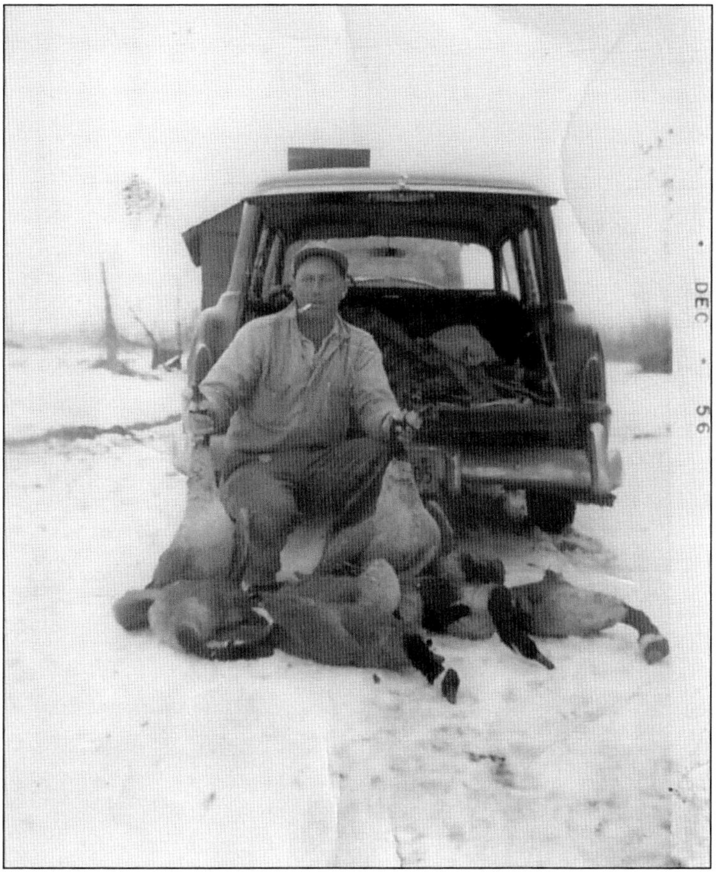

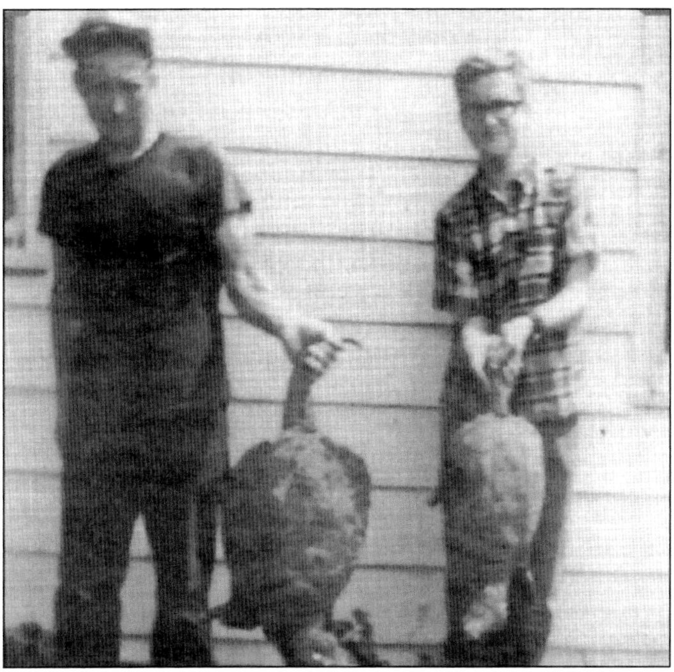

Beardstown resident Dick Krohe (left) and his son Jim are pictured with a pair of snapping turtles in this photograph taken around 1970.

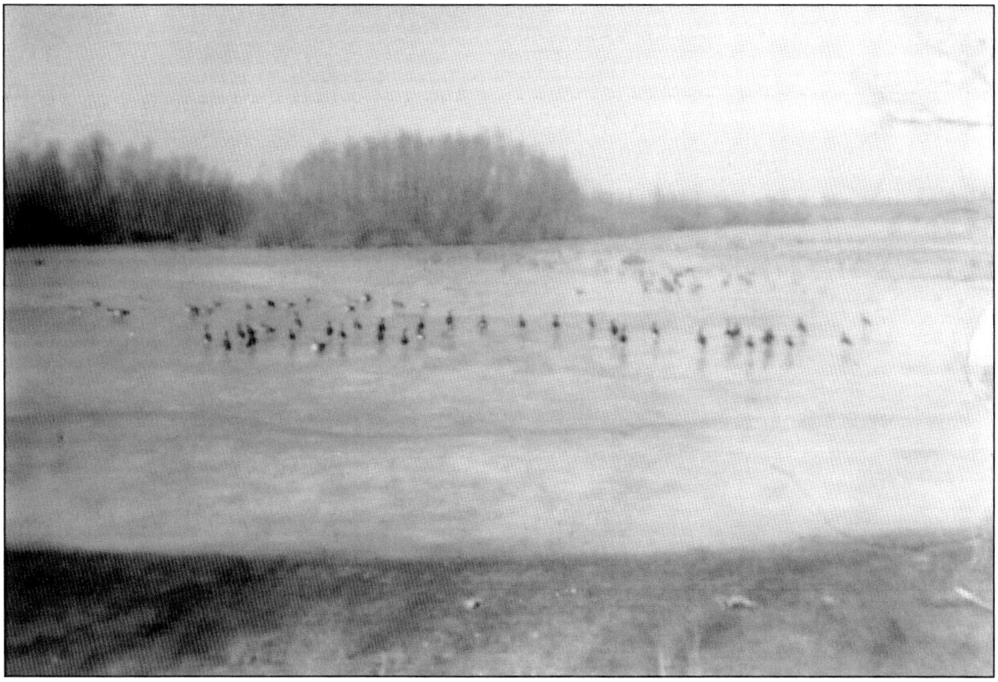

This is a 1956 picture of a flock of geese on a frozen Mascouten Bay.

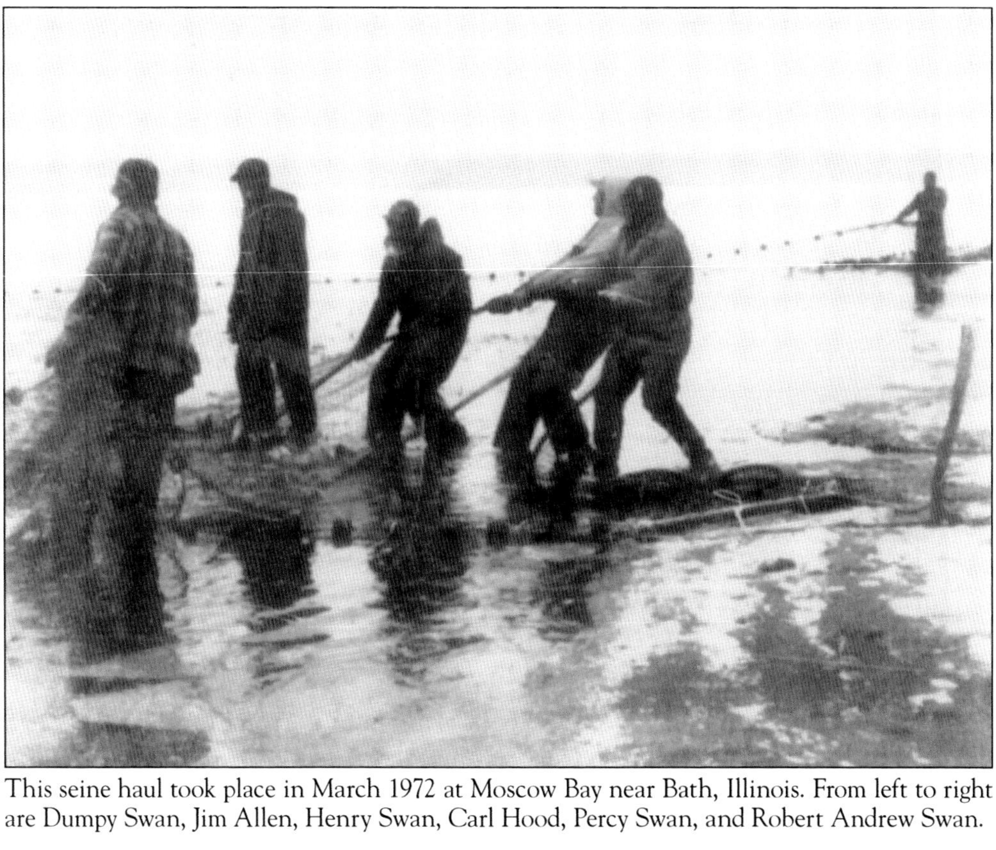

This seine haul took place in March 1972 at Moscow Bay near Bath, Illinois. From left to right are Dumpy Swan, Jim Allen, Henry Swan, Carl Hood, Percy Swan, and Robert Andrew Swan.

One of the Swan boys poses for this picture with enough fish for his family's supper.

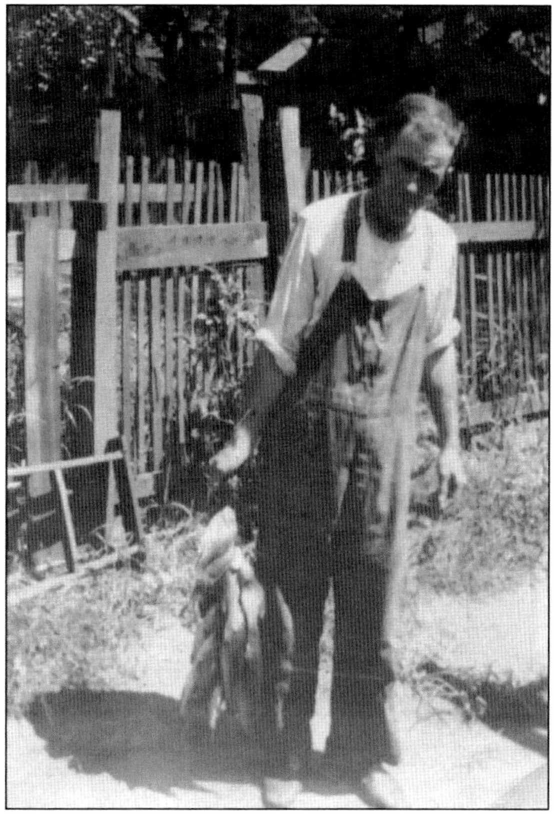

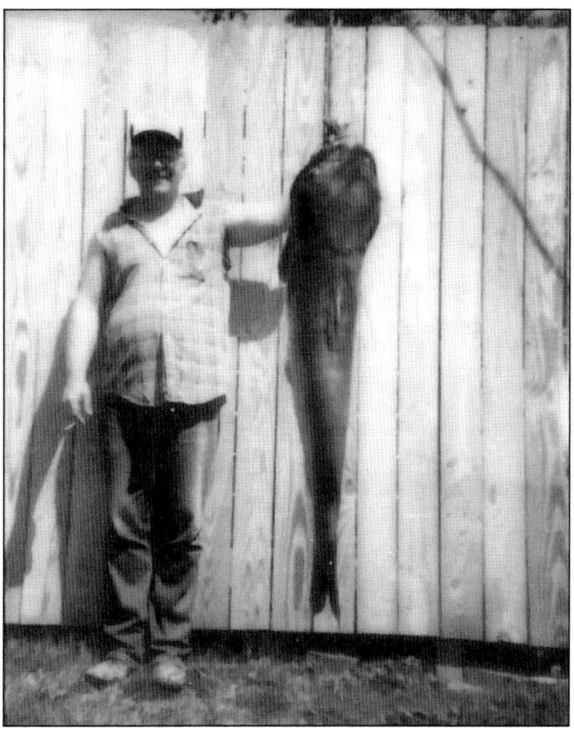

Ric Dawson is pictured with the 80-pound catfish he caught in 1996. He caught the fish on a pole with a 10-pound test line at the La Grange Locks. Dawson was in a small flatboat. A couple of old-timers came to his aid with a net. Needless to say, there was a big fish fry in the neighborhood that night! (Author's note: Every time this story gets told, the fish gets bigger!)

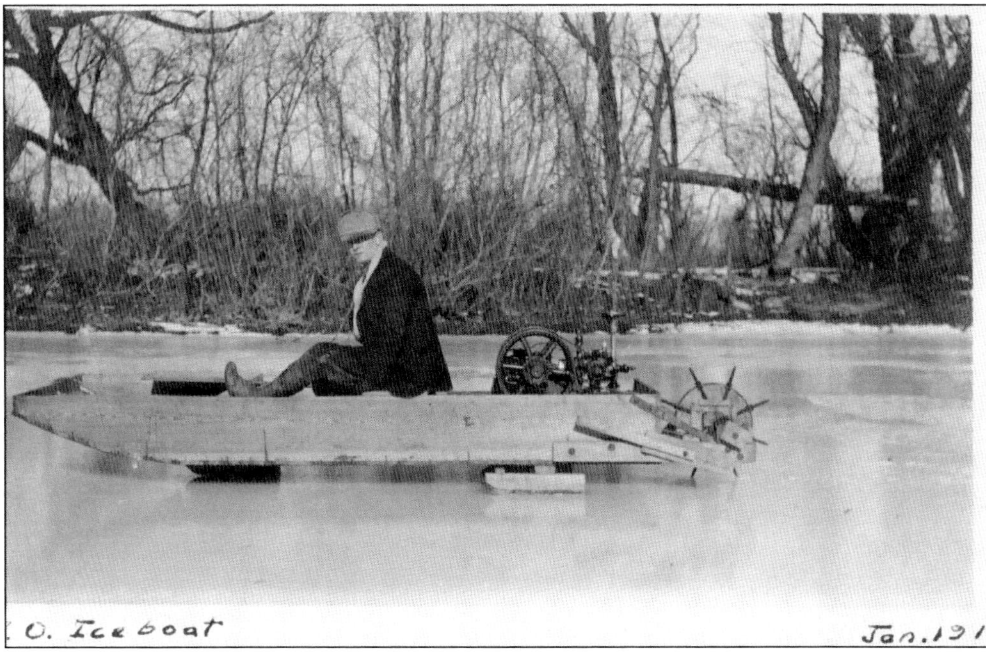

This January 1913 photograph features a man sitting in an iceboat used for duck hunting. Note the motor and the paddle that has cleats that grabbed the ice.

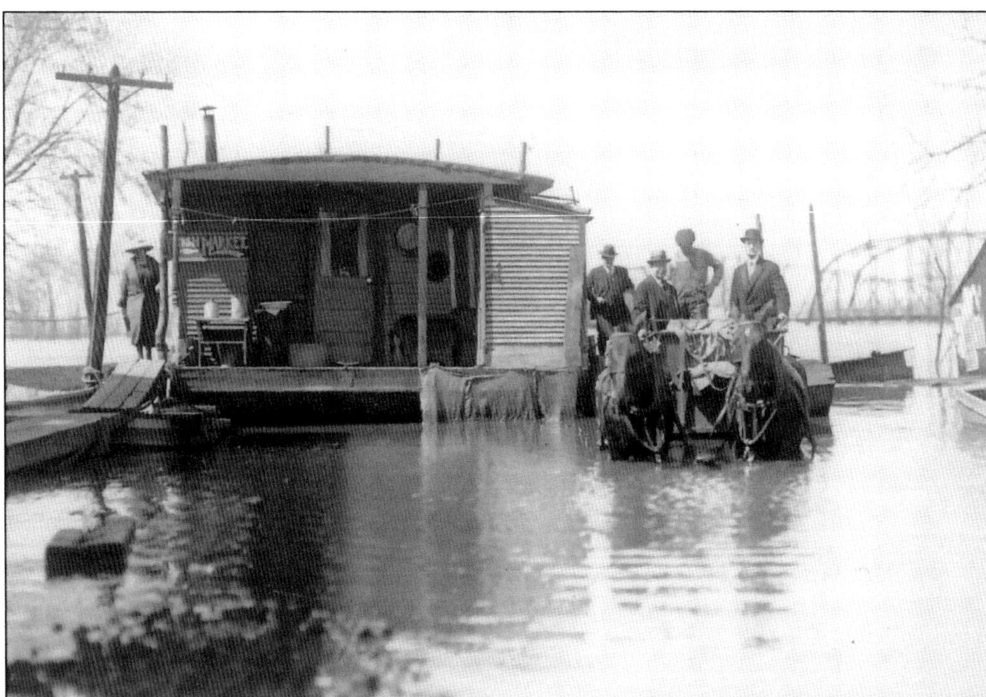

This horse and cart crew was delivering ice to the fish market at the end of Adams or Jackson Street.

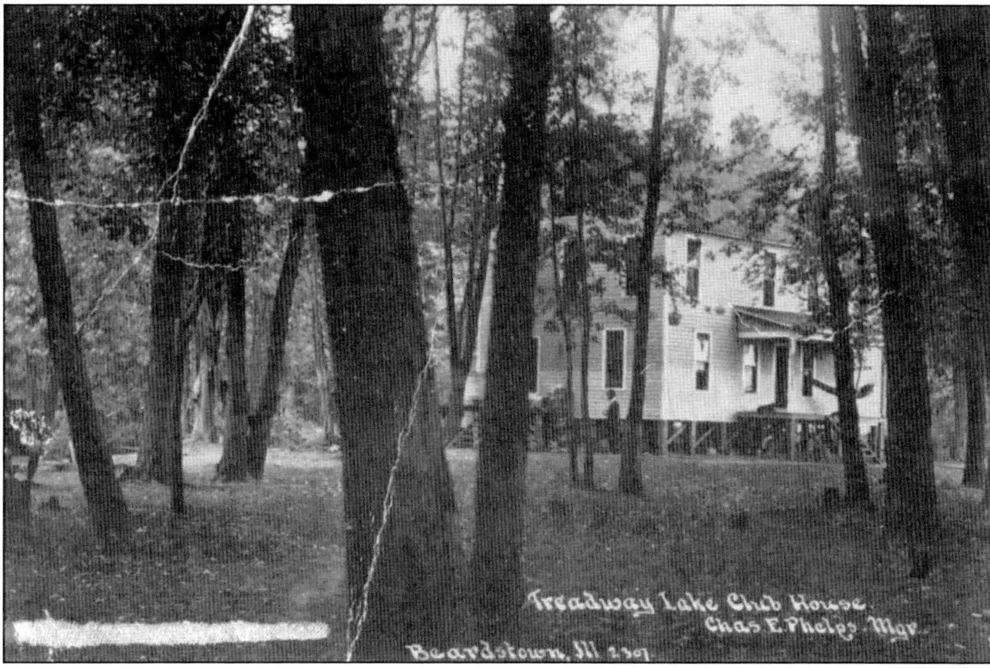

This postcard shows the Treadway Lake Duck Hunting Club House. Charles Phelps was the manager.

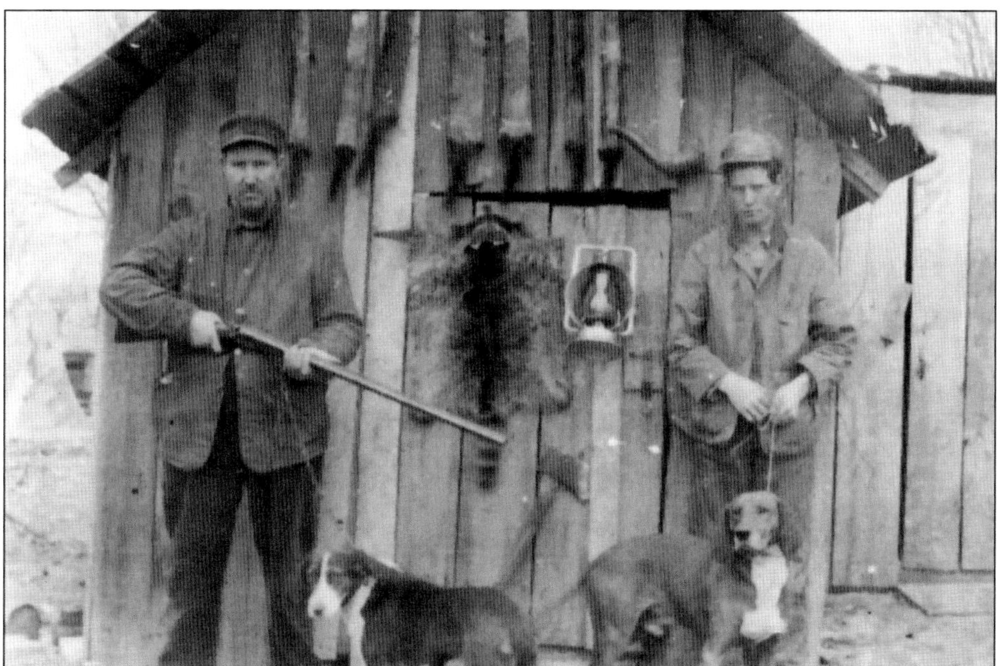
Frank Sommers (left) is pictured with his son Lloyd. Note the tanned coonskin and the mink pelts behind them. The horn on the wall was used to call in the dogs.

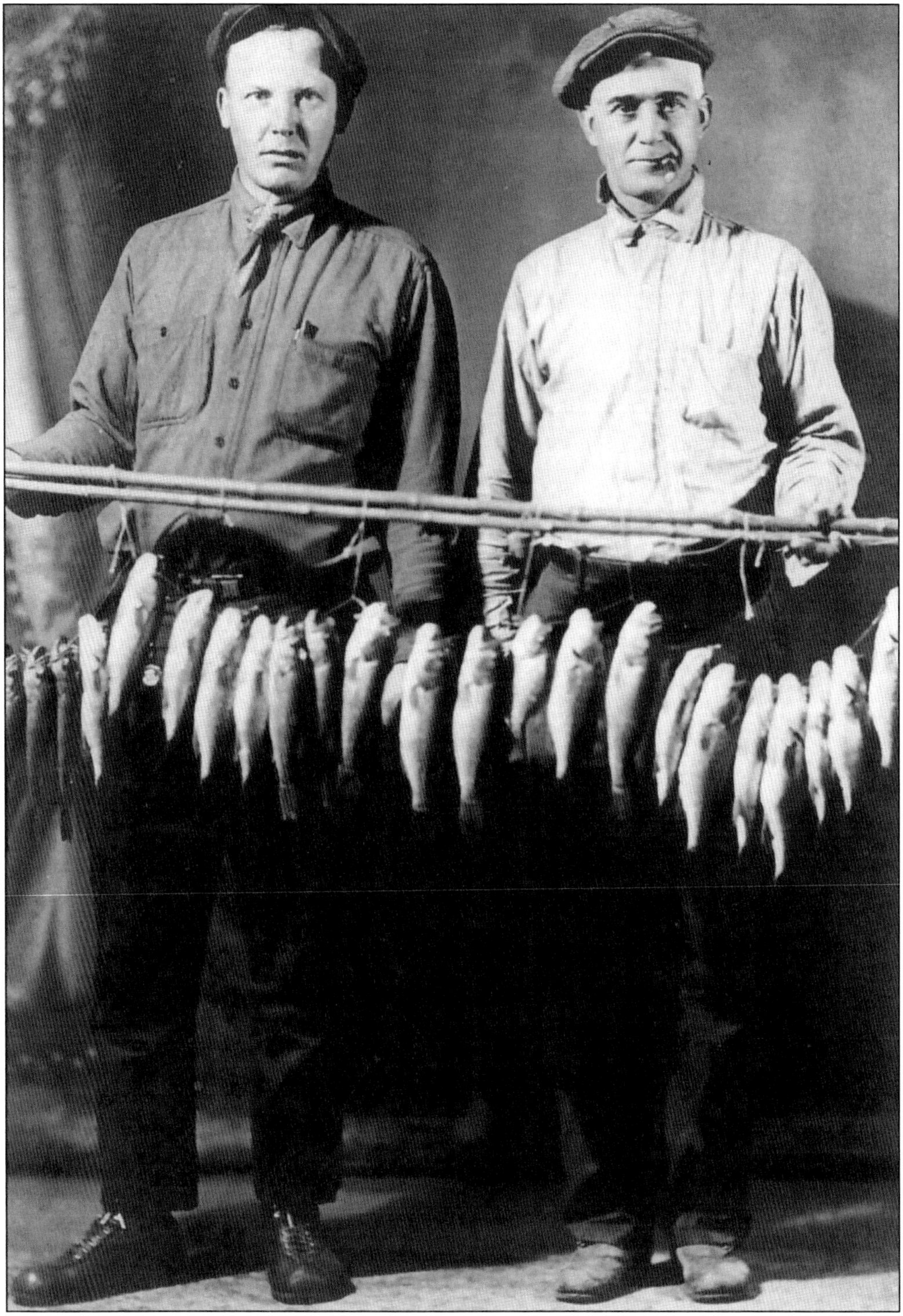

Showing off a good day's catch are Charles Hood (left), who worked at the Hood Blacksmith and Repair Shop, and Nick Leocis, who ran the Sugar Bowl ice-cream and candy shop.

Six

ADVERTISING

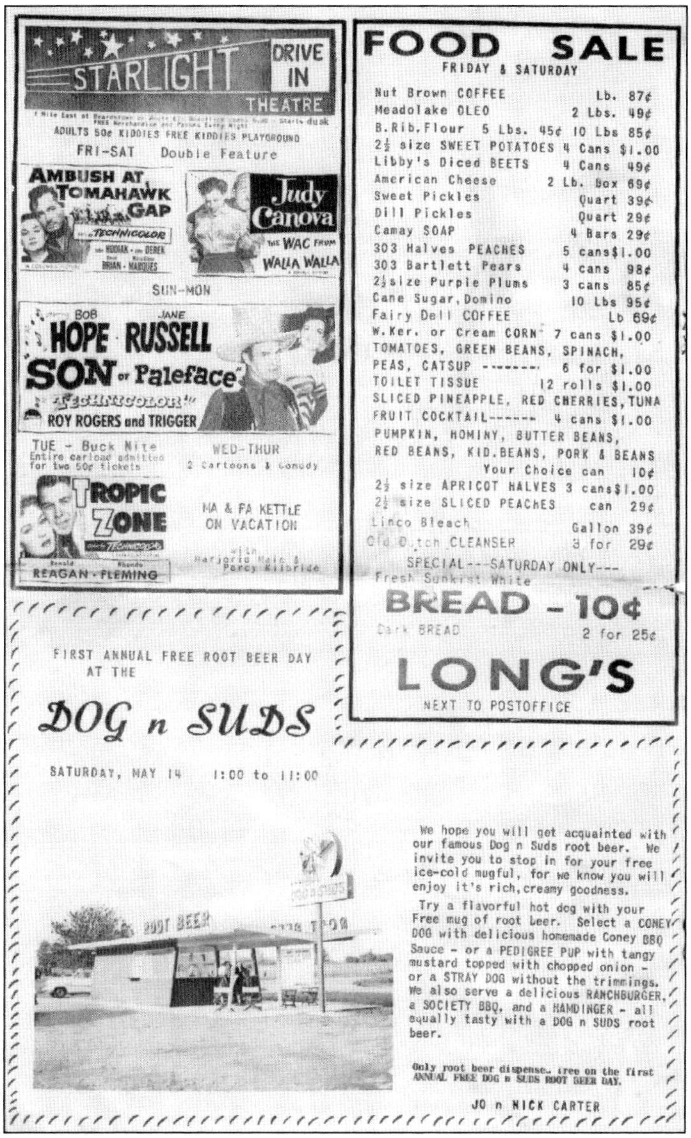
STARLIGHT DRIVE IN THEATRE

ADULTS 50¢ KIDDIES FREE KIDDIES PLAYGROUND

FRI-SAT Double Feature

AMBUSH AT TOMAHAWK GAP

TECHNICOLOR

HODIAK · DEREK

BRIAN · MARQUES

Judy Canova

THE WAC FROM WALLA WALLA

SUN-MON

BOB HOPE · JANE RUSSELL

"SON OF Paleface"

TECHNICOLOR

ROY ROGERS and TRIGGER

TUE - Buck Nite
Entire carload admitted
for two 50¢ tickets

TROPIC ZONE

TECHNICOLOR

Ronald REAGAN · Rhonda FLEMING

WED-THUR
2 Cartoons & Comedy

MA & PA KETTLE
ON VACATION
with
Marjorie Main &
Percy Kilbride

FOOD SALE
FRIDAY & SATURDAY

Nut Brown COFFEE	Lb. 87¢
Meadolake OLEO	2 Lbs. 49¢
B.Rib.Flour 5 Lbs. 45¢	10 Lbs 85¢
2½ size SWEET POTATOES	4 Cans $1.00
Libby's Diced BEETS	4 Cans 49¢
American Cheese	2 Lb. Box 69¢
Sweet Pickles	Quart 39¢
Dill Pickles	Quart 29¢
Camay SOAP	4 Bars 29¢
303 Halves PEACHES	5 cans $1.00
303 Bartlett Pears	4 cans 98¢
2½ size Purple Plums	3 cans 85¢
Cane Sugar, Domino	10 Lbs 95¢
Fairy Dell COFFEE	Lb 69¢
W.Ker. or Cream CORN	7 cans $1.00
TOMATOES, GREEN BEANS, SPINACH, PEAS, CATSUP	6 for $1.00
TOILET TISSUE	12 rolls $1.00
SLICED PINEAPPLE, RED CHERRIES, TUNA FRUIT COCKTAIL	4 cans $1.00
PUMPKIN, HOMINY, BUTTER BEANS, RED BEANS, KID.BEANS, PORK & BEANS Your Choice	can 10¢
2½ size APRICOT HALVES	3 cans $1.00
2½ size SLICED PEACHES	can 29¢
Linco Bleach	Gallon 39¢
Old Dutch CLEANSER	3 for 29¢

SPECIAL---SATURDAY ONLY---
Fresh Sunkrist White
BREAD - 10¢
Dark BREAD 2 for 25¢

LONG'S
NEXT TO POSTOFFICE

FIRST ANNUAL FREE ROOT BEER DAY
AT THE

DOG n SUDS

SATURDAY, MAY 14 1:00 to 11:00

We hope you will get acquainted with our famous Dog n Suds root beer. We invite you to stop in for your free ice-cold mugful, for we know you will enjoy it's rich, creamy goodness.

Try a flavorful hot dog with your Free mug of root beer. Select a CONEY DOG with delicious homemade Coney BBQ Sauce - or a PEDIGREE PUP with tangy mustard topped with chopped onion - or a STRAY DOG without the trimmings. We also serve a delicious RANCHBURGER, a SOCIETY BBQ, and a HAMDINGER - all equally tasty with a DOG n SUDS root beer.

Only root beer dispense.. free on the first ANNUAL FREE DOG n SUDS ROOT BEER DAY.

JO n NICK CARTER

This page of advertising from the mid-1950s features the Starlight Drive-In Theater.

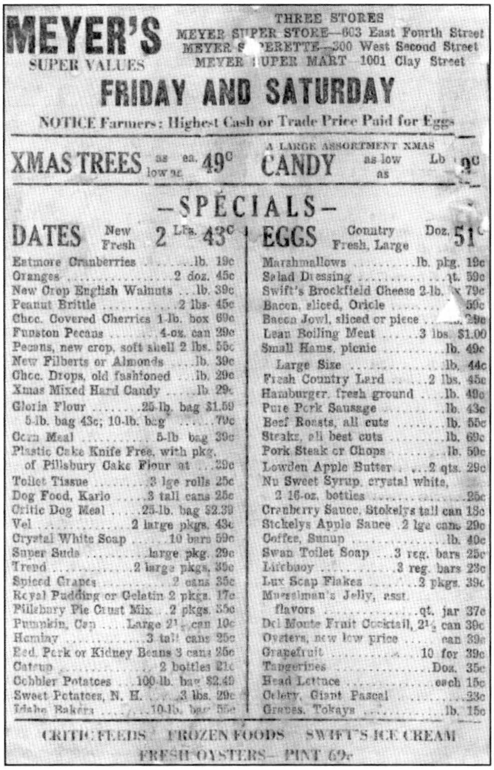

This is an early Meyer's Grocery Store advertisement.

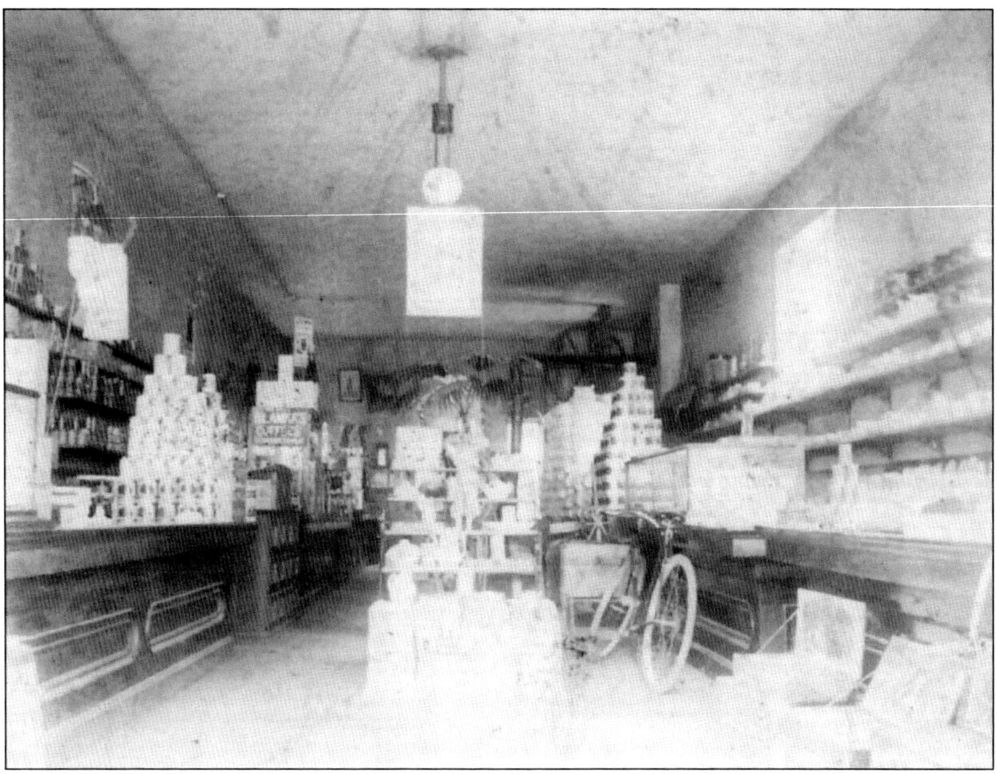

This picture was taken inside of Frey Hardware on East Main Street east of the post office.

These advertisements are for the Schmoldt Lumber Yard. A.E. Schmoldt had a sawmill near where the railroad bridge crosses the Illinois River. The Schmoldt lumberyard stood where the Vredenburg Lumber Co. is currently located on Fourth and Wall Streets.

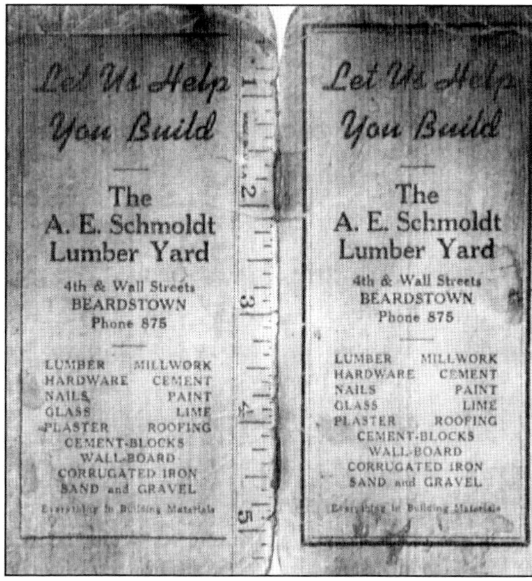

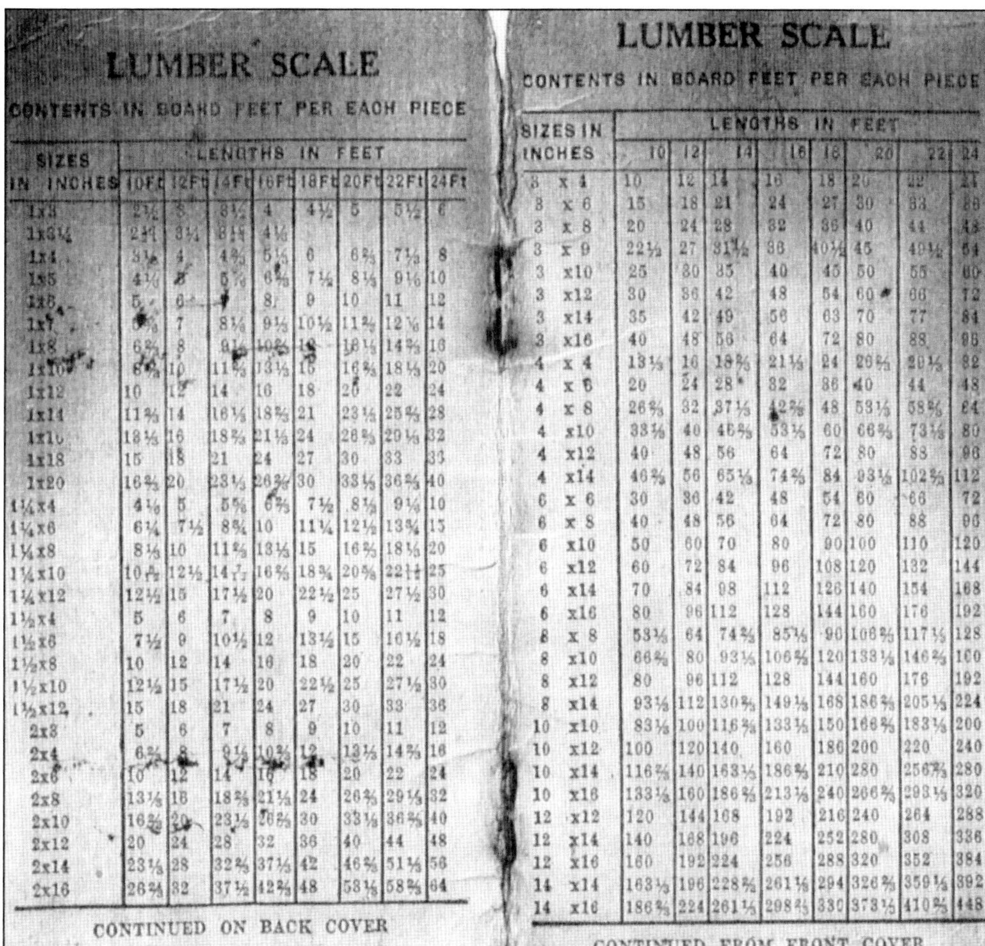

LUMBER SCALE

CONTENTS IN BOARD FEET PER EACH PIECE

SIZES IN INCHES	LENGTHS IN FEET 10Ft	12Ft	14Ft	16Ft	18Ft	20Ft	22Ft	24Ft
1x3	2½	3	3½	4	4½	5	5½	6
1x3¼	[illegible]	3¼	[illegible]	4⅓				
1x4	3⅓	4	4⅔	5⅓	6	6⅔	7⅓	8
1x5	4⅙	5	5⅚	6⅔	7½	8⅓	9⅙	10
1x6	5	6	[illegible]	8	9	10	11	12
1x7	5⅚	7	8⅙	9⅓	10½	11⅔	12⅚	14
1x8	6⅔	8	9⅓	10⅔	12	13⅓	14⅔	16
1x10	8⅓	10	11⅔	13⅓	15	16⅔	18⅓	20
1x12	10	12	14	16	18	20	22	24
1x14	11⅔	14	16⅓	18⅔	21	23⅓	25⅔	28
1x16	13⅓	16	18⅔	21⅓	24	26⅔	29⅓	32
1x18	15	18	21	24	27	30	33	36
1x20	16⅔	20	23⅓	26⅔	30	33⅓	36⅔	40
1¼x4	4⅙	5	5⅚	6⅔	7½	8⅓	9⅙	10
1¼x6	6¼	7½	8¾	10	11¼	12½	13¾	15
1¼x8	8⅓	10	11⅔	13⅓	15	16⅔	18⅓	20
1¼x10	10 5/12	12½	14 7/12	16⅔	18¾	20⅚	22 11/12	25
1¼x12	12½	15	17½	20	22½	25	27½	30
1½x4	5	6	7	8	9	10	11	12
1½x6	7½	9	10½	12	13½	15	16½	18
1½x8	10	12	14	16	18	20	22	24
1½x10	12½	15	17½	20	22½	25	27½	30
1½x12	15	18	21	24	27	30	33	36
2x3	5	6	7	8	9	10	11	12
2x4	6⅔	8	9⅓	10⅔	12	13⅓	14⅔	16
2x6	10	12	14	16	18	20	22	24
2x8	13⅓	16	18⅔	21⅓	24	26⅔	29⅓	32
2x10	16⅔	20	23⅓	26⅔	30	33⅓	36⅔	40
2x12	20	24	28	32	36	40	44	48
2x14	23⅓	28	32⅔	37⅓	42	46⅔	51⅓	56
2x16	26⅔	32	37⅓	42⅔	48	53⅓	58⅔	64

CONTINUED ON BACK COVER

LUMBER SCALE

CONTENTS IN BOARD FEET PER EACH PIECE

SIZES IN INCHES	LENGTHS IN FEET 10	12	14	16	18	20	22	24
3 x 4	10	12	14	16	18	20	22	24
3 x 6	15	18	21	24	27	30	33	36
3 x 8	20	24	28	32	36	40	44	48
3 x 9	22½	27	31½	36	40½	45	49½	54
3 x10	25	30	35	40	45	50	55	60
3 x12	30	36	42	48	54	60	66	72
3 x14	35	42	49	56	63	70	77	84
3 x16	40	48	56	64	72	80	88	96
4 x 4	13⅓	16	18⅔	21⅓	24	26⅔	29⅓	32
4 x 6	20	24	28	32	36	40	44	48
4 x 8	26⅔	32	37⅓	42⅔	48	53⅓	58⅔	64
4 x10	33⅓	40	46⅔	53⅓	60	66⅔	73⅓	80
4 x12	40	48	56	64	72	80	88	96
4 x14	46⅔	56	65⅓	74⅔	84	93⅓	102⅔	112
6 x 6	30	36	42	48	54	60	66	72
6 x 8	40	48	56	64	72	80	88	96
6 x10	50	60	70	80	90	100	110	120
6 x12	60	72	84	96	108	120	132	144
6 x14	70	84	98	112	126	140	154	168
6 x16	80	96	112	128	144	160	176	192
8 x 8	53⅓	64	74⅔	85⅓	96	106⅔	117⅓	128
8 x10	66⅔	80	93⅓	106⅔	120	133⅓	146⅔	160
8 x12	80	96	112	128	144	160	176	192
8 x14	93⅓	112	130⅔	149⅓	168	186⅔	205⅓	224
10 x10	83⅓	100	116⅔	133⅓	150	166⅔	183⅓	200
10 x12	100	120	140	160	186	200	220	240
10 x14	116⅔	140	163⅓	186⅔	210	280	256⅔	280
10 x16	133⅓	160	186⅔	213⅓	240	266⅔	293⅓	320
12 x12	120	144	168	192	216	240	264	288
12 x14	140	168	196	224	252	280	308	336
12 x16	160	192	224	256	288	320	352	384
14 x14	163⅓	196	228⅔	261⅓	294	326⅔	359⅓	392
14 x16	186⅔	224	261⅓	298⅔	330	373⅓	410⅔	448

CONTINUED FROM FRONT COVER

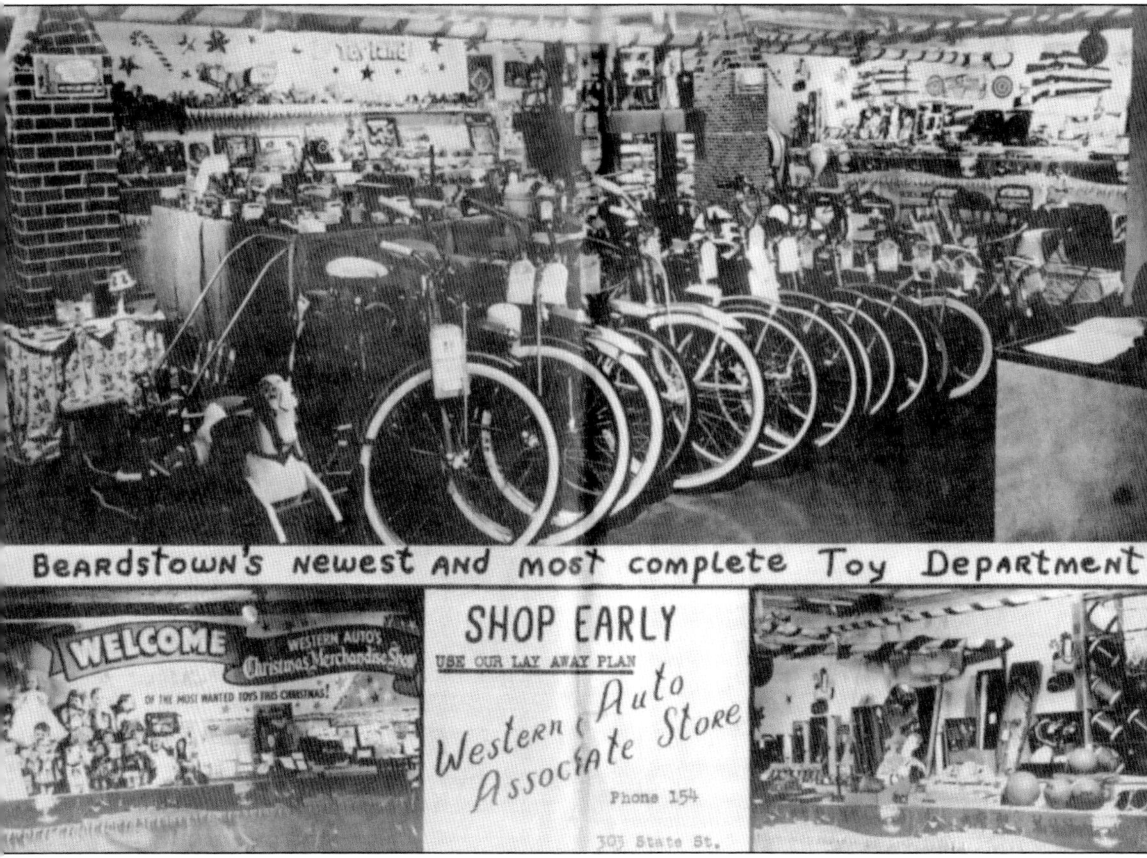

Pictured here is the Christmas display at the Western Auto store. The store was owned and managed by Charlie Soer and was located at 303 State Street, where the Beardstown Savings Bank now stands.

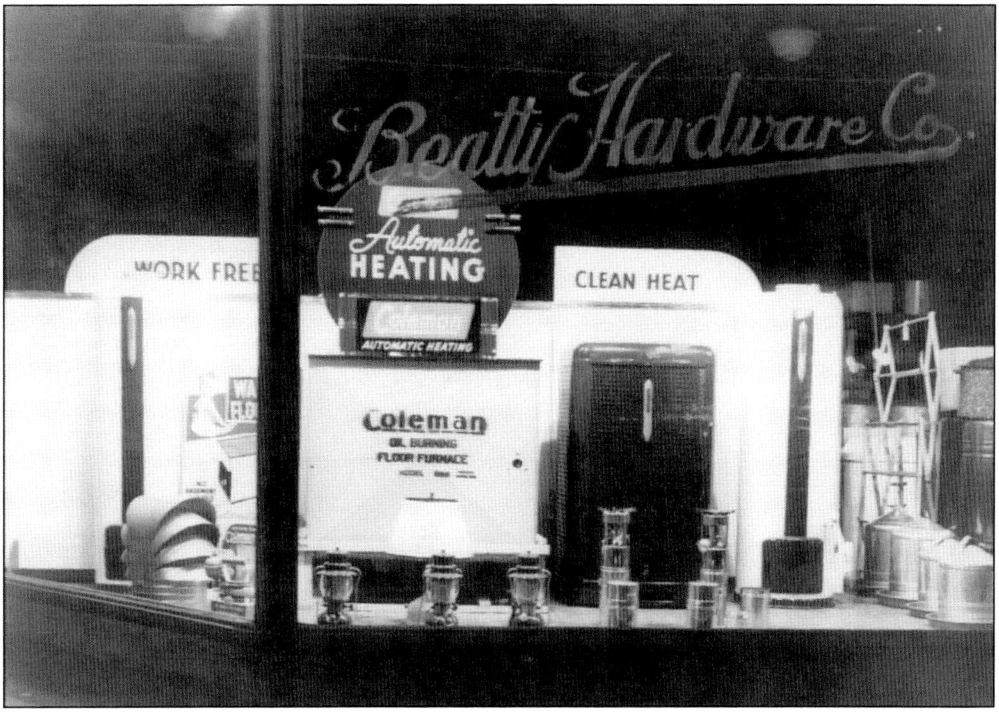

This front-window display at Beatty Hardware Company features Coleman Heating. The building was located at Main and Washington Streets on the river side.

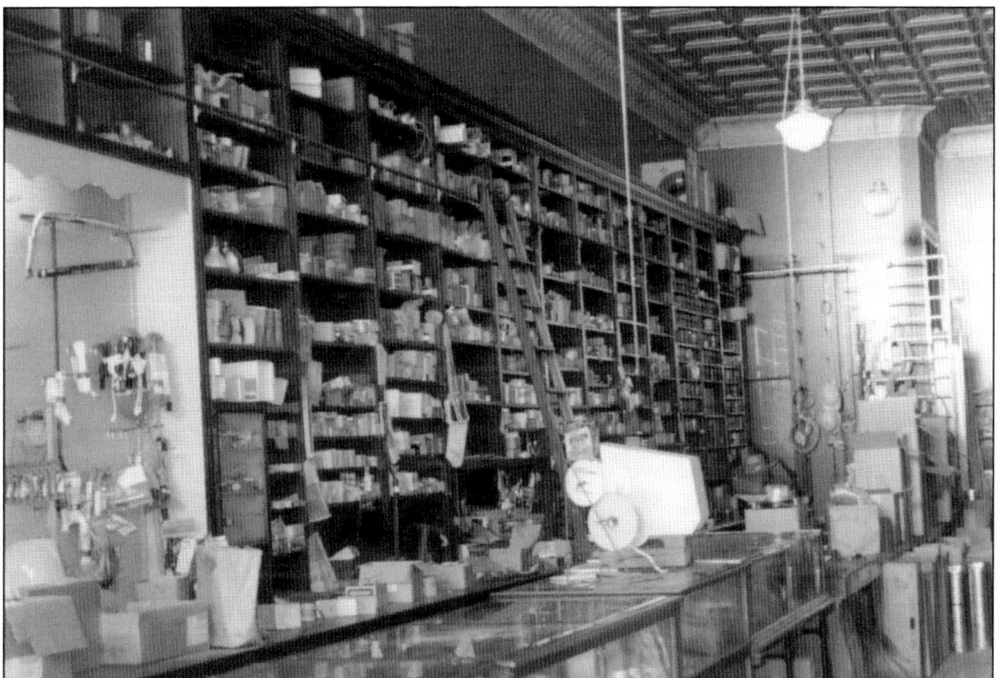

This image shows the west wall of Beatty Hardware. Owner John Beatty knew what was on every shelf!

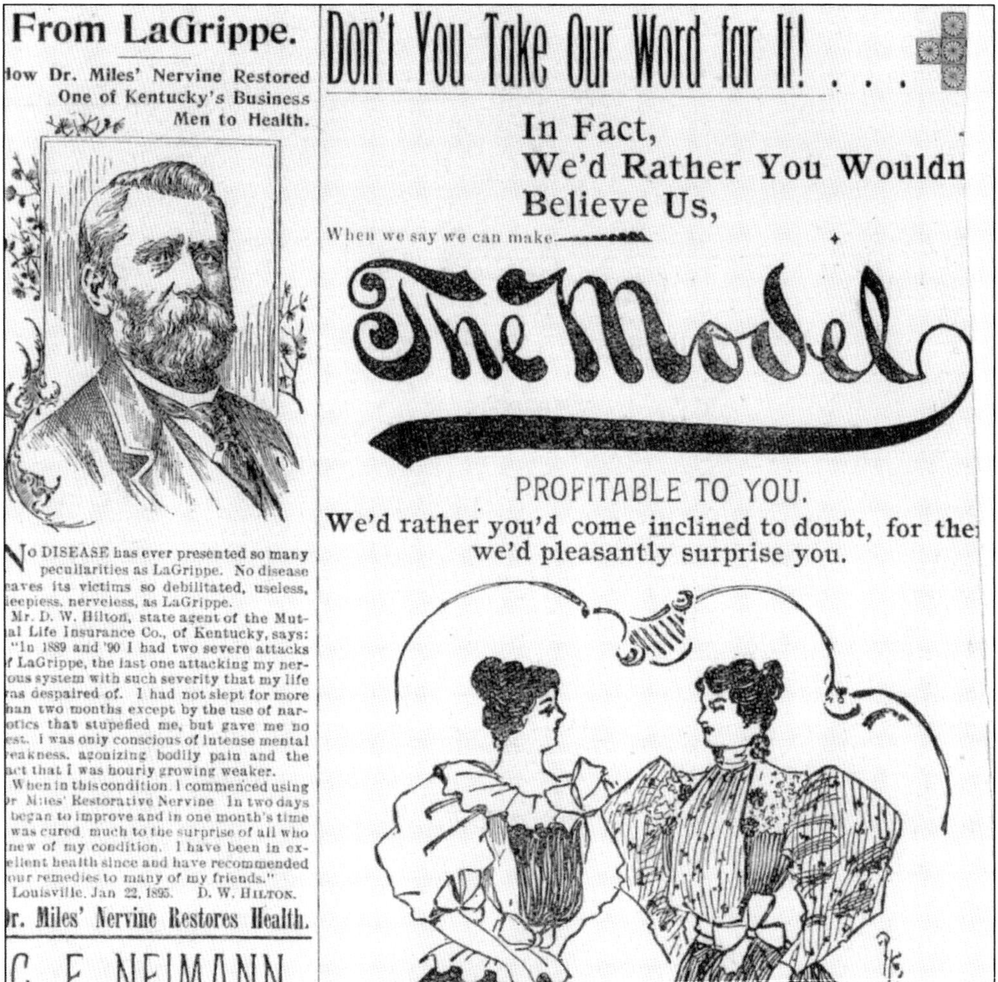

From LaGrippe.

low Dr. Miles' Nervine Restored One of Kentucky's Business Men to Health.

NO DISEASE has ever presented so many peculiarities as LaGrippe. No disease eaves its victims so debilitated, useless, leepless, nerveless, as LaGrippe.

Mr. D. W. Hilton, state agent of the Mutal Life Insurance Co., of Kentucky, says: "In 1889 and '90 I had two severe attacks f LaGrippe, the last one attacking my nerous system with such severity that my life as despaired of. I had not slept for more han two months except by the use of narotics that stupefied me, but gave me no est. I was only conscious of intense mental eakness, agonizing bodily pain and the act that I was hourly growing weaker. When in this condition I commenced using r Miles' Restorative Nervine In two days began to improve and in one month's time was cured much to the surprise of all who new of my condition. I have been in exellent health since and have recommended our remedies to many of my friends."

Louisville, Jan 22, 1895. D. W. Hilton.

r. Miles' Nervine Restores Health.

C. F. NEIMANN,

Corner Main and Washington, BEARDSTOWN, ILL.

DEALER in FINE WINE, LIQUOR AND CIGARS.

gent for Pabst's Celebrated Milwaukee Beer.

Don't You Take Our Word for It! . . .

In Fact,
We'd Rather You Wouldn
Believe Us,

When we say we can make

The Model

PROFITABLE TO YOU.

We'd rather you'd come inclined to doubt, for the we'd pleasantly surprise you.

THE MODEL POLICY is to make your interests our interests and treat you so you'll want to come again

We are now

CLEARING UP STOCK, SELLING OUT REMNANTS, CUTTING DOWN QUANTITY, PREPARING FOR BIG FALL TRADE.

Summer Goods must go.
Other seasonable goods go with them.

Look at the daisy Duck Suits.
The Calico Wrappers and Waists, all at first cost.
Best Swivel Silks, worth 60c now 40c. Wool Challies, worth 20c now 15c.
Good Jersey Vests, 5c. Better Jersey Vests 9c worth 15c.
Gauntlet Silk Mitts 25c worth 50c. Ladies Black Hose 12½c extra good for 25c.
Carpet Samples and Remnants are selling freely at the reduced prices.
August Delineators, Sheets and Patterns are now in.

The Model

This sheet of advertising from the *Illinoisan Star* dates to 1915.

Frey Hardware, pictured here, was located on East Main Street.

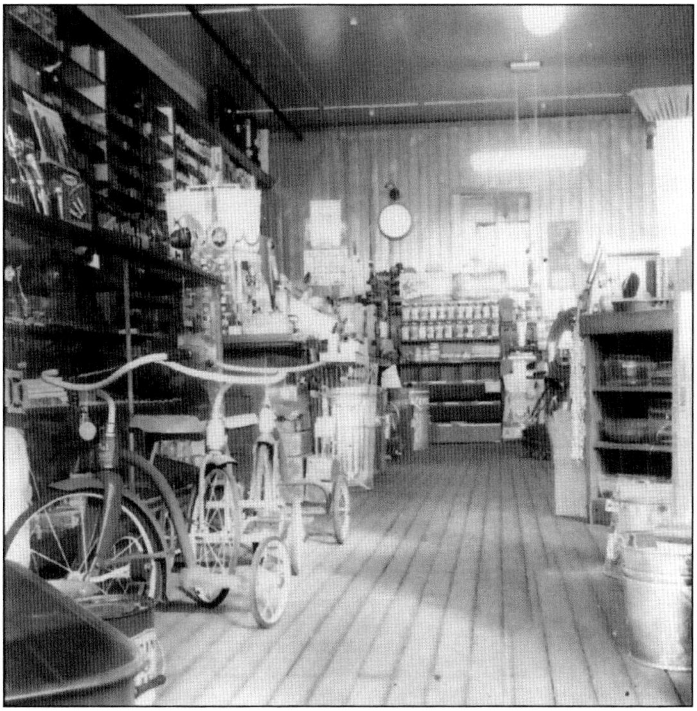

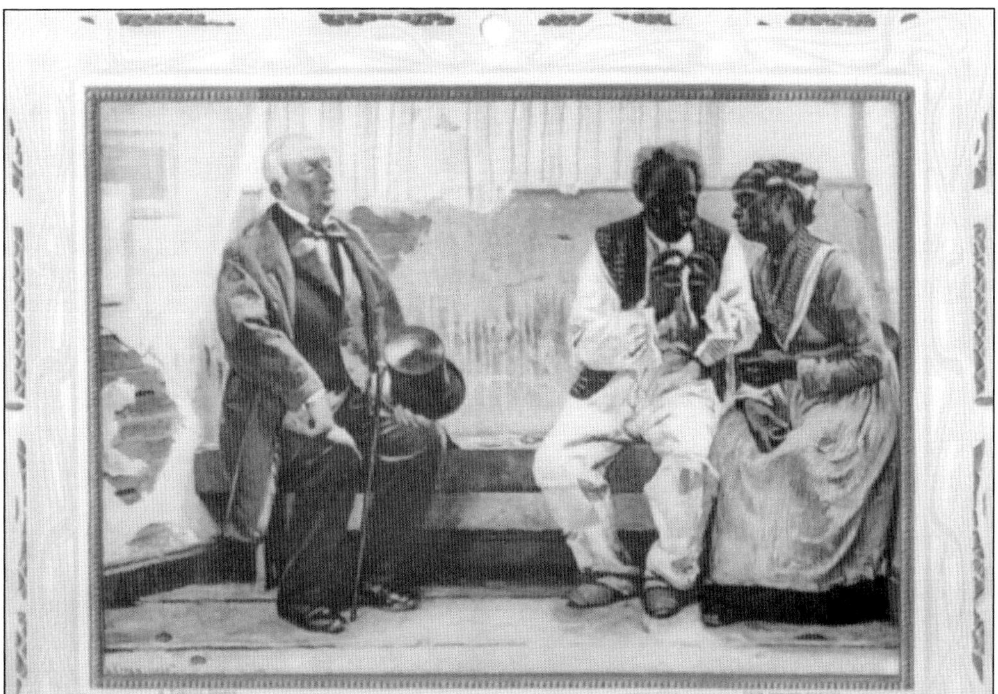

This image is from a W.M. Frey Hardware Store calendar. Frey was the founding owner of the Frey Hardware Store.

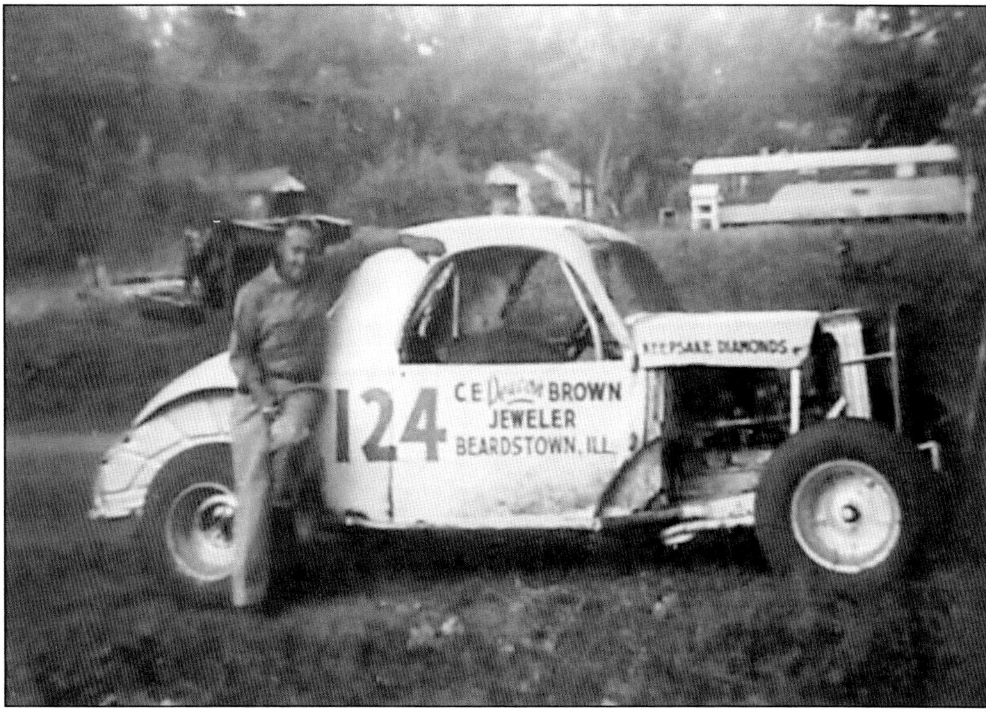

C.E. "Deacon" Brown and his race car are pictured here. Brown owned and operated Brown's Jewelry and Gift Shop at 115 State Street.

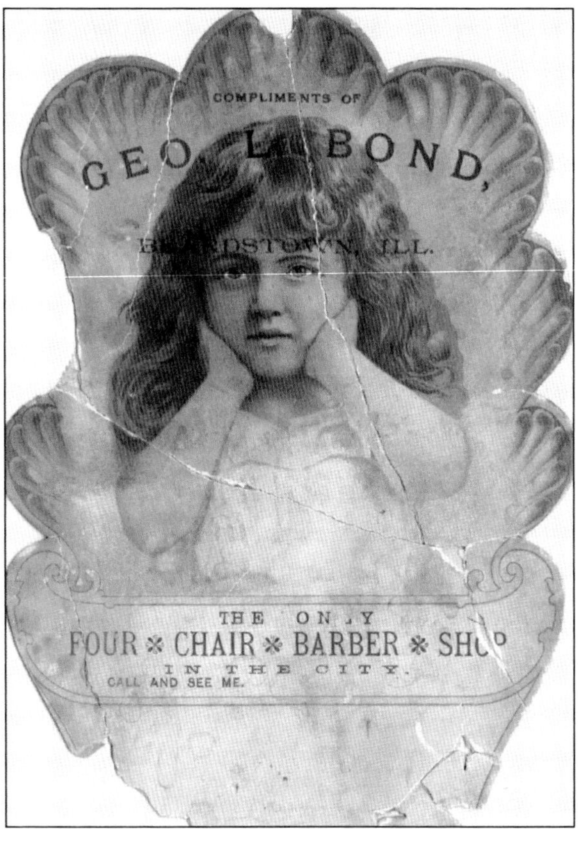

Shown here is an advertising card for the George Bond barbershop, which was located at 415 West Sixth Street.

Seven

Business and Infrastructure

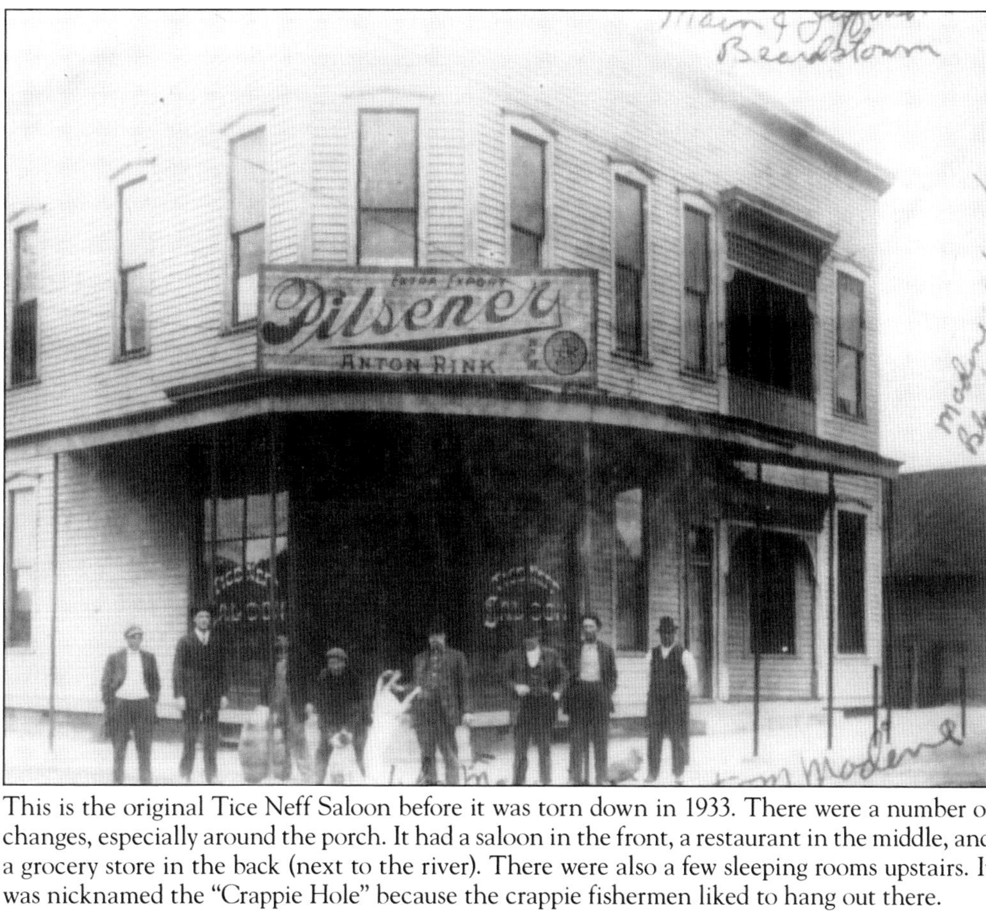

This is the original Tice Neff Saloon before it was torn down in 1933. There were a number of changes, especially around the porch. It had a saloon in the front, a restaurant in the middle, and a grocery store in the back (next to the river). There were also a few sleeping rooms upstairs. It was nicknamed the "Crappie Hole" because the crappie fishermen liked to hang out there.

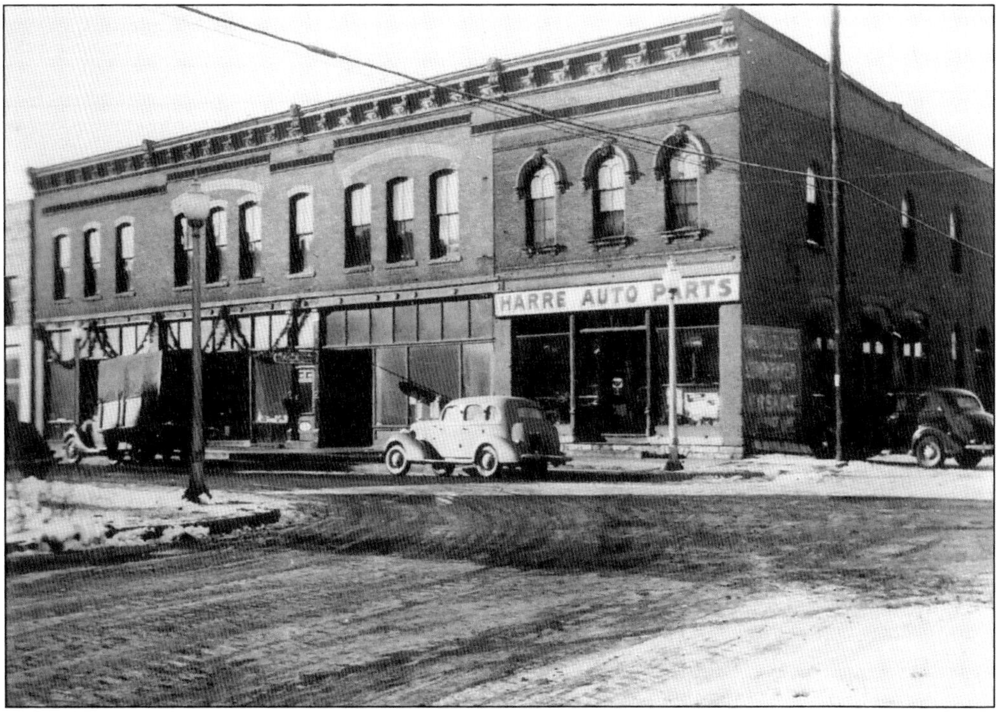

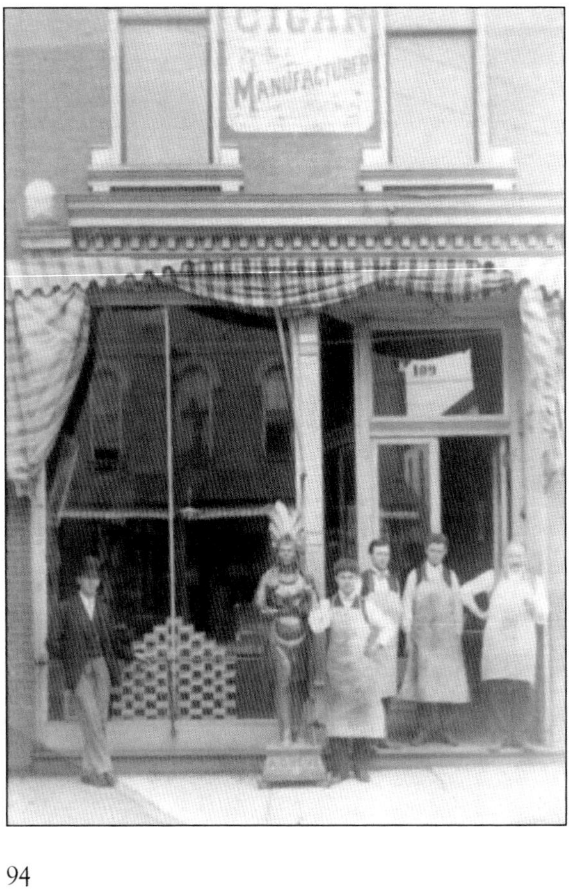

The Harre Auto Parts store was located on the 100 block of East Main Street in the 1950s. It later became R&S Auto Parts.

The Greve Cigar Store was located at 109 State Street. Mr. Greve is on the far right. The store and the cigar-store Indian were later sold to Charles Hunter, who ran a cigar store for many years.

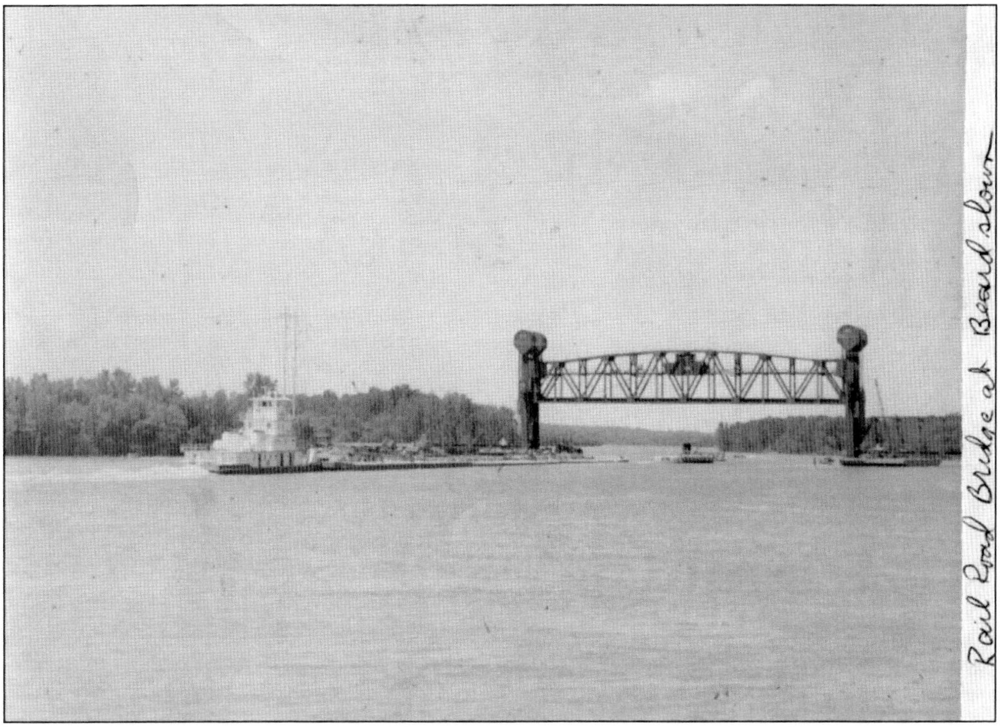

This photograph from the 1970s is of the lift span railroad bridge at Beardstown. It was built during 1971 and 1972 upstream from Beardstown and floated into place.

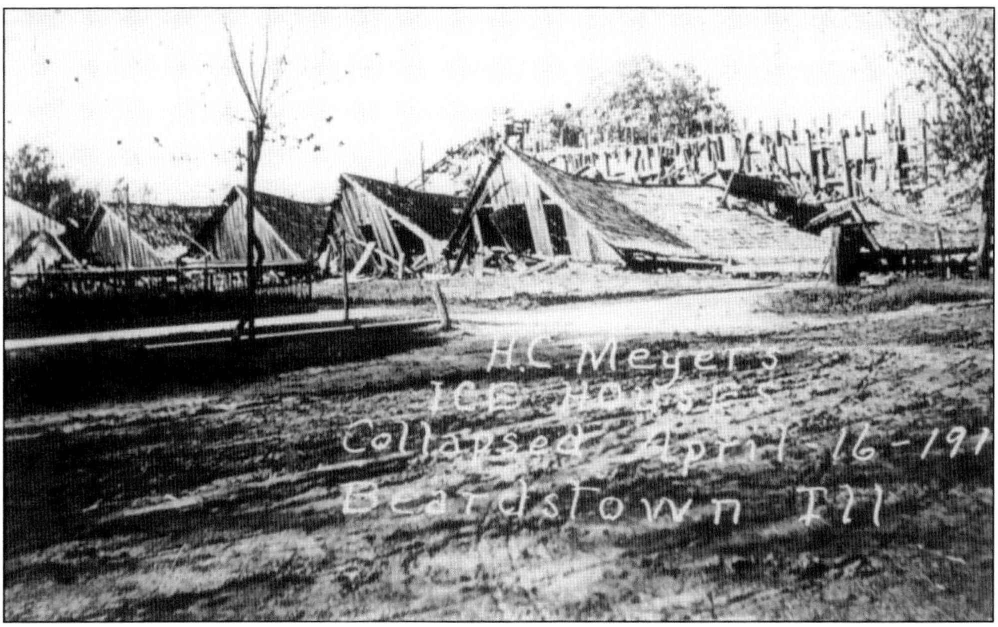

These icehouses were located where the levee now stands at the north end of Schmoldt Park. They were used to store ice taken from Mascouten Bay. The railroad used the ice to keep food and vegetables fresh on their journey between Chicago and St. Louis. Walter Myer became wealthy selling ice to the railroad for 25¢ per ton.

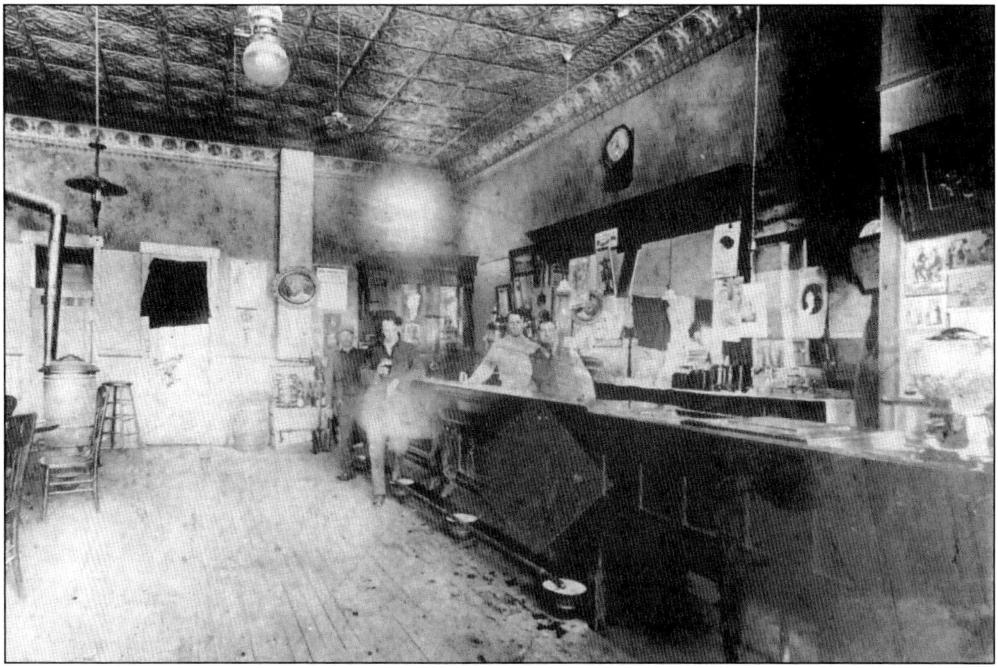

This is the Anton Knippenburg Saloon located at 207 State Street. It opened in the early 1900s and closed during Prohibition. Note the spittoons—and the number of times the spitters missed! The picture was taken in 1915 at 4:00 in the afternoon. Knippenburg is the man in the vest.

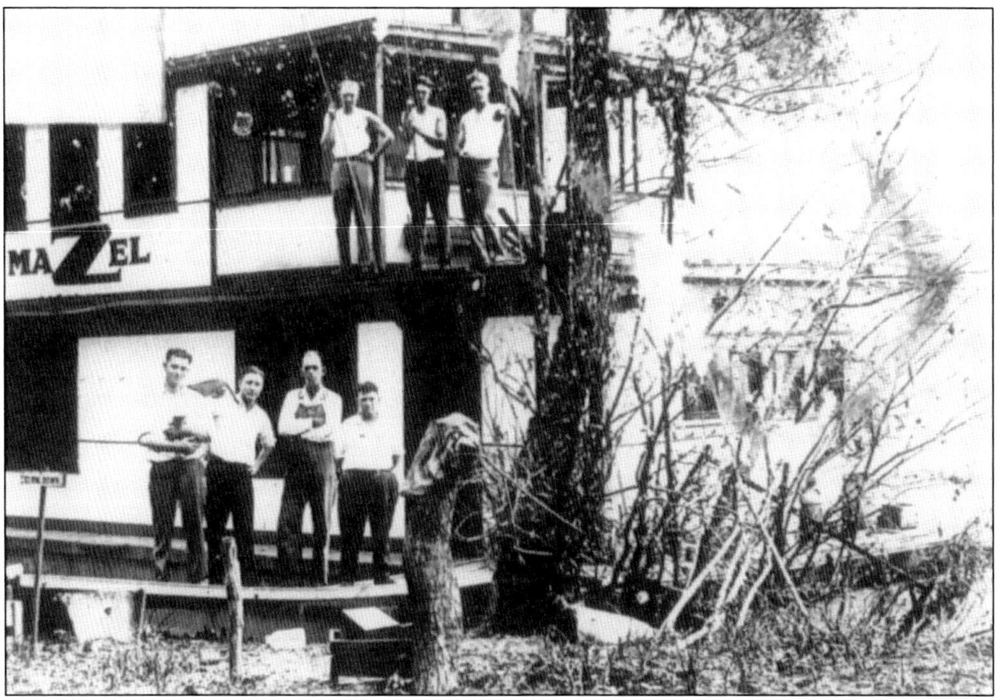

The gambling boat *Mazel* was owned and operated by Ferrial "Screwy" Lane. It was tied up at the river end of Jefferson Street. It finally ended up at Knapp Island across the river from Browning. The boat was later sold and moved to Joliet, Illinois, where it burned.

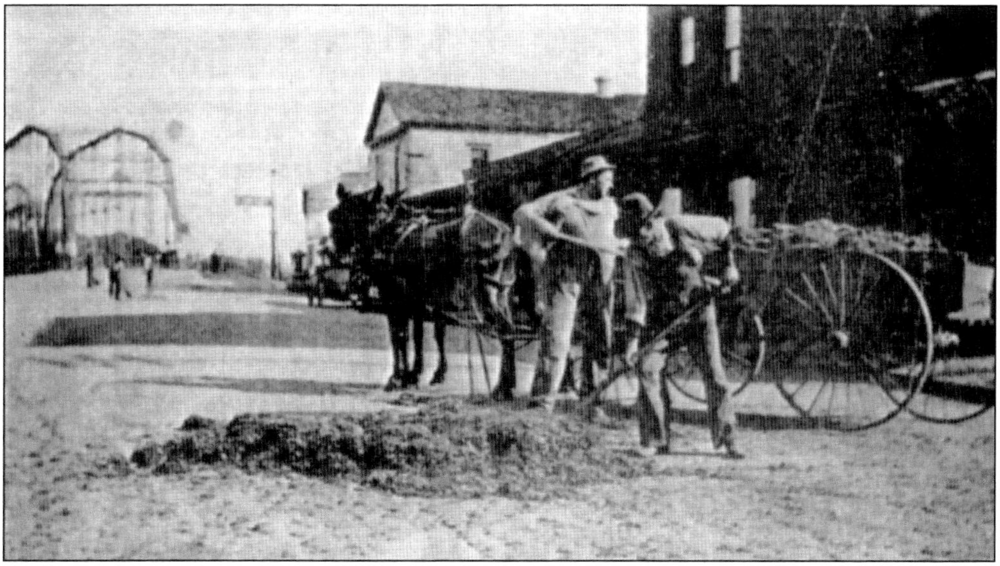

The willow bugs hit Beardstown. This was an annual event. Willow bugs are also known as mayflies and require good quality water in which to breed. They are much rarer today. This photograph was taken on State Street, with the wagon bridge on the far left.

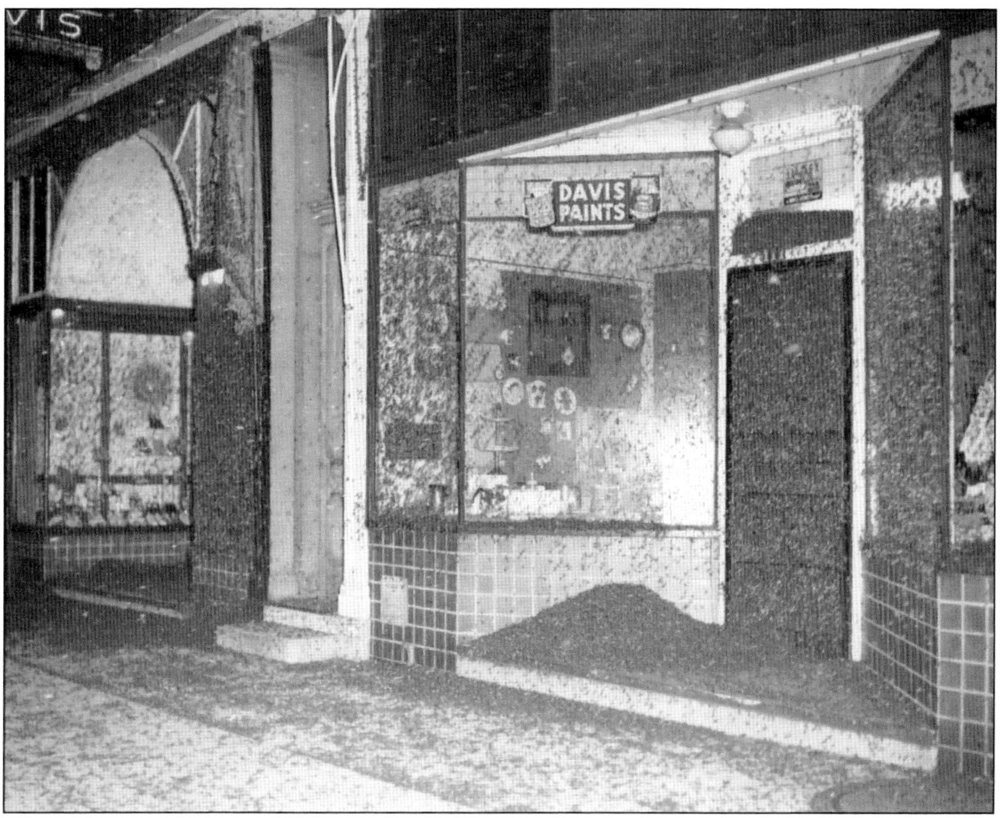

This is a 1947 photograph of the Howard Davis Paint Store, which later became the Davis Shoe Store on State Street. If there was a light on at night, the swarm of mayflies would be worse!

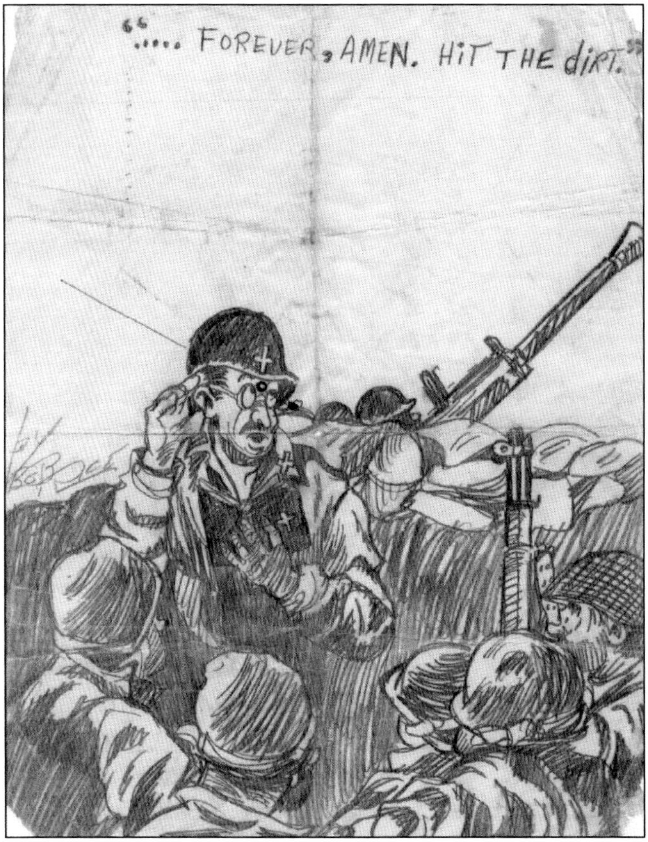

This cartoon was drawn by Bob Rice, who worked for the US Army Corps of Engineers at the La Grange Lock and Dam. His favorite pastime was drawing cartoons.

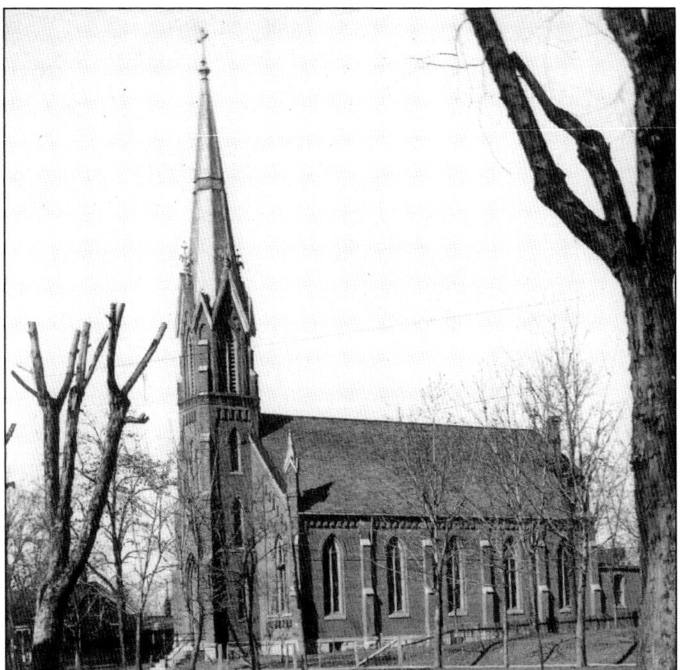

This is a photograph of the brand-new St. Alexius Catholic Church. The church was organized in 1855. This building was constructed in 1889.

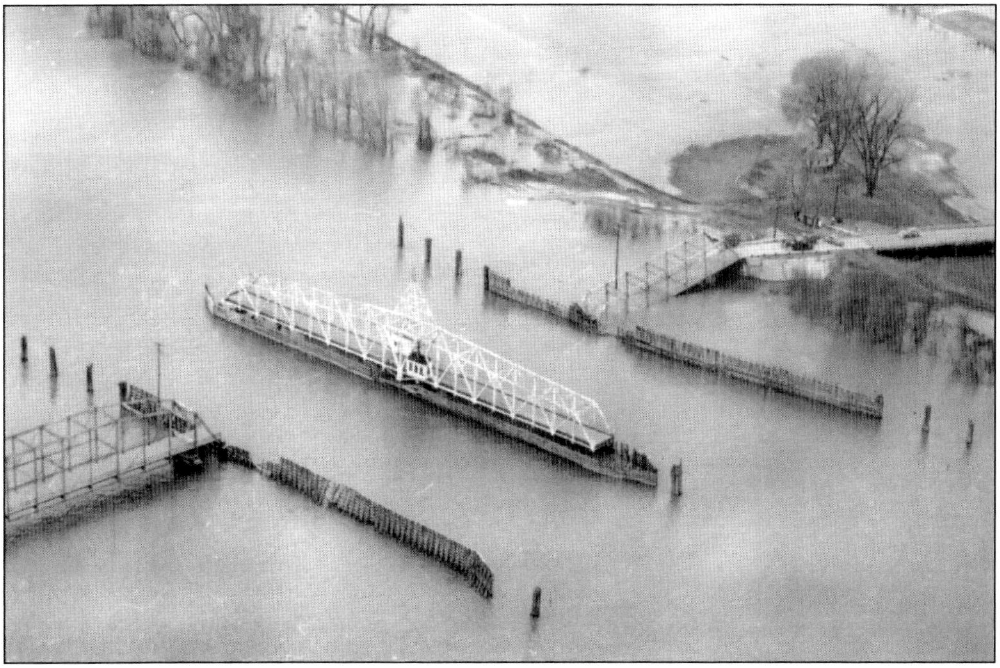

On April 5, 1950, the tugboat *Ferdinand* struck the swing span bridge at Beardstown. The boat veered and knocked the bridge approach off the pilings. This AP photograph taken after the fact shows the approach clearly in the river. The Illinois River makes a 90-degree turn at the Sangamon River at Beardstown, which makes it very difficult for river captains still today.

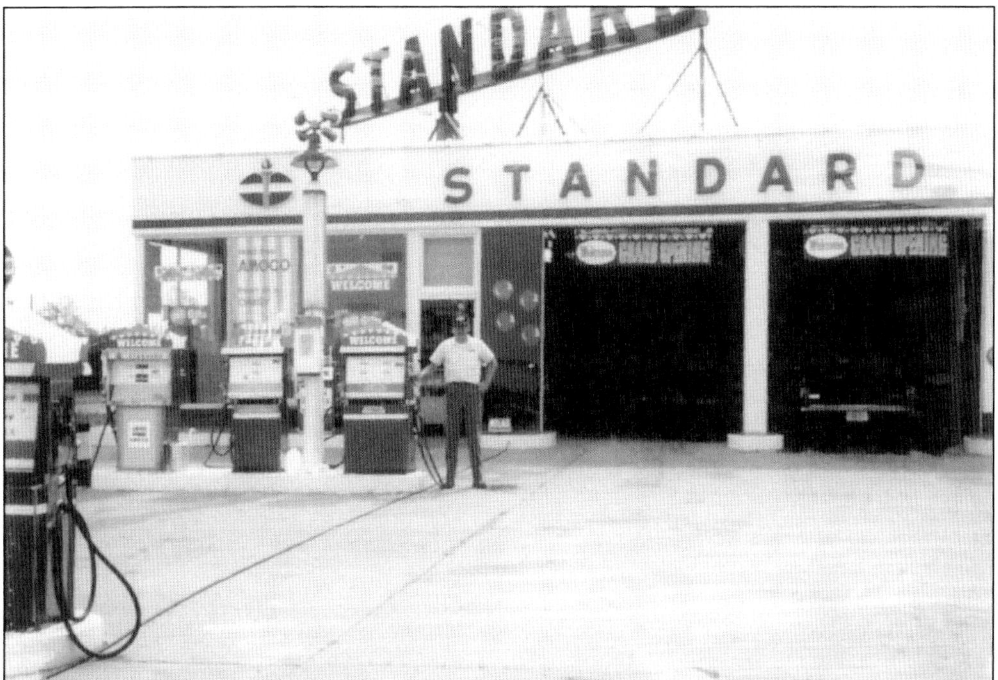

Pictured here is Jim Givens Standard Service Station at the junction of US Route 67 and Illinois Route 100. This site is currently home to a Hardee's.

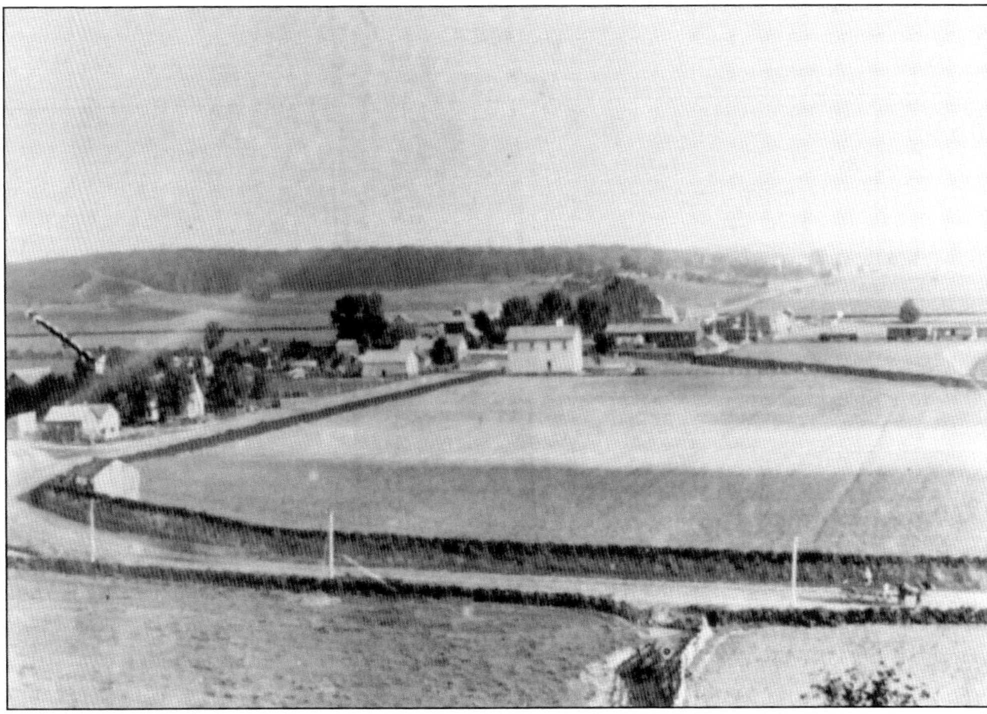

This aerial view is of Bluff Springs from the north long before the paved highway was created. The white building is the old Odd Fellows Hall.

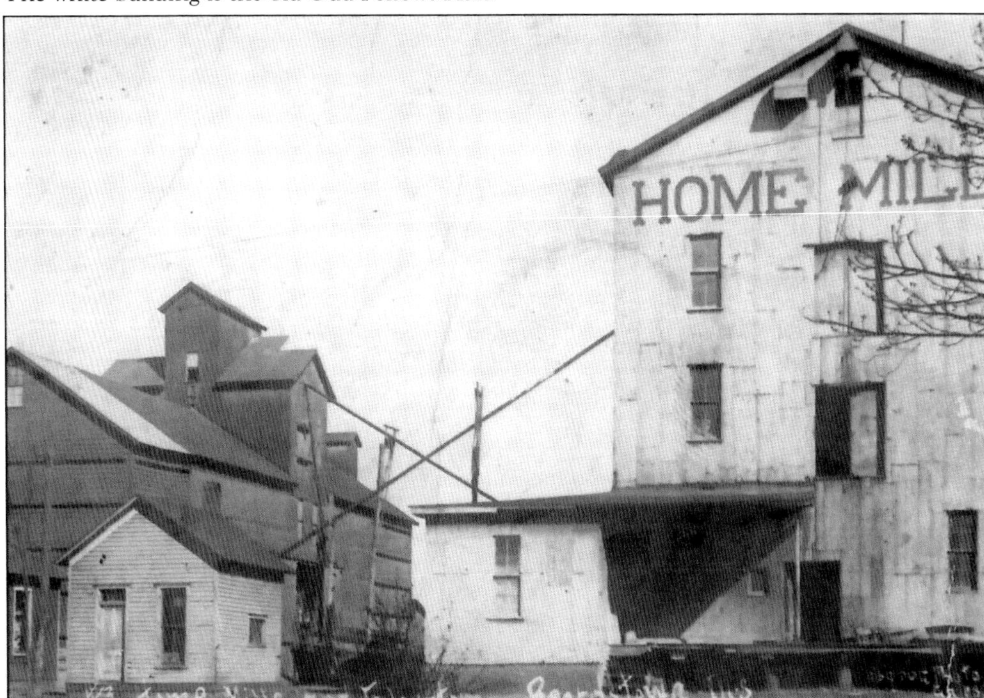

The Home Mills Flour Mill was built in the early 1870s and burned to the ground in 1917. It could produce 50 barrels of flour per day.

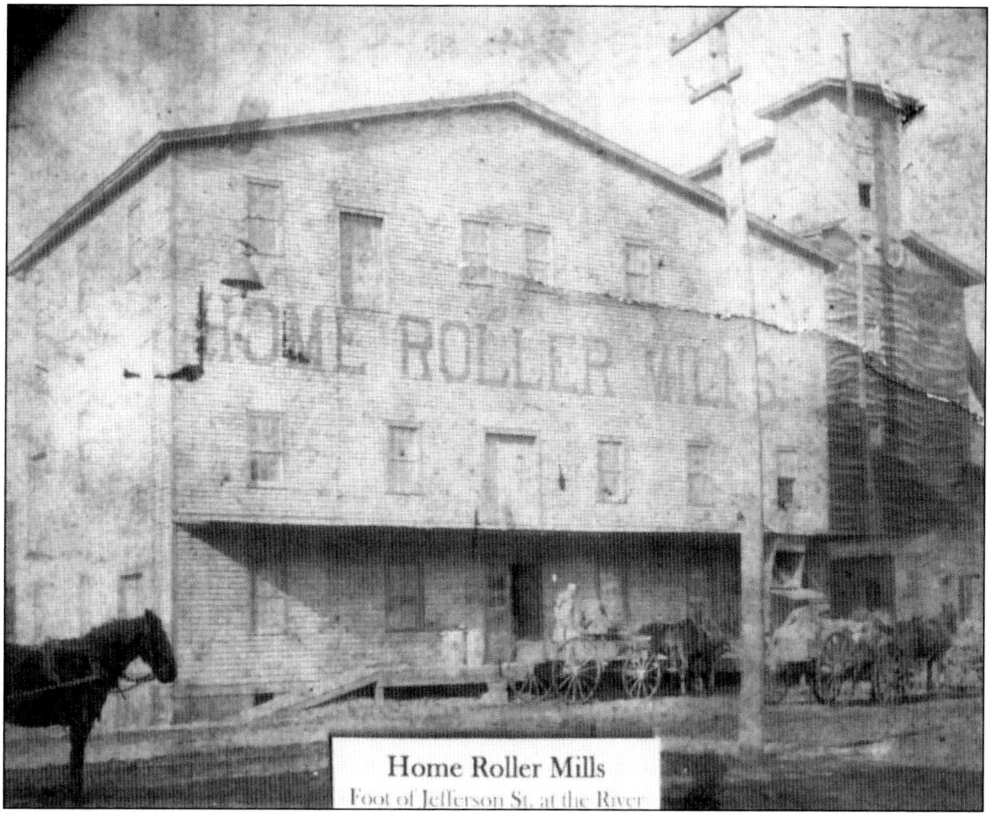

This is a riverside view of the Home Mills Flour Mill at the end of Jefferson Street.

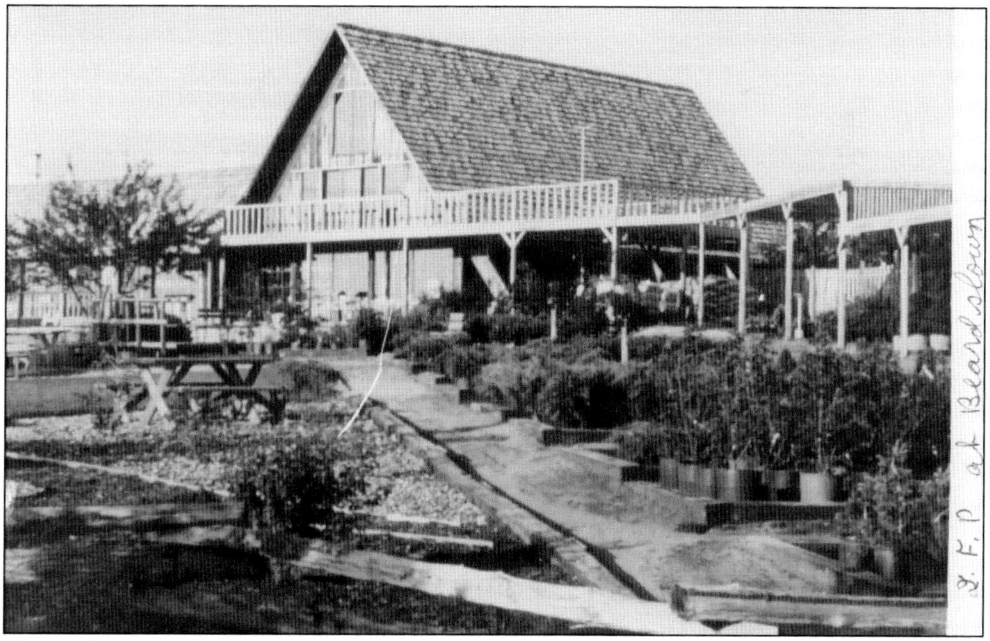

Illinois Forest Products Company was started when Cass Wood Products Company split up in 1964. IFP, as it was known, was started by Glen Massey and located on the Arenzville Road.

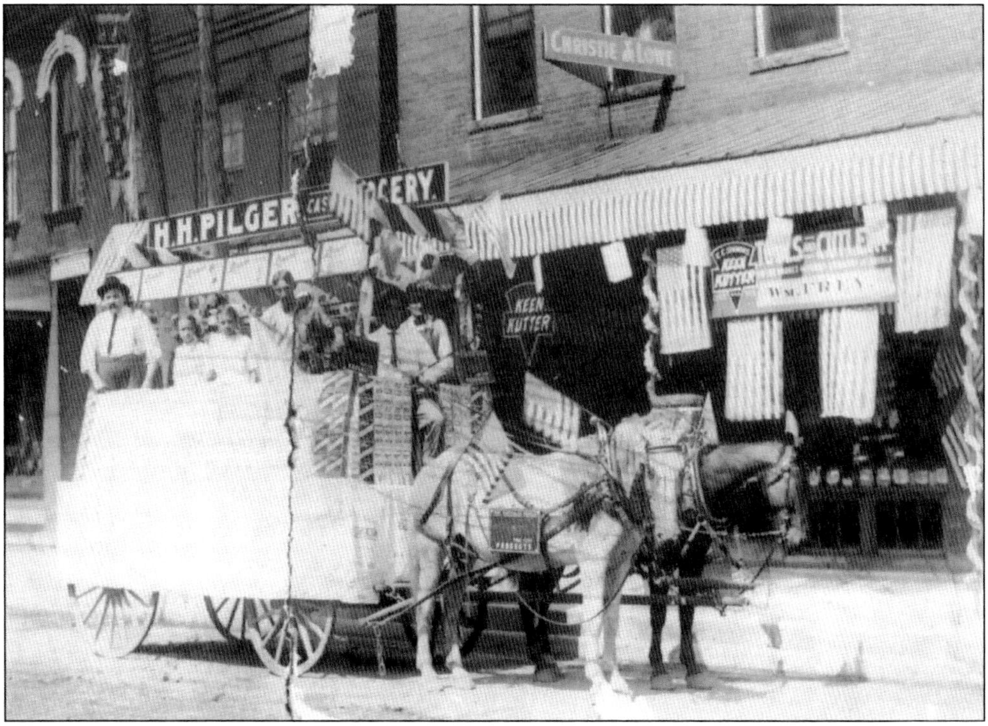

This Fourth of July float advertising Wilson Products is shown on the 100 block of East Main Street.

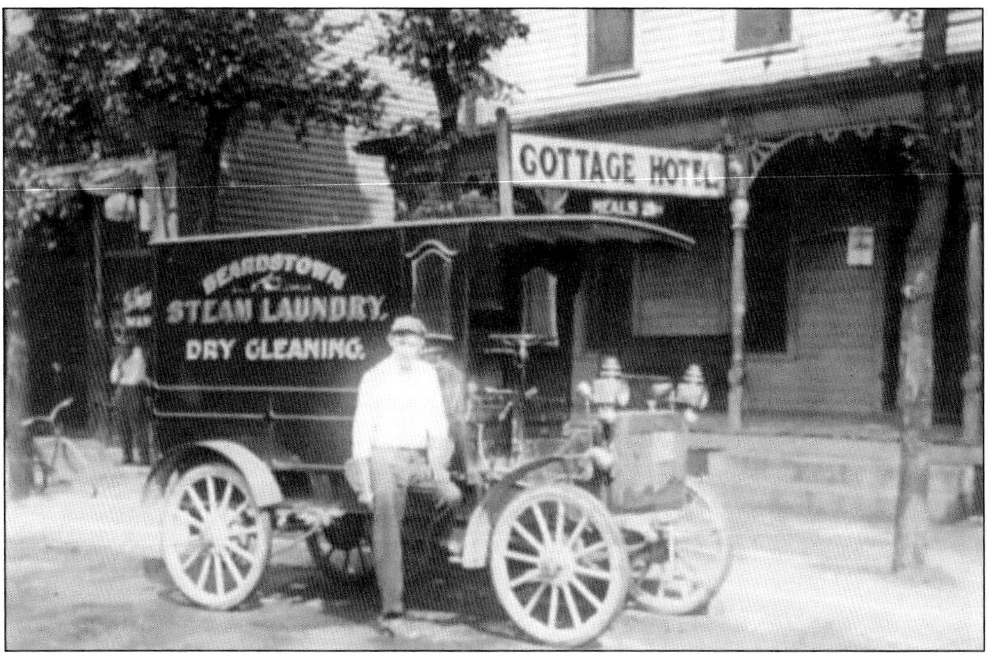

This Beardstown Steam Laundry driver is making a delivery to the Cottage Hotel. The hotel was located at 619 East Fourth Street, next to the Chicago, Burlington & Quincy Railroad station. The laundry was located at 201 East Second Street and owned by Charles and Herman Bolhorst.

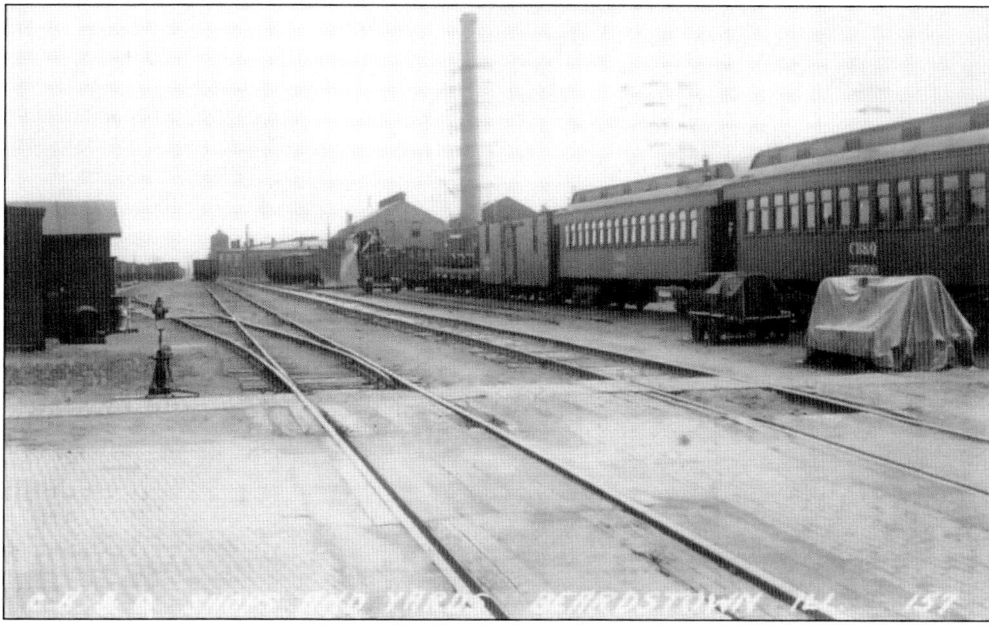

The Chicago, Burlington & Quincy Railroad repair shops and yard are pictured in this view looking south from the Eighth Street crossing.

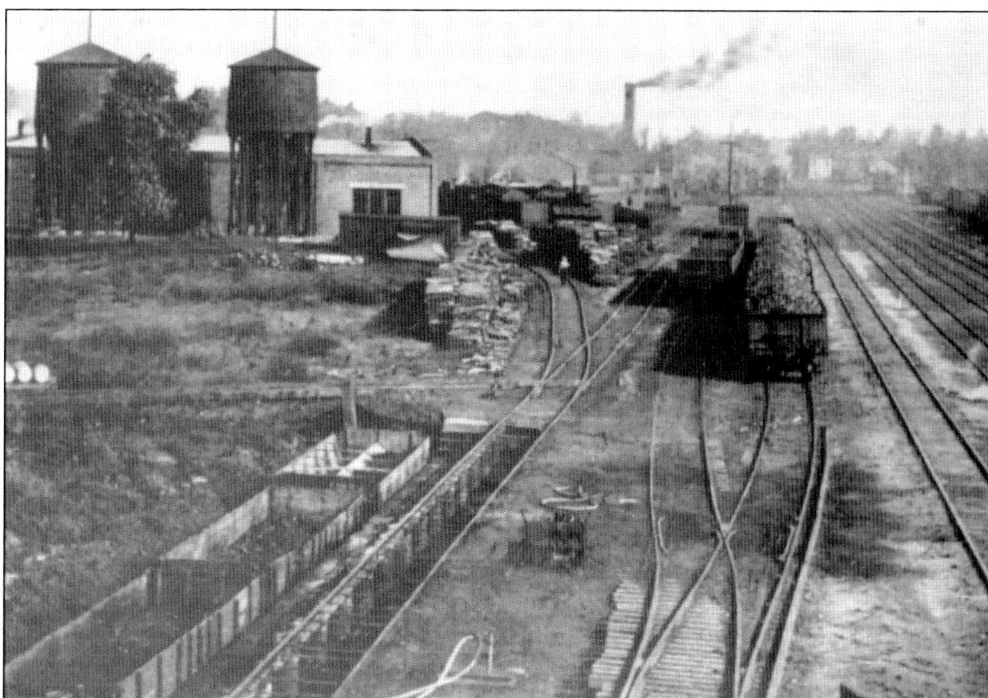

This photographer was looking north toward the Chicago, Burlington & Quincy Railroad yard at Beardstown.

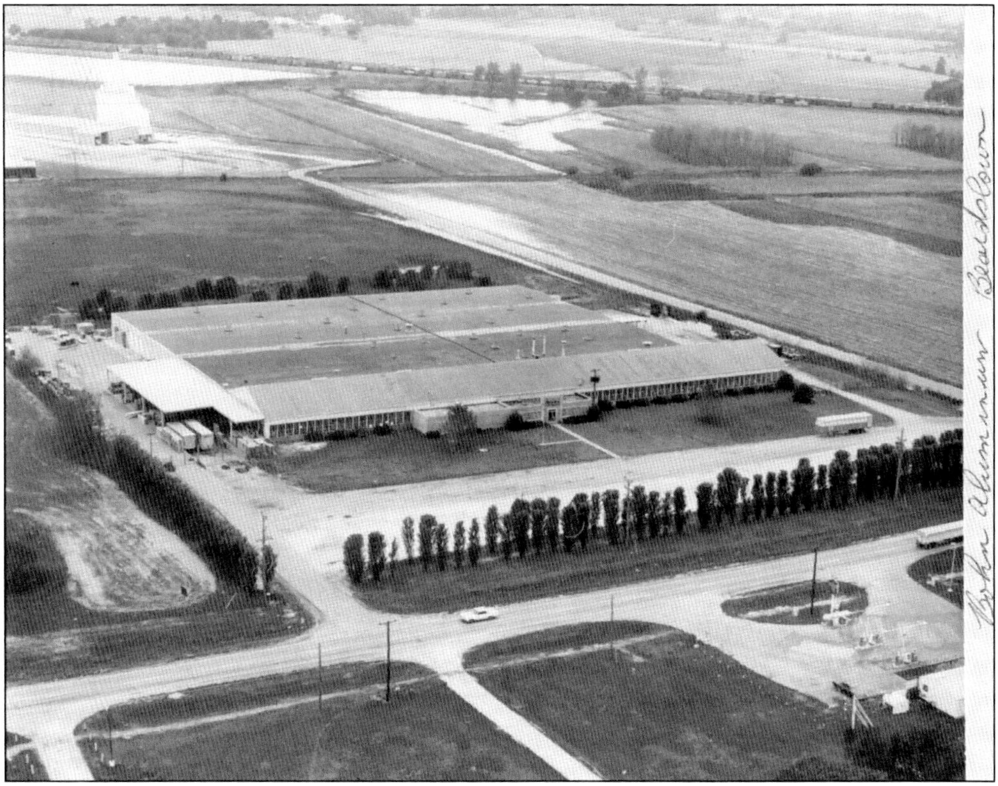

The Bohn Aluminum Plant at Beardstown faced Illinois Route 125. The company manufactured custom air-cooling units.

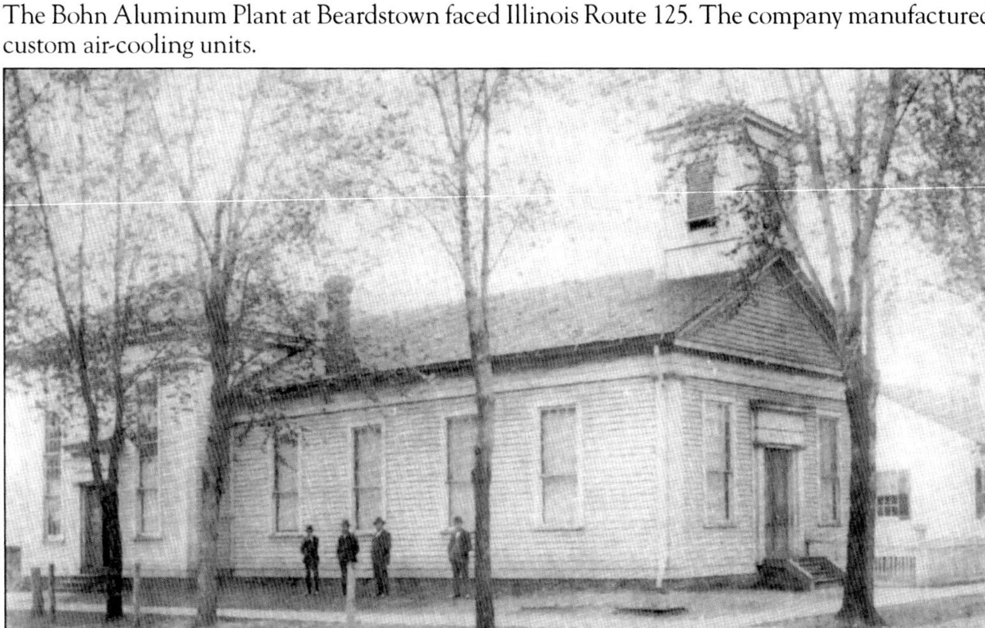

In the 1840s, the German Methodist church was located at Fifth and State Streets. In 1848, the minister and 32 members withdrew and built the First Evangelical Lutheran Church (seen here) on Fourth and Lafayette Streets. This church was built in 1851.

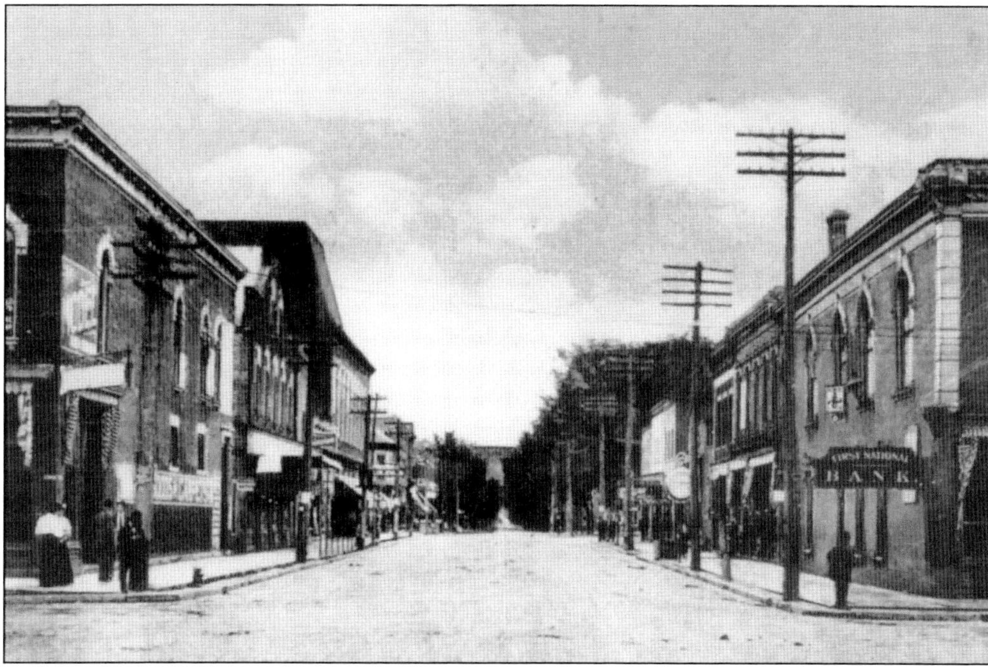

This image shows State Street from Main Street in a view looking south.

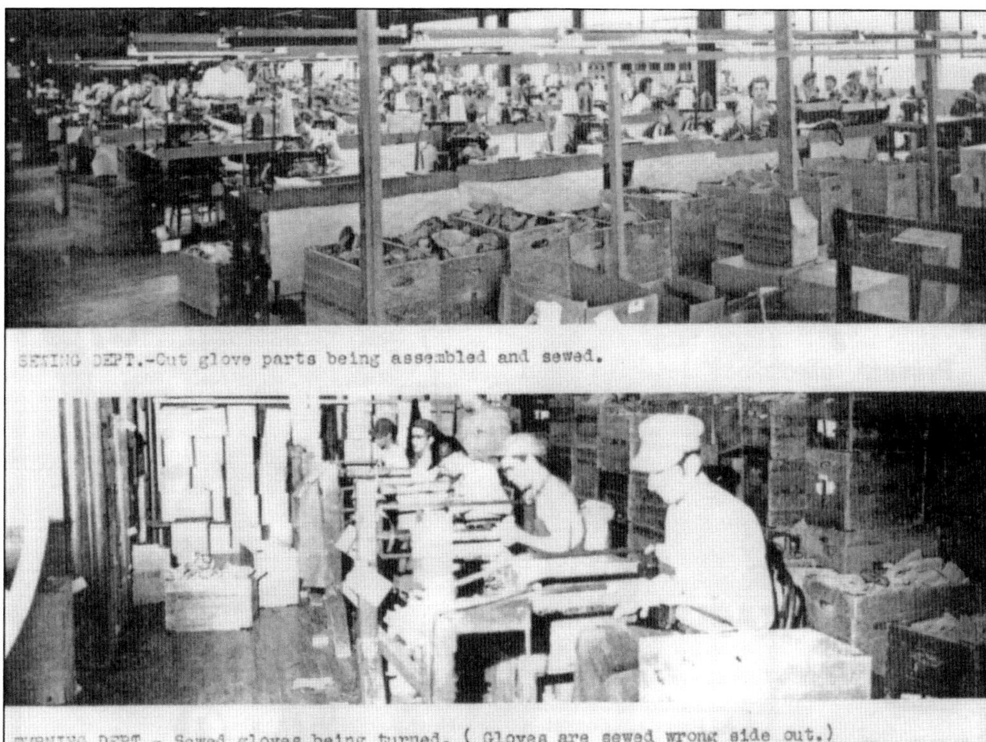

These pictures offer a peek at the inside of the Wells-Lamont-Smith glove factory, located on East Main Street, in 1939.

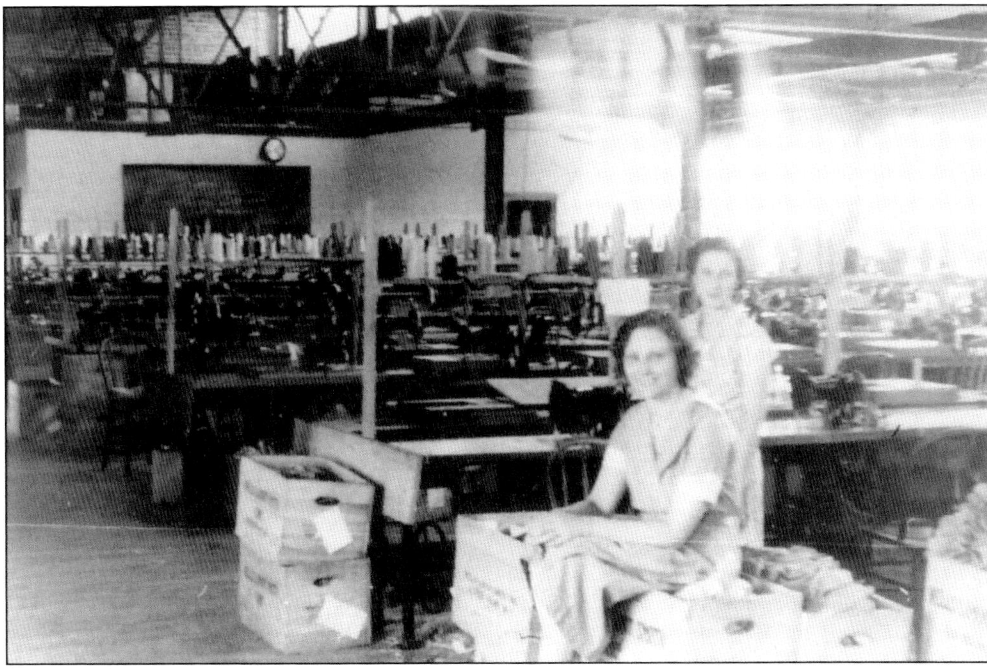

A couple of Wells-Lamont-Smith glove factory employees are shown resting after a hard day's work in 1939.

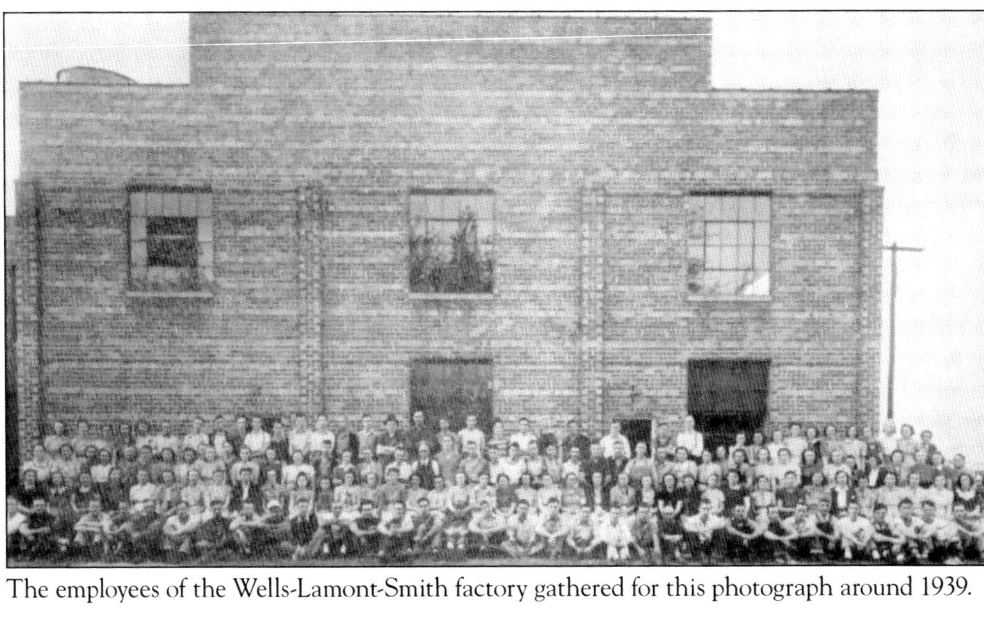

The employees of the Wells-Lamont-Smith factory gathered for this photograph around 1939.

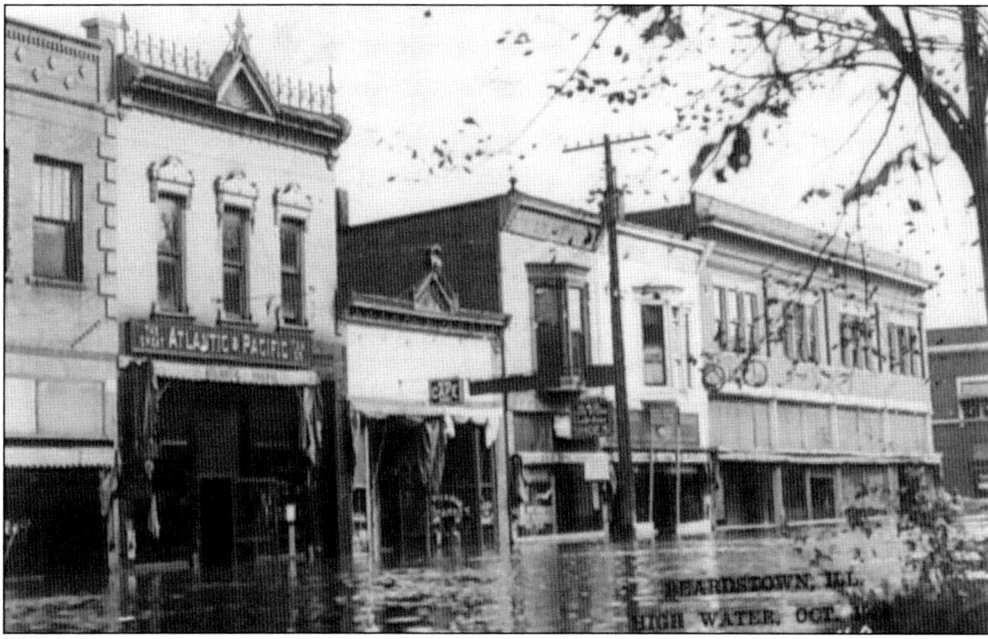

The 200 block of State Street is shown during the 1926 flood. The buildings in this block are still there today! The edge of the Woolworth building is pictured on the left, and Cline's Department Store is on the right.

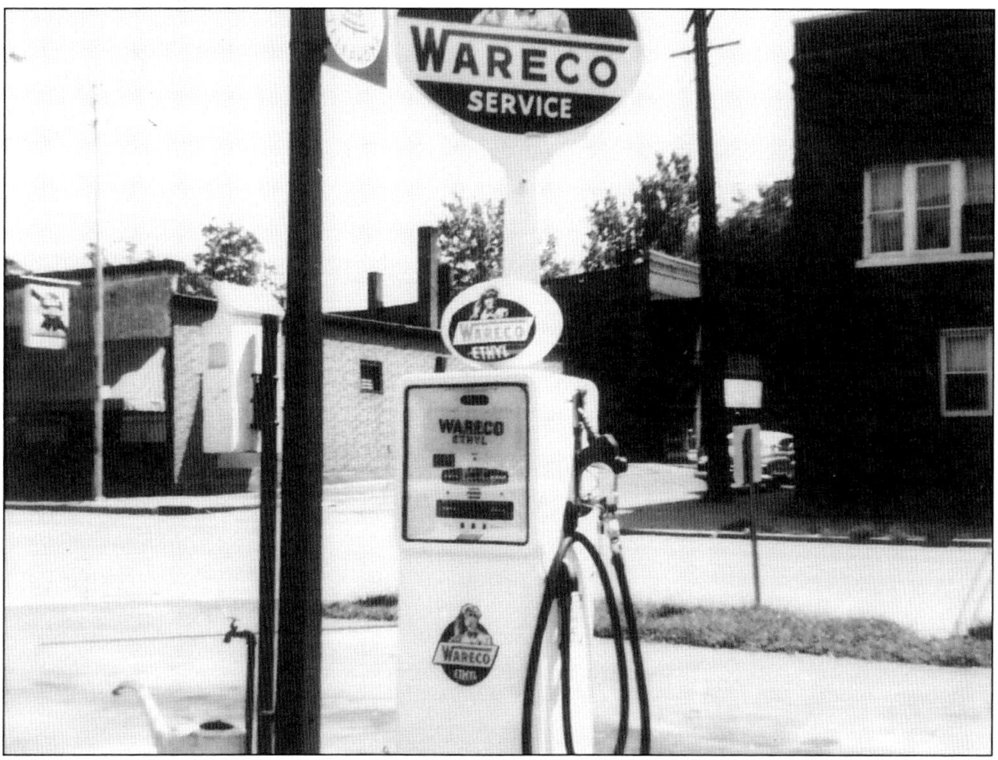

This picture of a Wareco Station gas pump was taken in the 1960s. Across the street, below the Pabst Blue Ribbon sign, is Leo and Bud's Tavern.

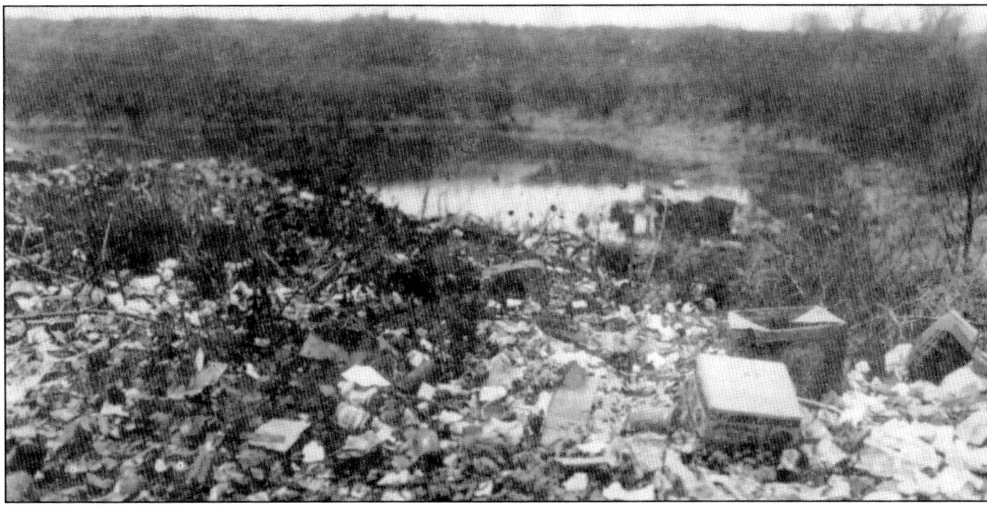

Here is a view of the Schmoldt Park site before the Works Progress Administration transformed it.

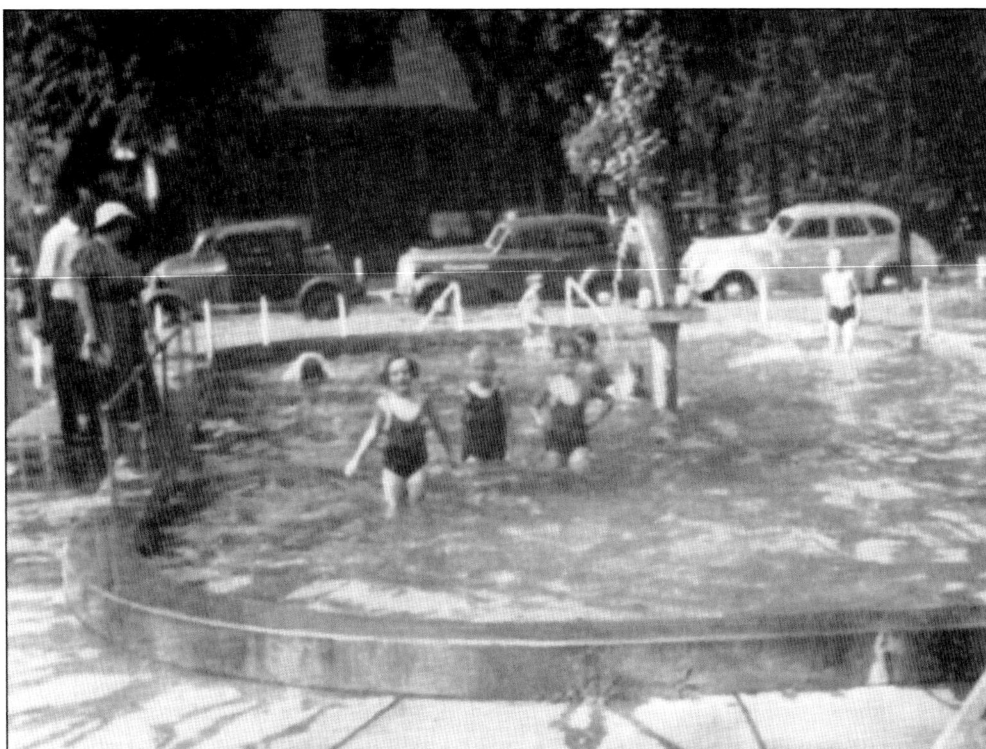

This children's wading pool was located on East Third Street near where the Elks Lodge is currently located.

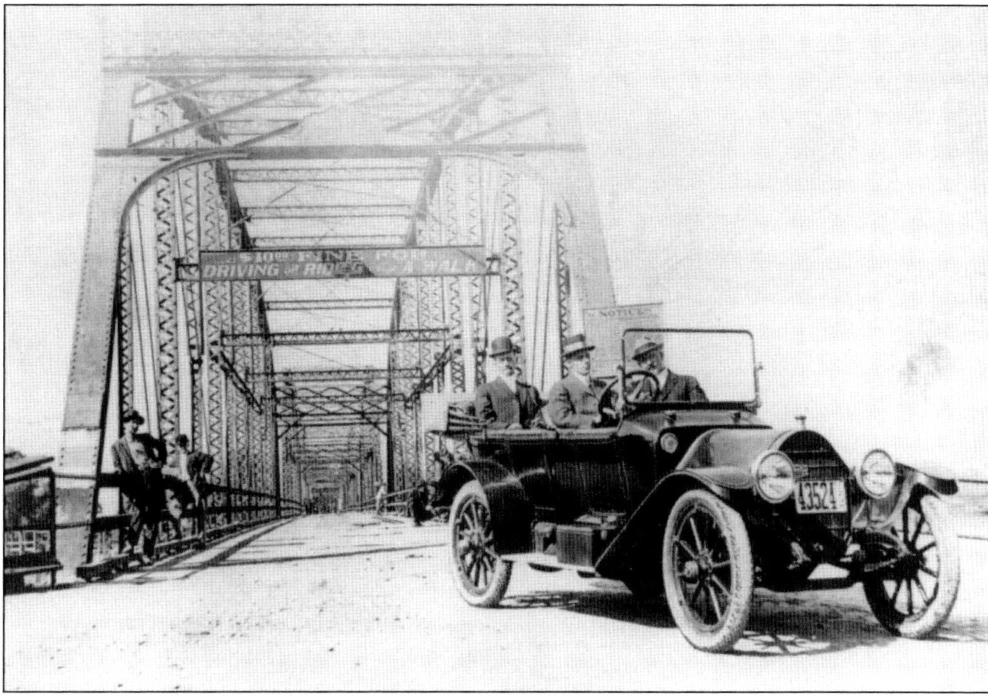

There was a $10 fine for driving or running on the bridge faster than a walk.

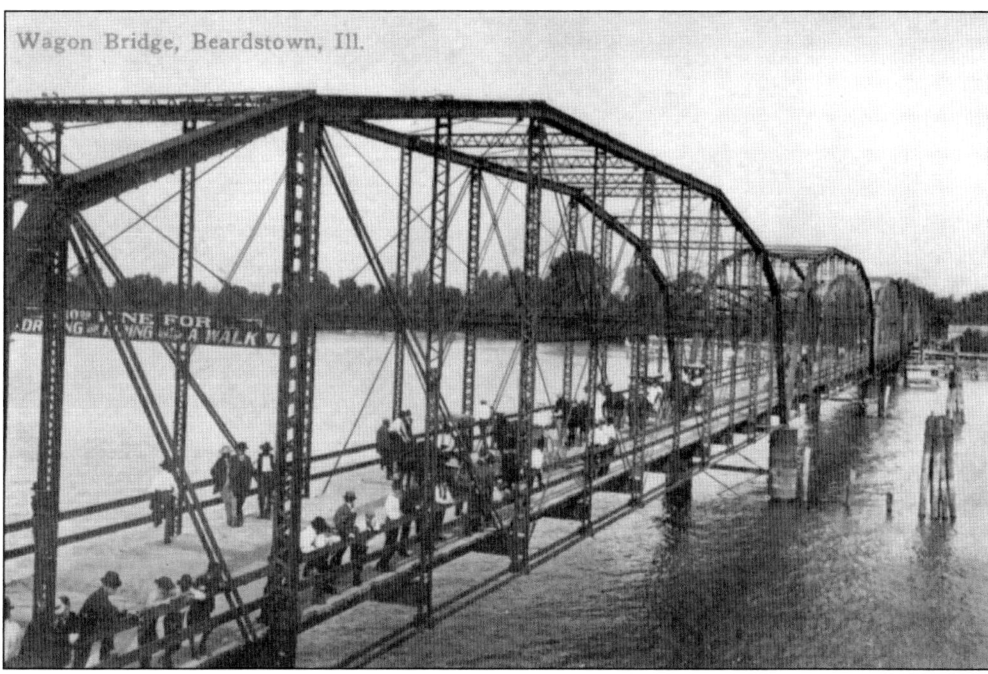

This 1910 postcard features the Wagon Bridge at the end of State Street.

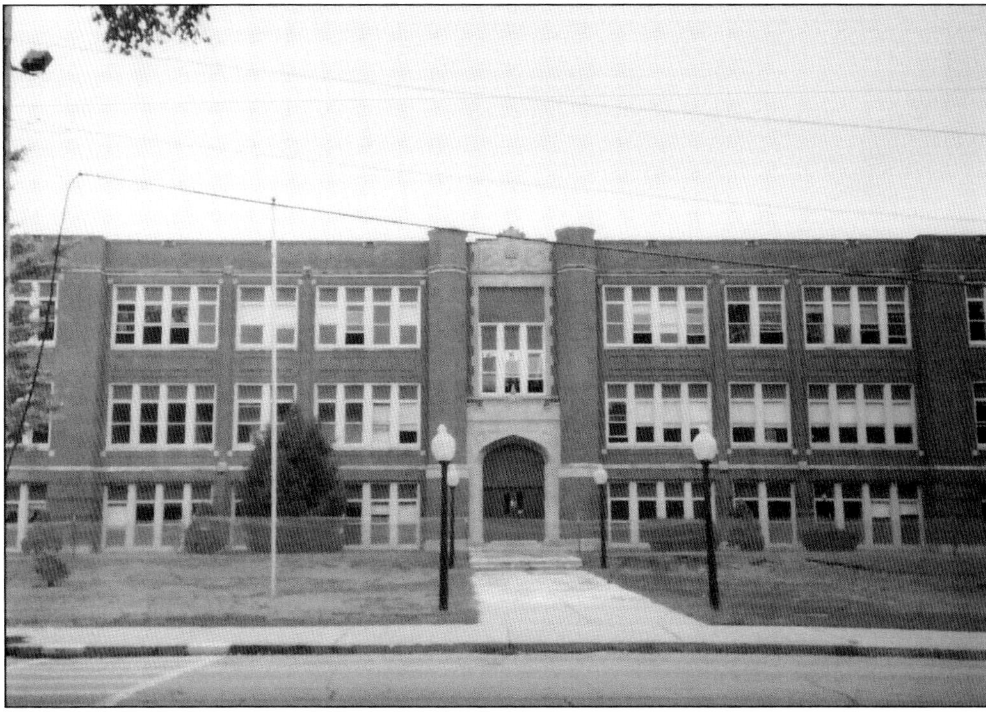

This is the front of the old Beardstown High School, which was built in 1920.

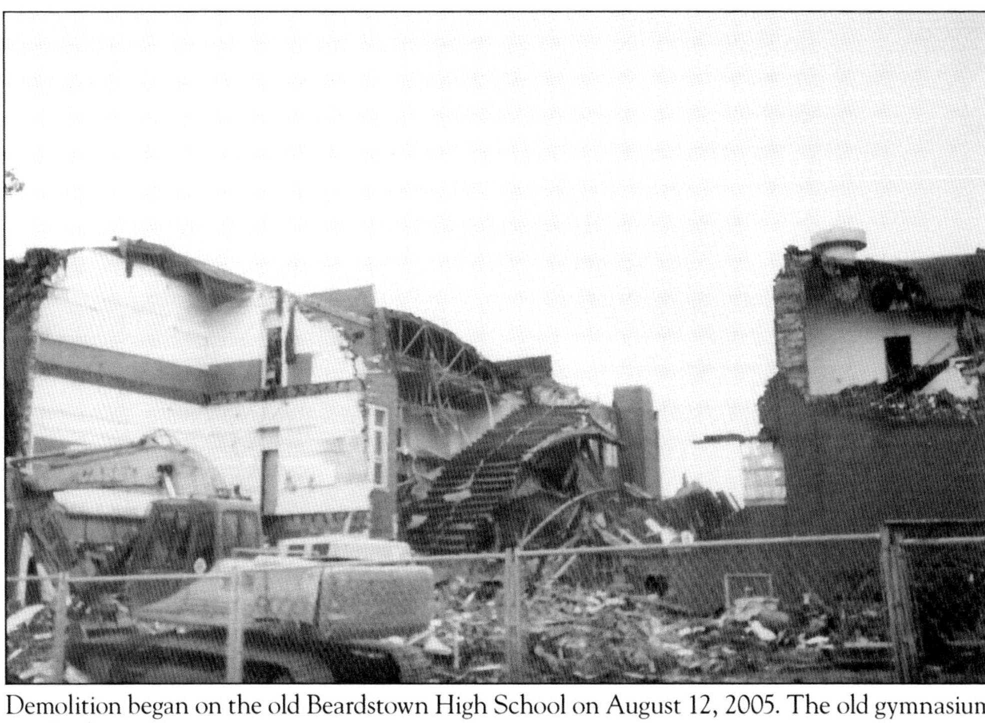

Demolition began on the old Beardstown High School on August 12, 2005. The old gymnasium was in the center.

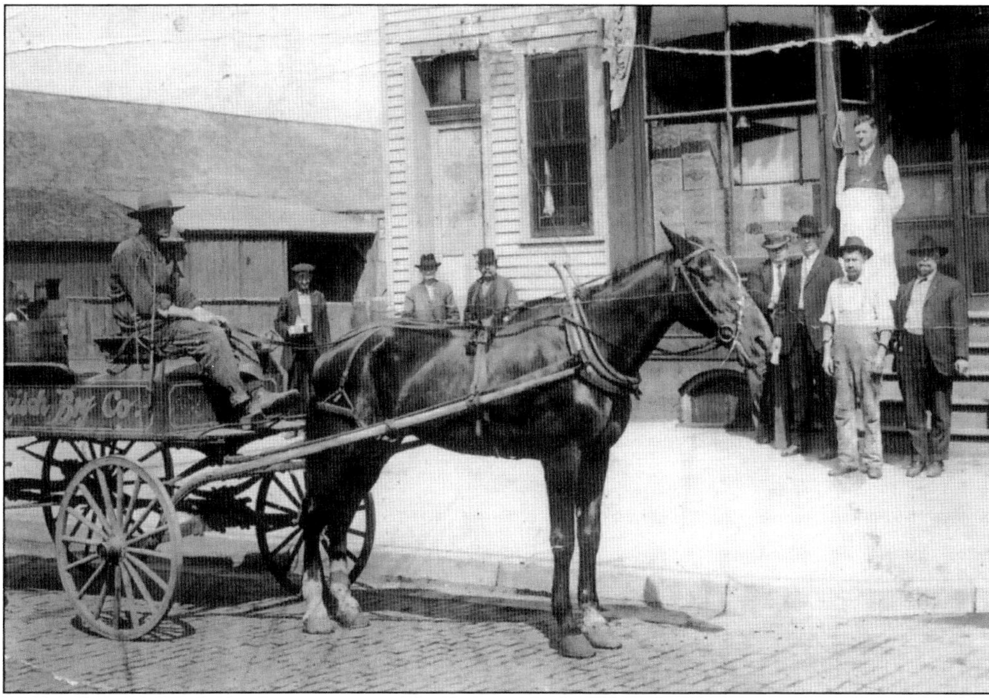

In this 1915 photograph, a worker from the Reisch Brewing Company, owned by John McCain and Harry Buck, is shown delivering a barrel of beer to the tavern owned by Al Brocker and Jim Scullion. The J.T. Kessling stable is behind the delivery wagon.

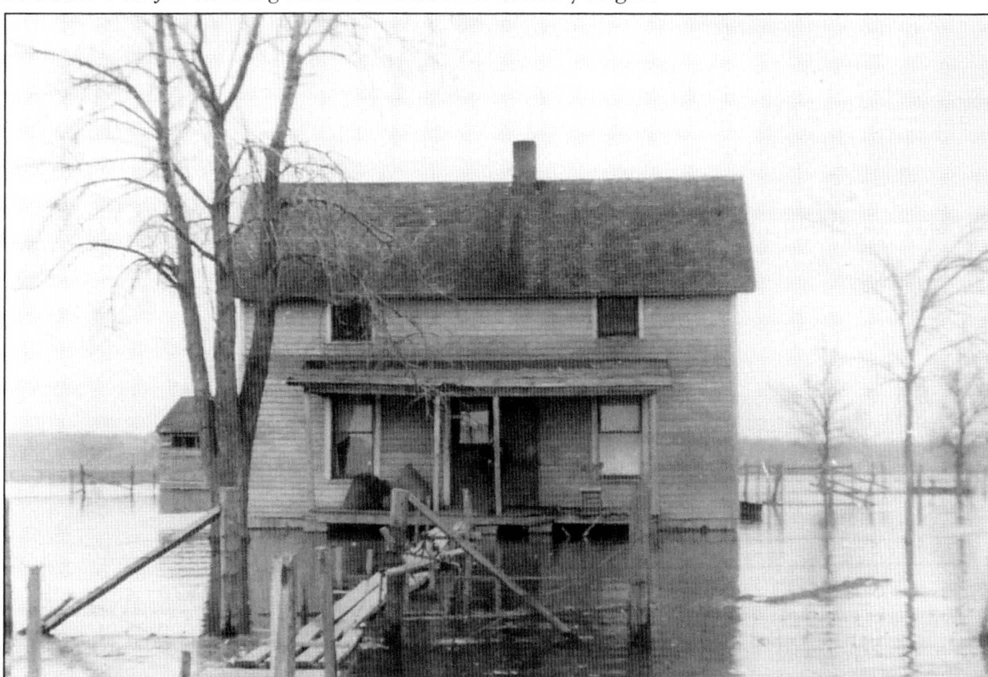

Floodwaters surrounded this country home during the dry flood of 1943. Note the levee in the background; it was not so dry on this side.

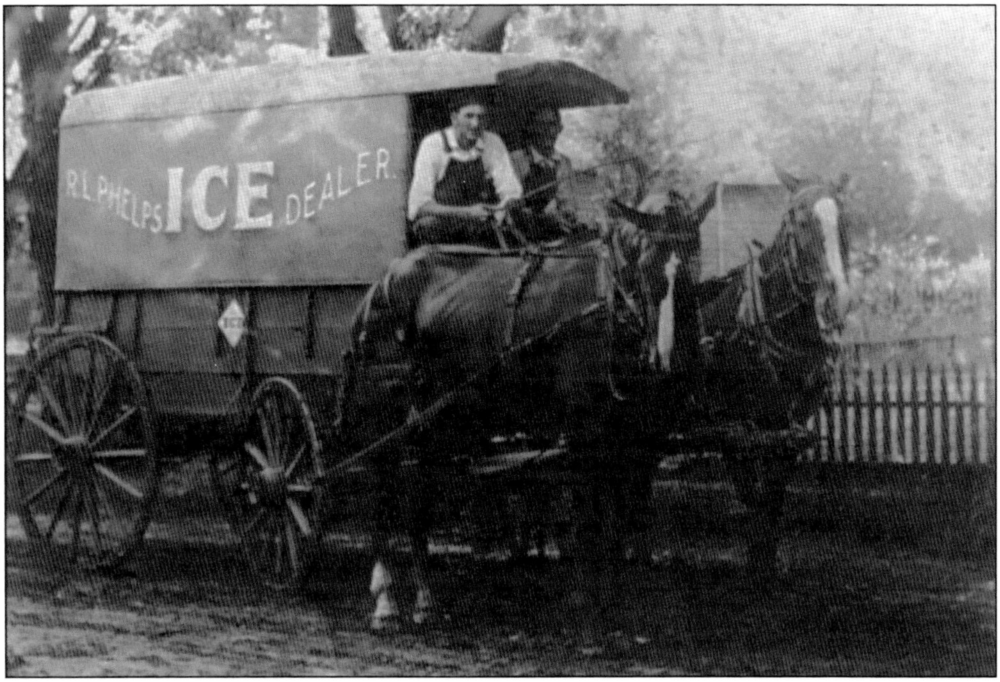

R.L. Phelps would buy ice from one of the icehouses in town and deliver it in his wagon.

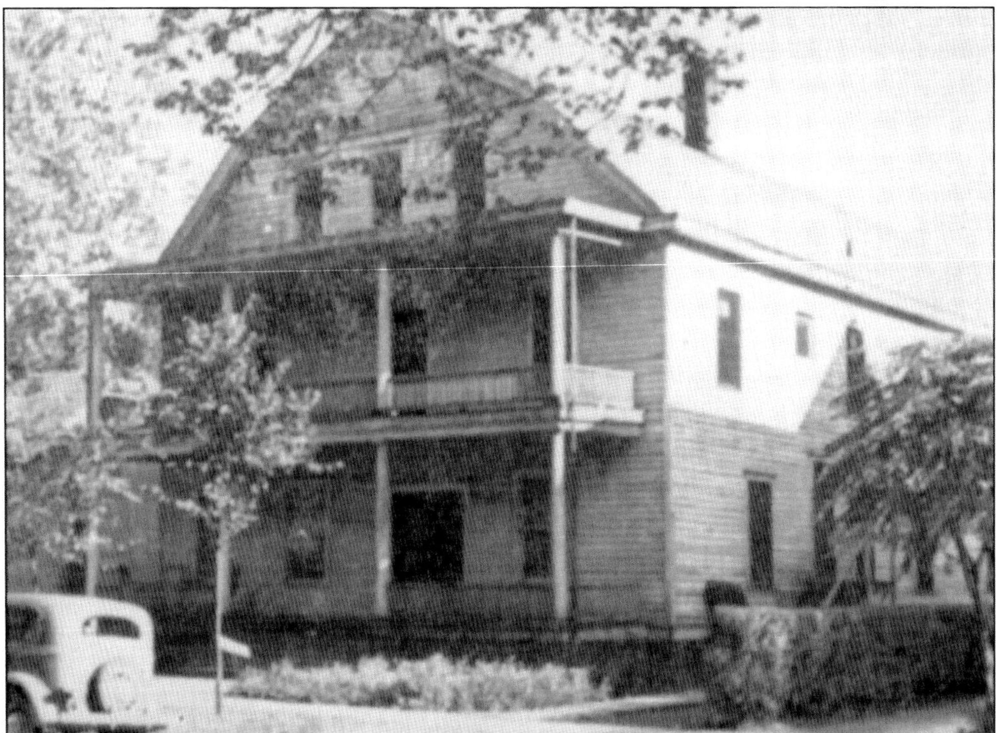

The Community House was on the 200 block of Second Street across from where the Elks Lodge is currently located.

These unidentified men are standing in front of the Wyatt and Ausmus Grocery. The location is not known.

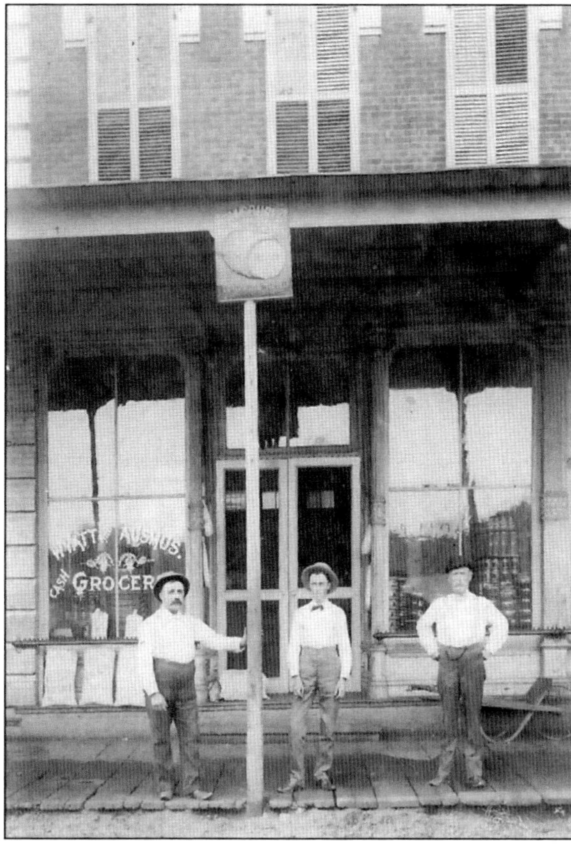

This home at the corner of Fourth and Washington Streets still stands. It has gone through many renovations and still is a beautiful home.

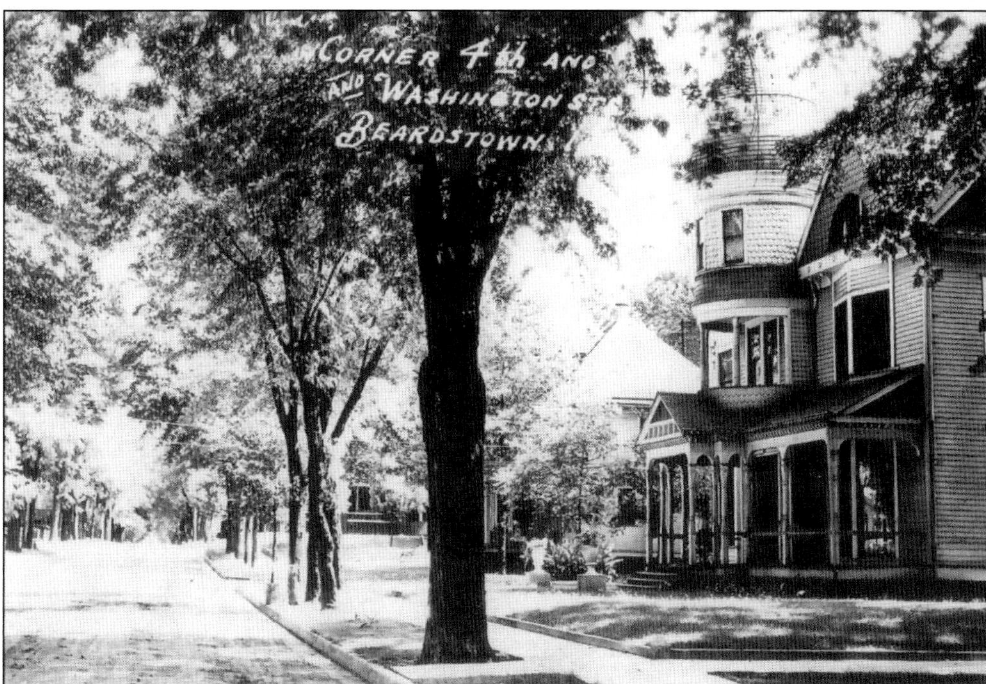

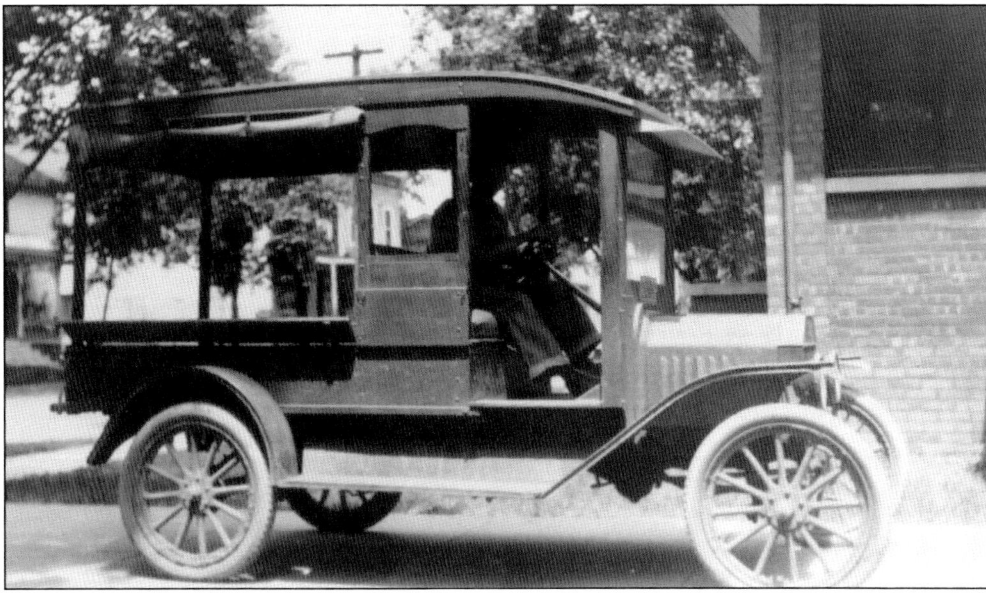

This is an old delivery truck.

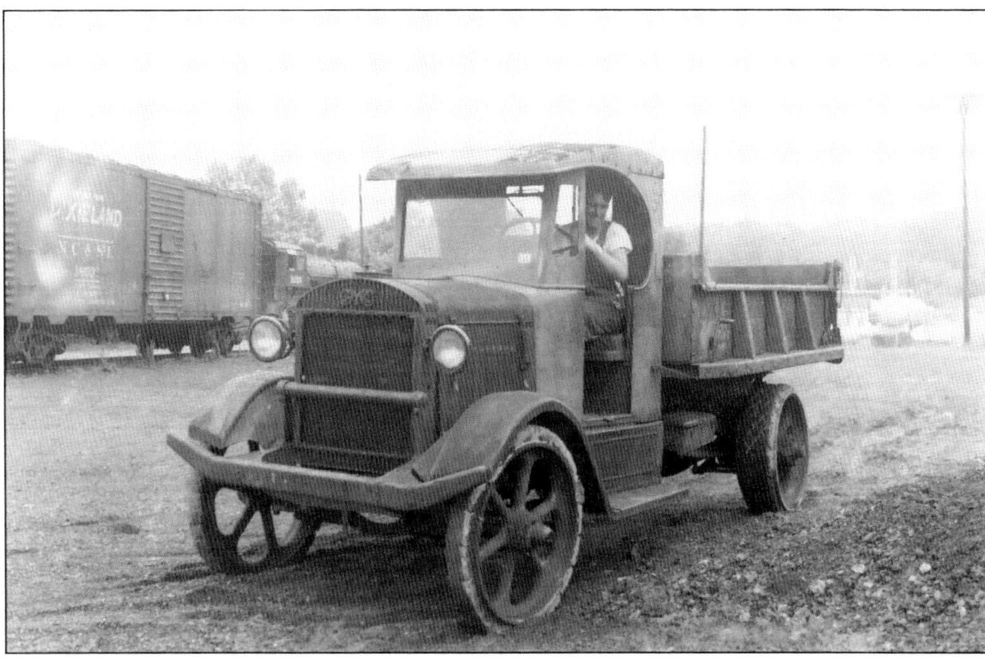

This is a railroad utility truck from the 1950s.

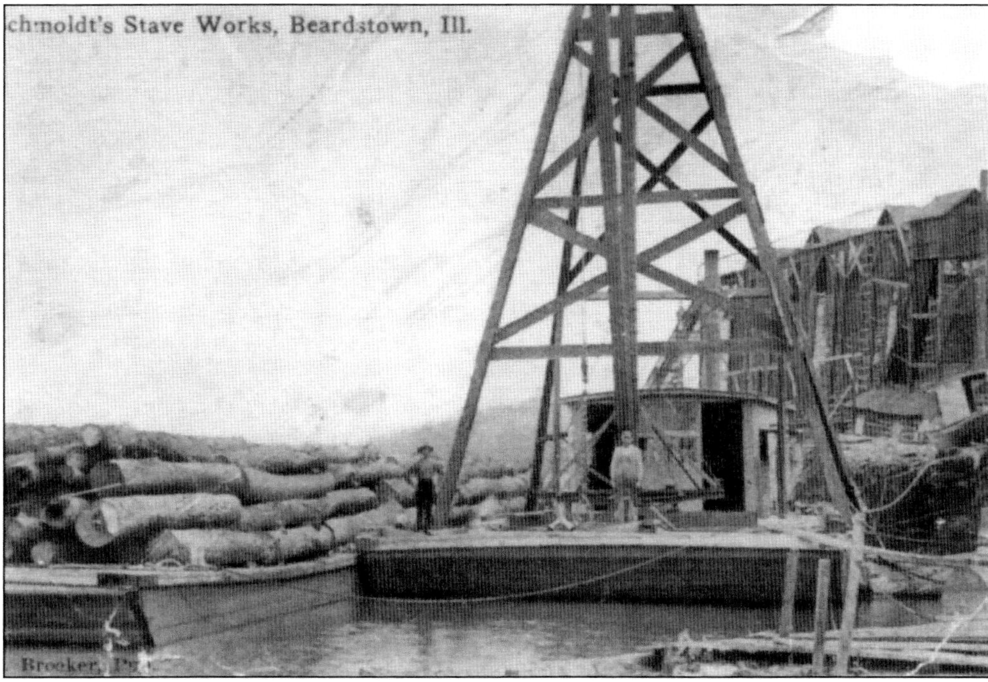

The Schmoldt Stave Works provided wood for the barrel-makers on Main Street. Nearly all the commodities shipped from Beardstown were transported in barrels. Note the icehouses in the background.

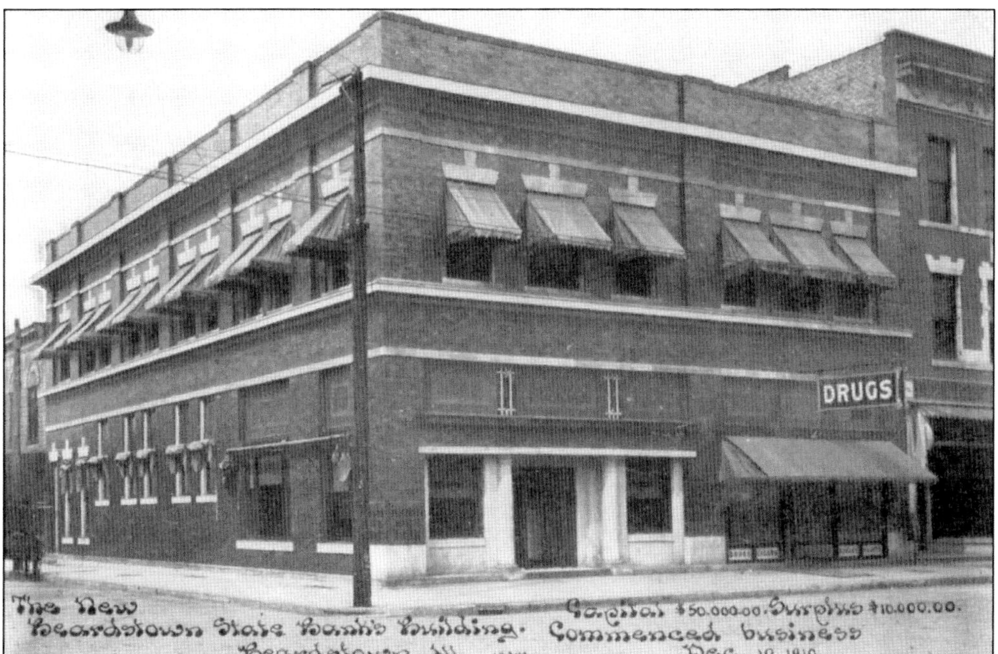

The new Beardstown State Bank building opened in December 1910. The J.W. Doyle drugstore was located next door.

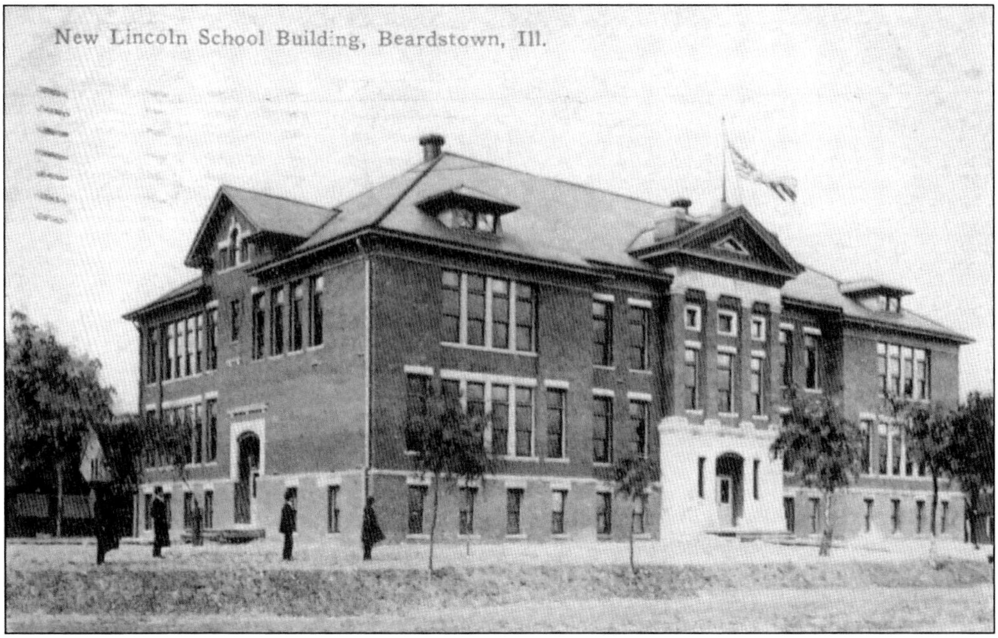

The Lincoln School was built in 1909 and served as a grade school and high school. The last Lincoln high school class graduated in 1924. The new high school opened in 1920.

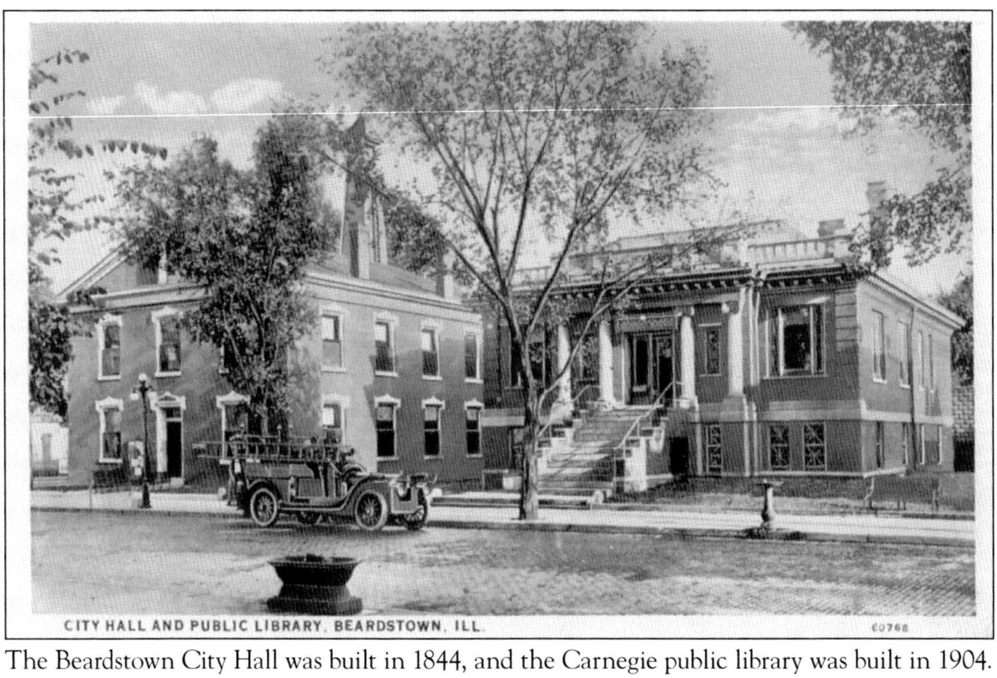

The Beardstown City Hall was built in 1844, and the Carnegie public library was built in 1904.

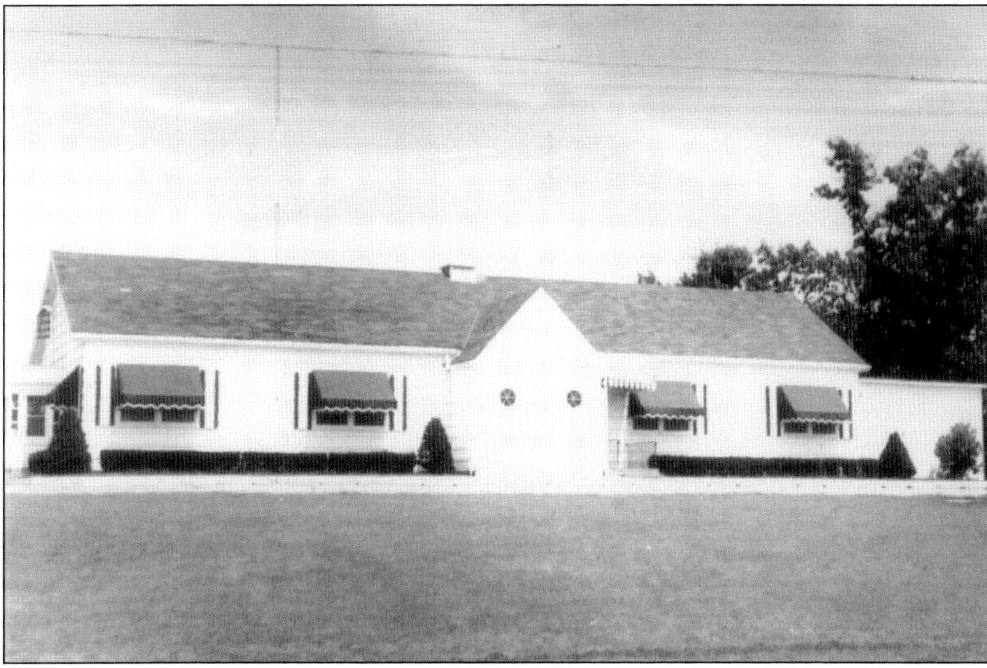

The Bel Taberan restaurant and bar was located on Illinois Route 125 east of town. It later became the Mallard Inn and was run by Frosty Kirchner.

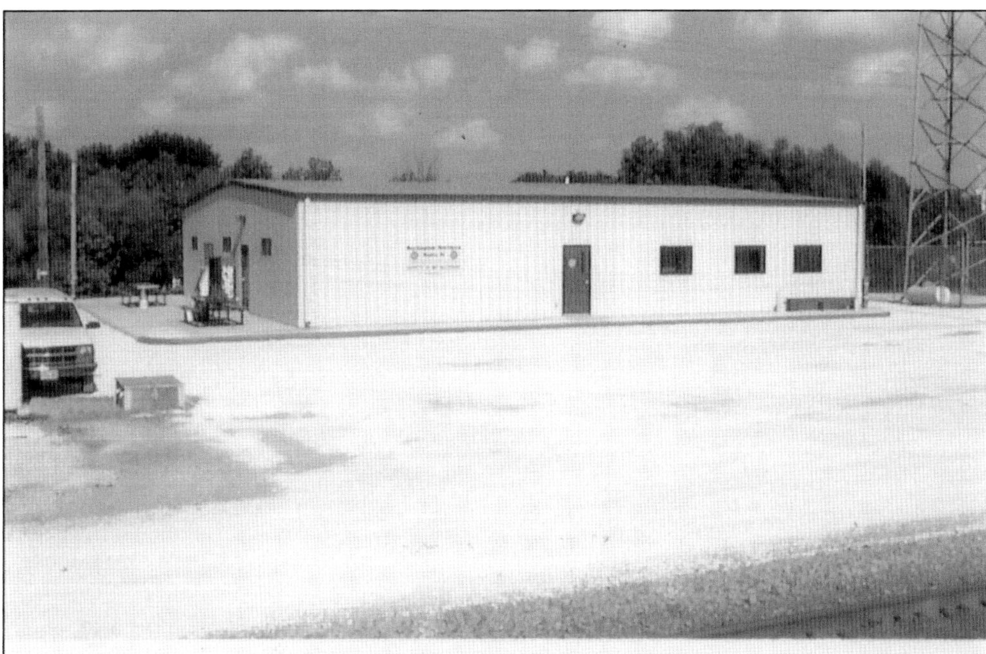

The new Burlington Northern Santa Fe (BNSF) office is located at the south end of the railroad yard.

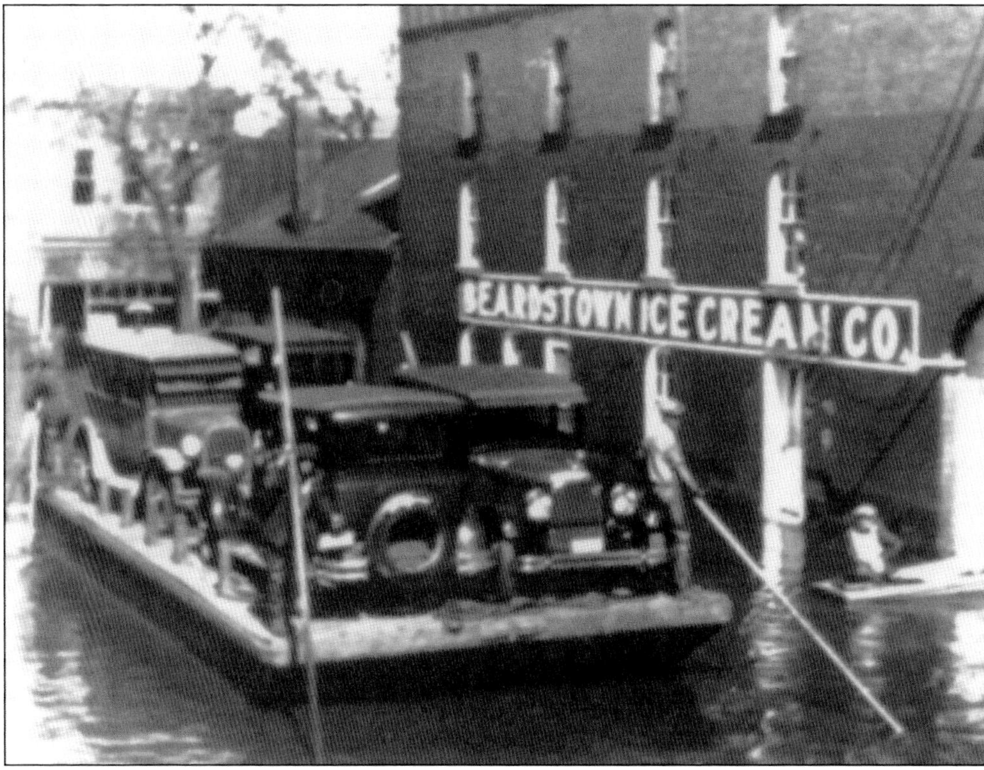

The Beardstown Ice Cream Company was located on Washington Street between Main and Second Streets. This photograph was taken during the 1926 flood.

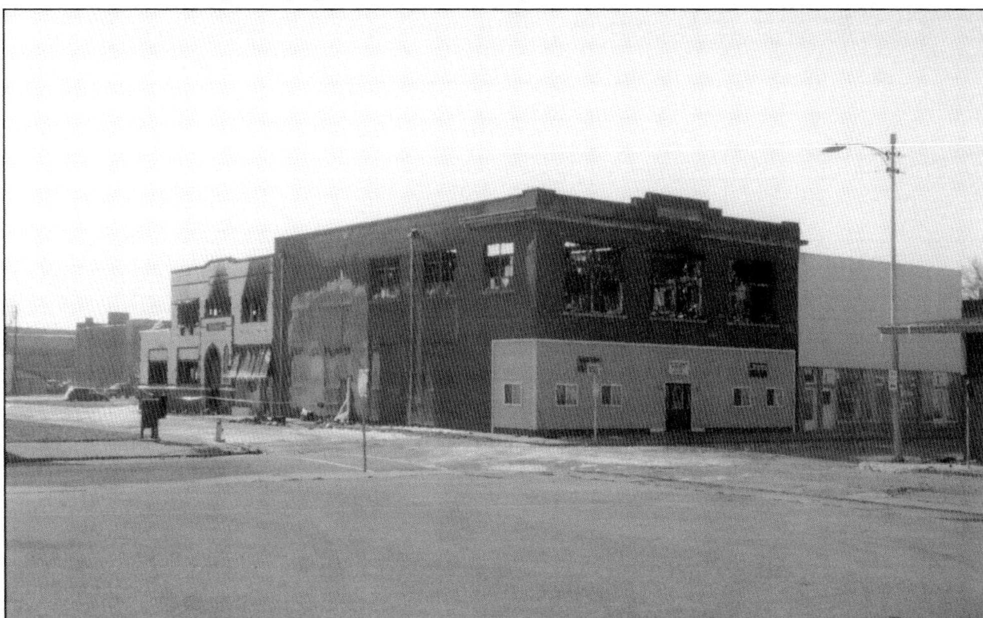

This photograph shows the Fred I. Cline Funeral Home and the Cline Furniture store after a fire destroyed them.

A winter scene near the wagon bridge is pictured in January 1915. The Smith Von Fossen Music Store is on the right.

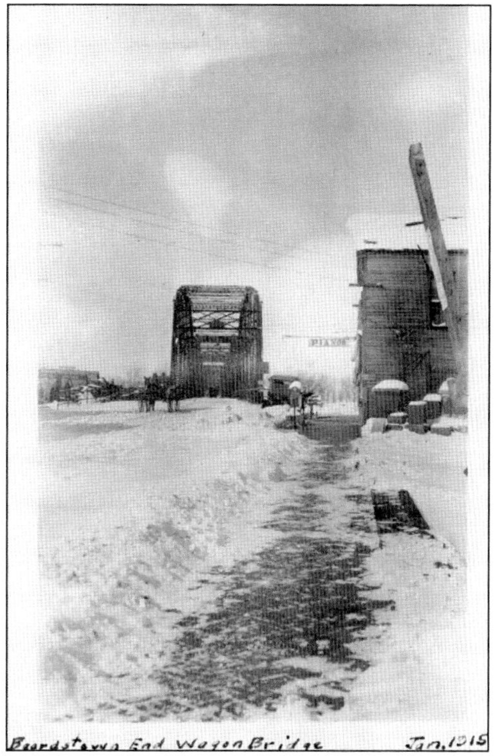

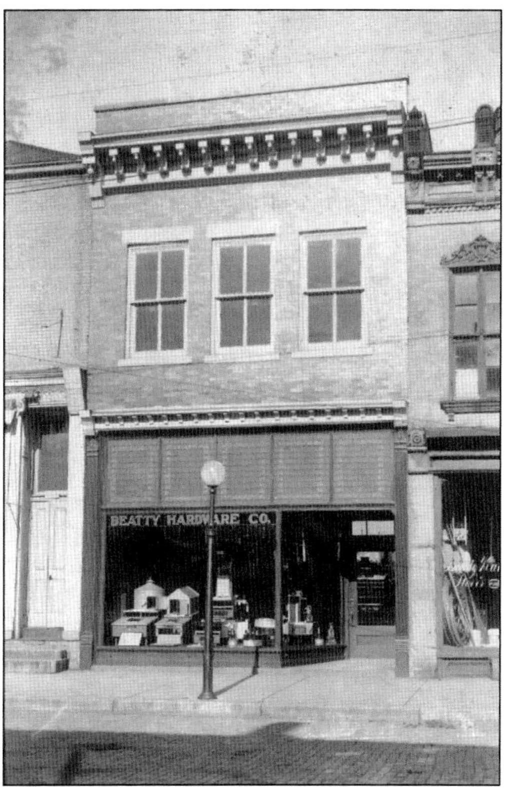

Beatty Hardware Company was located on West Main and Washington Streets.

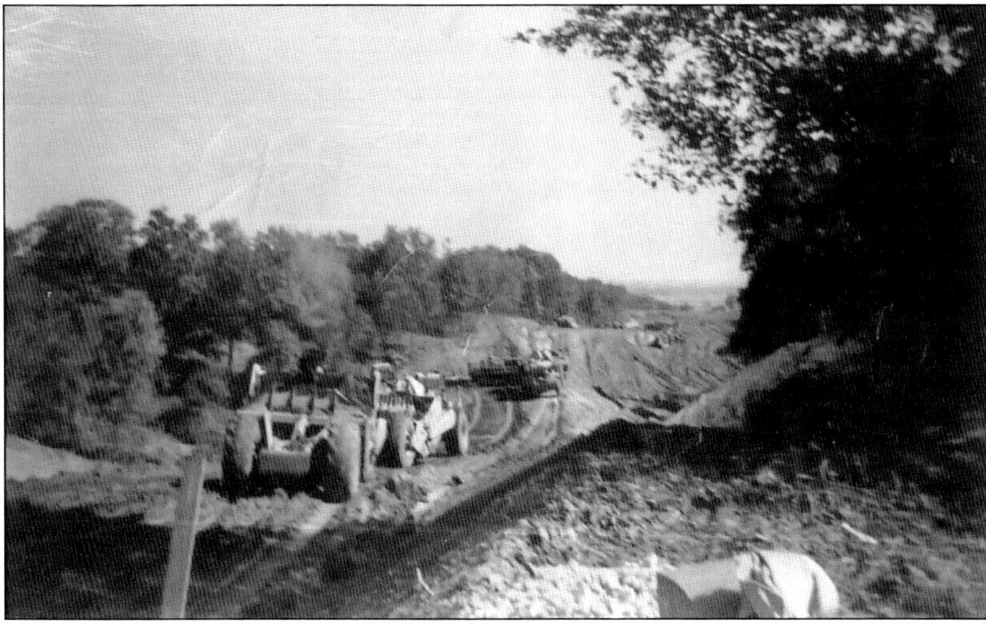

Workers began building the new US Route 67 on the bluff across the river from Beardstown in 1955. This was a big improvement, along with the new bridge at Beardstown. Previously, travelers had to go to Frederick, then up the bluff and on to Rushville.

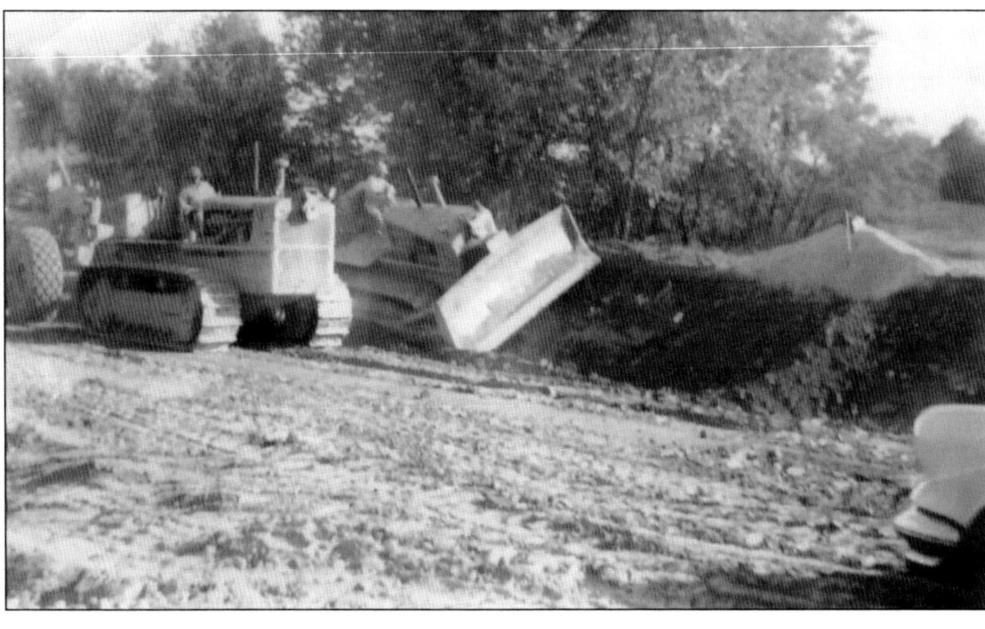

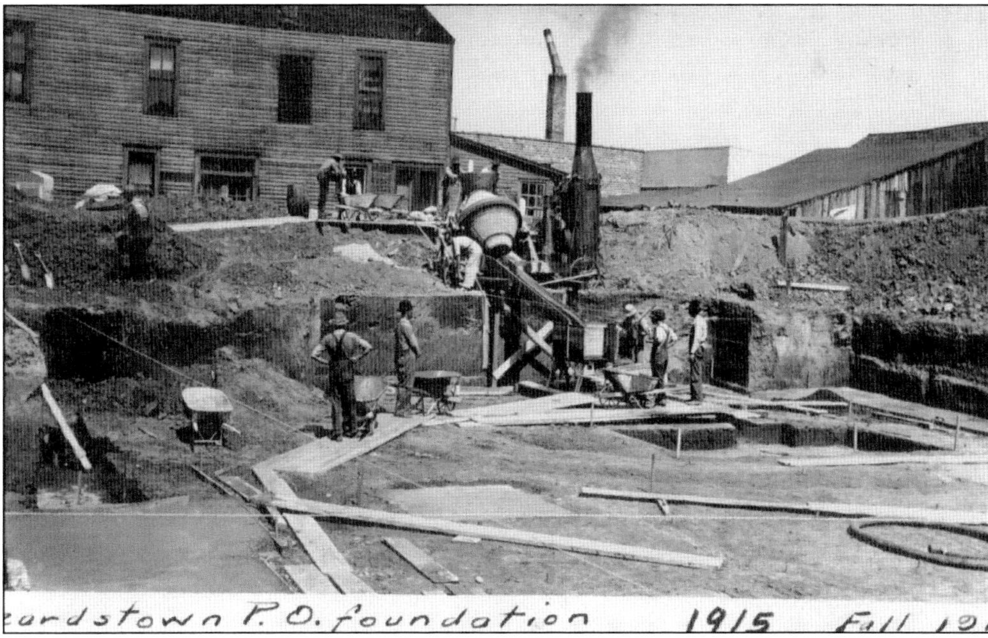

The foundation was poured for the post office at State and Main Streets in 1915. This post office is still in use today. This was originally the site of the Thomas Beard Hotel.

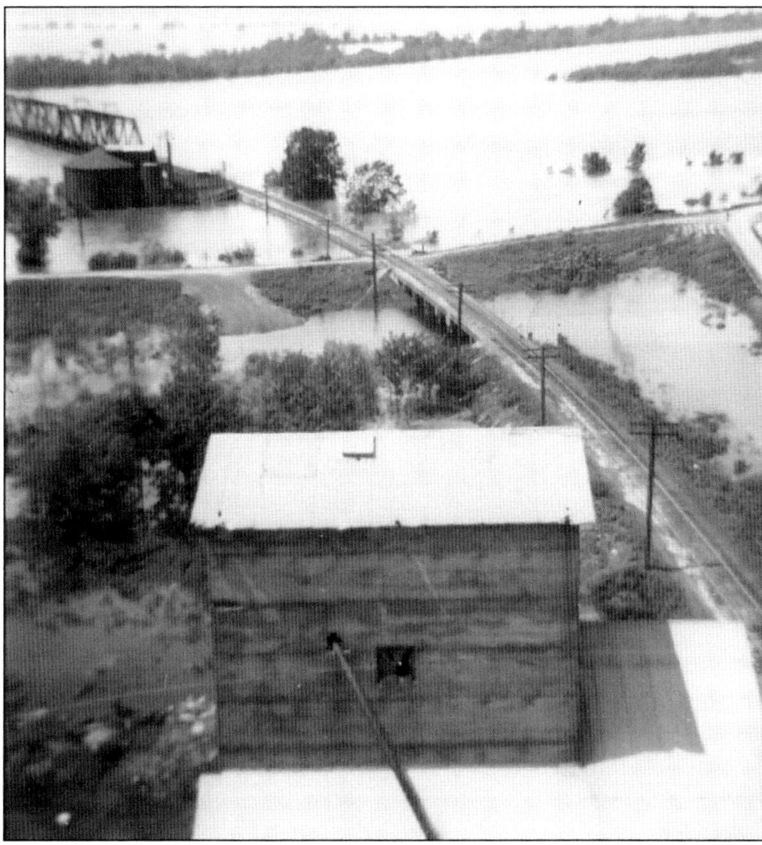

This picture of the old railroad bridge and levee was taken from the top of the Home Mills Elevator, which later became the Schultz-Baujan Flour Mill. This was taken during the high water of 1922.

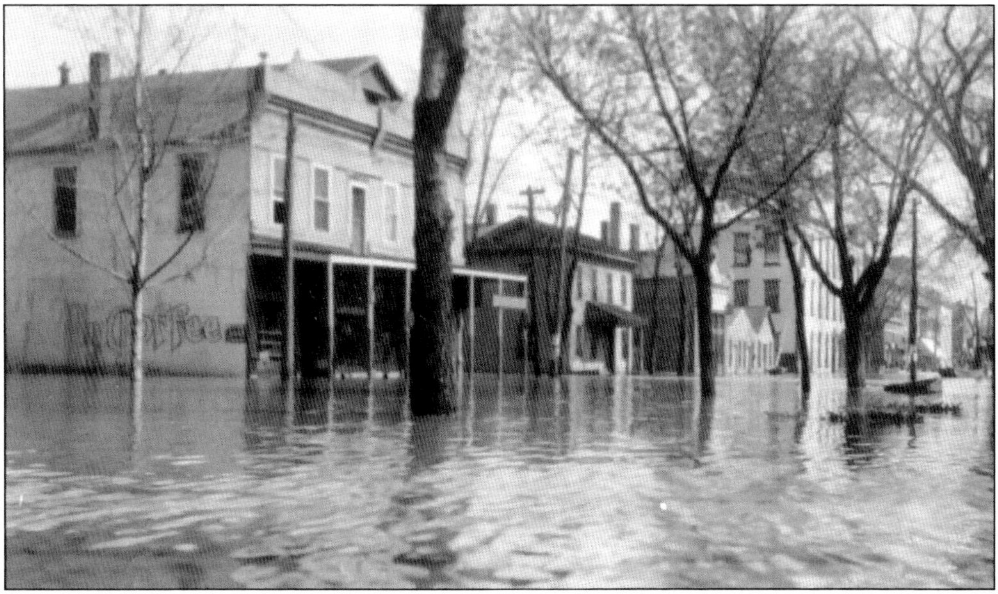

This the 300 block of the north side of West Second Street. The first building is the John Schaeffer Grocery Store, and next to it is the H.H. Pilger Grocery Store. The big building on the next block is the Park Hotel. This photograph was probably taken during the 1922 flood.

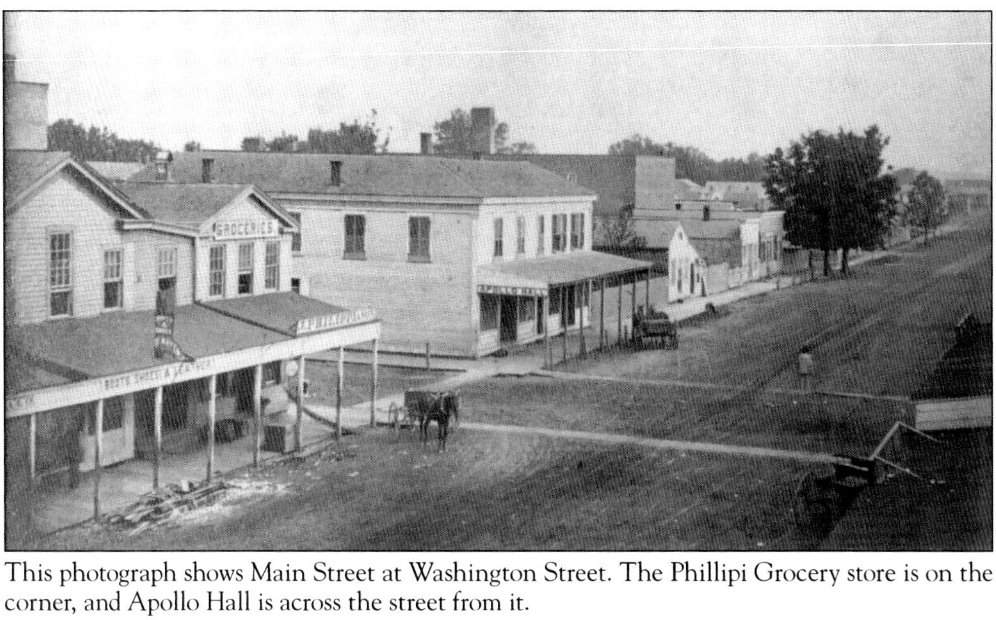

This photograph shows Main Street at Washington Street. The Phillipi Grocery store is on the corner, and Apollo Hall is across the street from it.

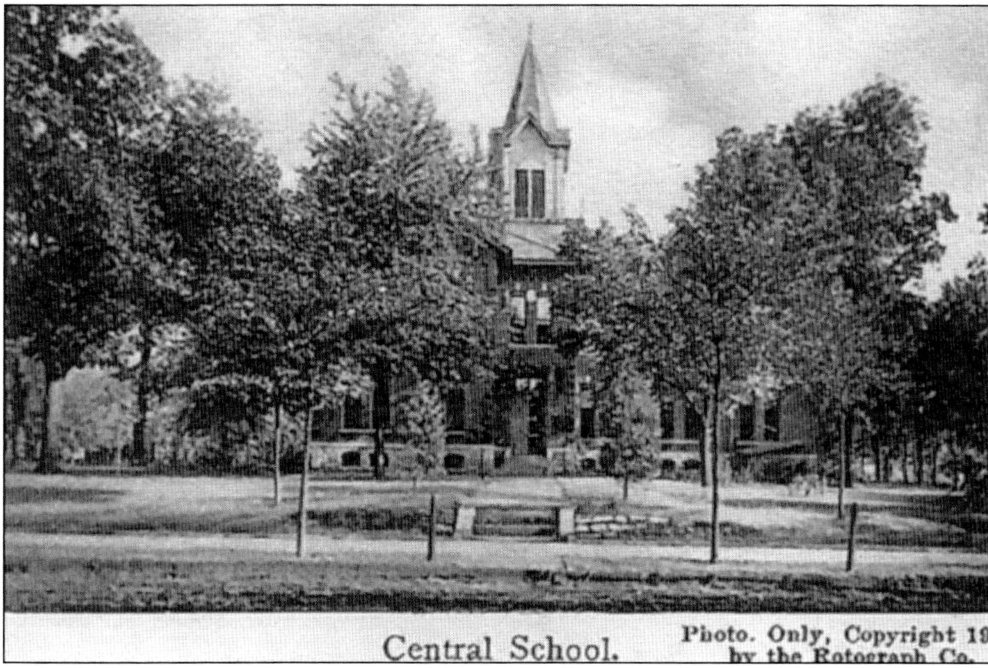

Central School was located on Fourth Street between Clay and Edwards Streets. This picture was taken in 1906. This site is now home to a Save-A-Lot grocery store and Family Video.

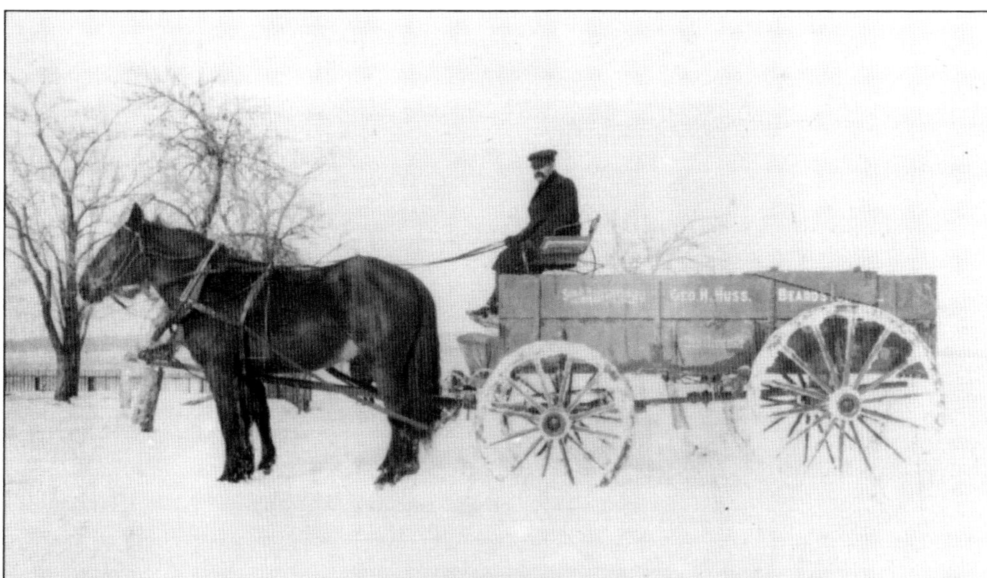

Christopher Huss is shown delivering a load of coal. In 1915, his business, Huss Coal Delivery, was located at 113 East Sixth Street.

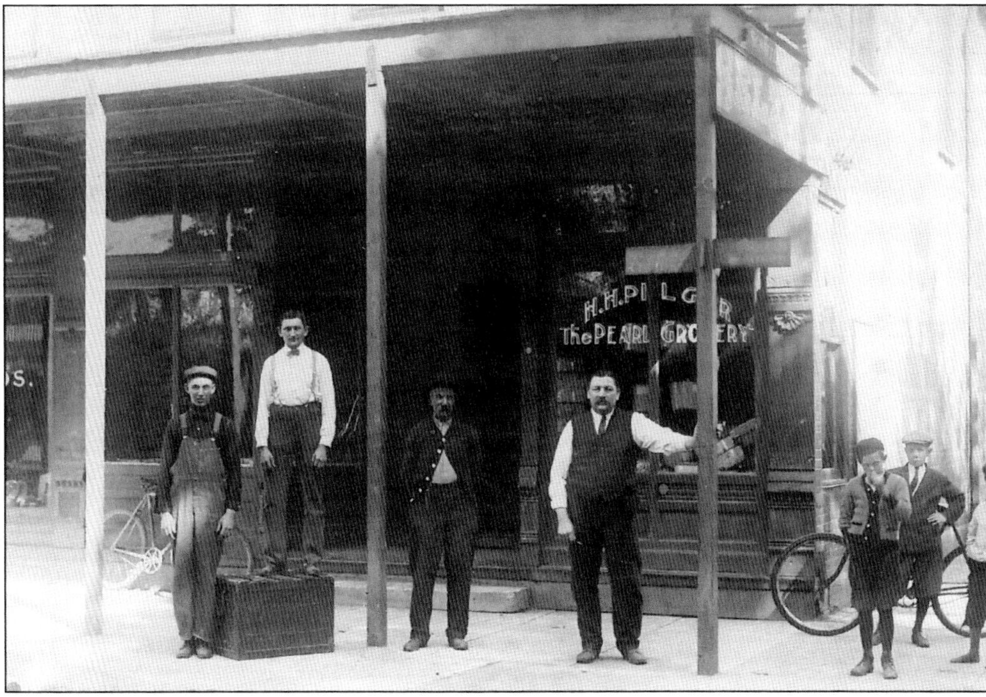

The H.H. Pilger Grocery was located on the north side of the 300 block of West Second Street. This photograph was taken in 1915.

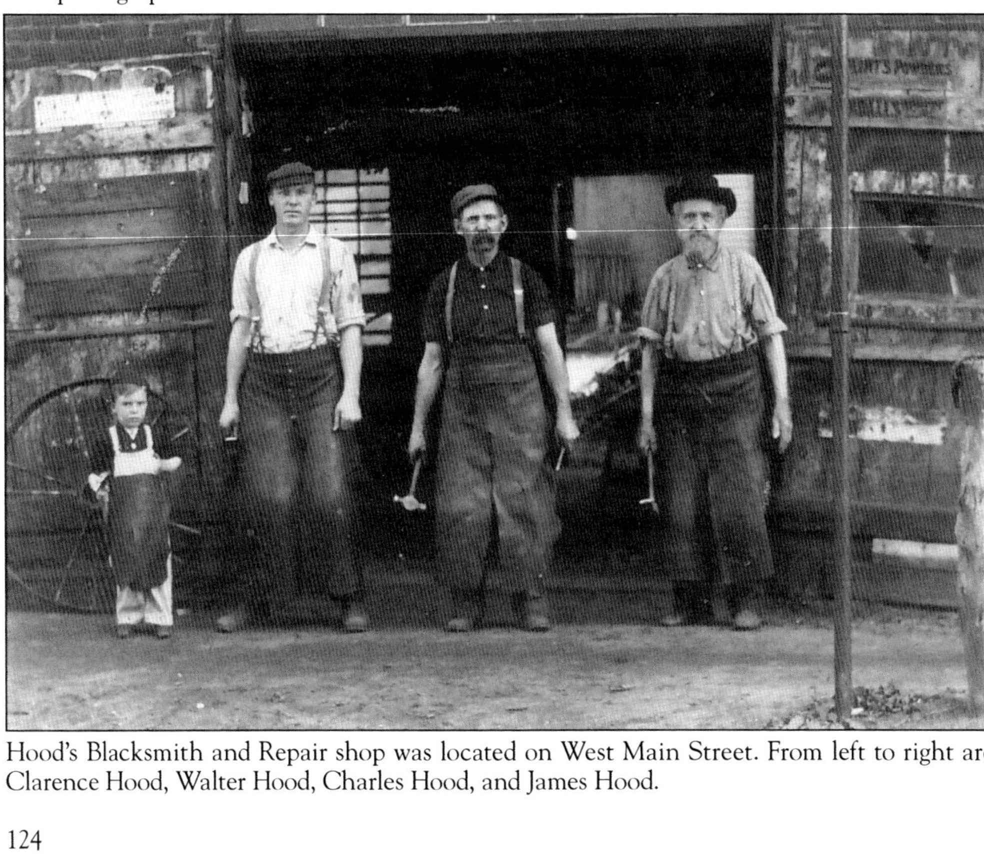

Hood's Blacksmith and Repair shop was located on West Main Street. From left to right are Clarence Hood, Walter Hood, Charles Hood, and James Hood.

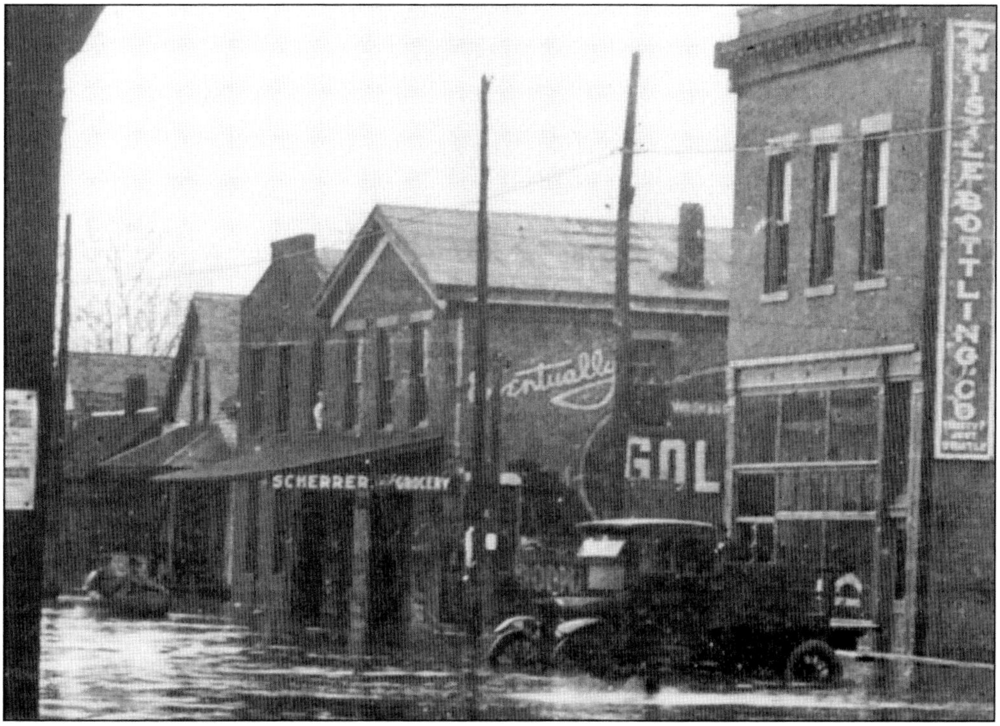

The 200 block of Main Street is shown here during the 1916 flood. Note the Whistle Bottling Company sign and the Scherrer Grocery Store.

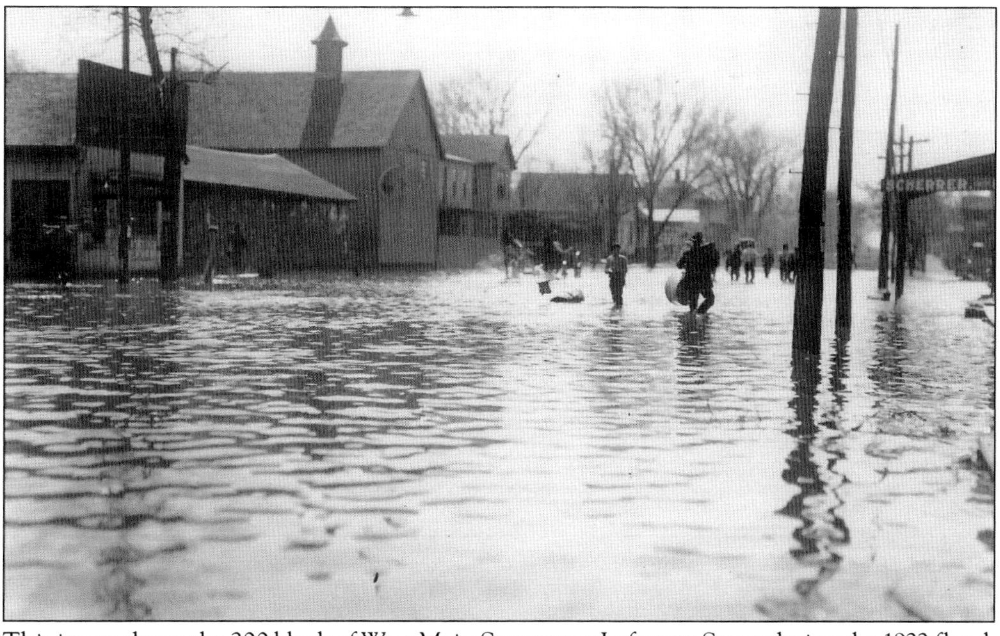

This image shows the 200 block of West Main Street near Lafayette Street during the 1922 flood. Note the Scherrer Grocery Store sign at far right.

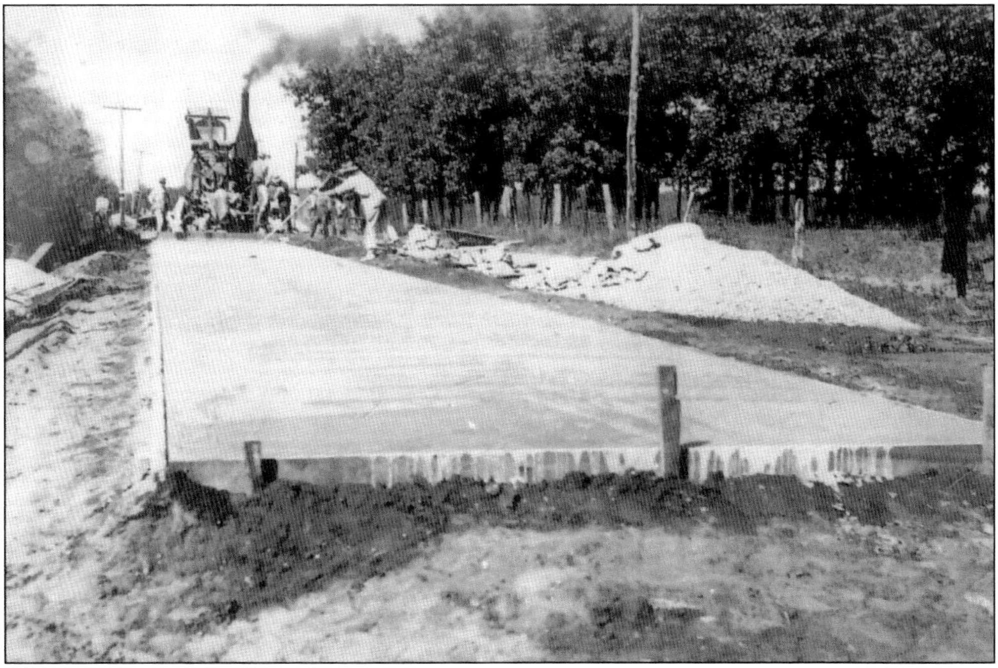

The Arenzville Road near the Beardstown City Cemetery is pictured here during the paving of the road in 1916.

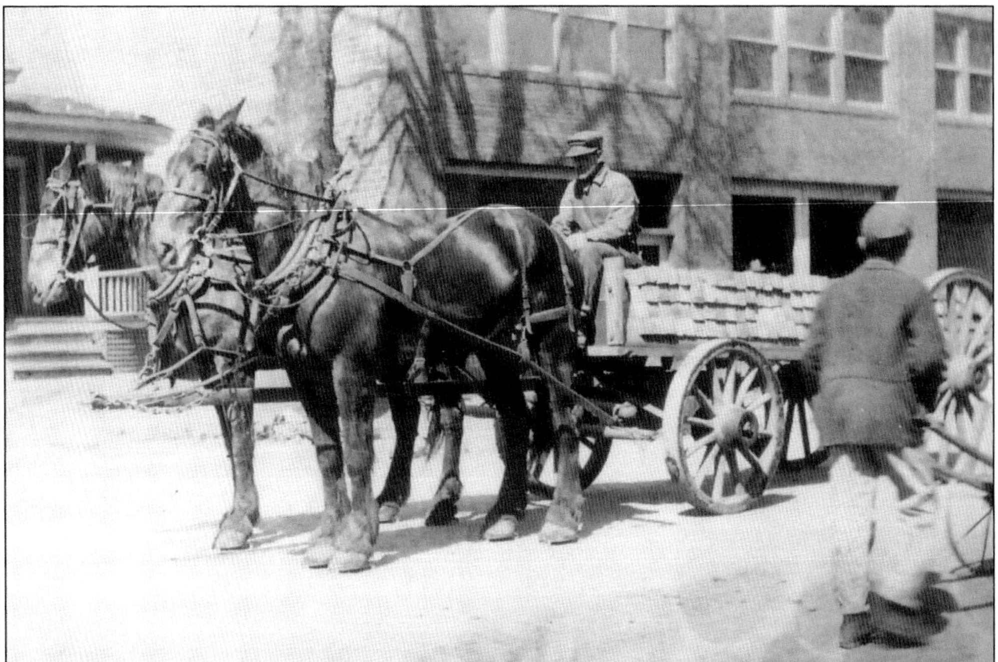

This horse-drawn carriage transporting a wagonload of bricks from the Meyer Brickyard is pictured in front of the Modern Chevrolet Building on Fourth Street between Jefferson and Monroe Streets.

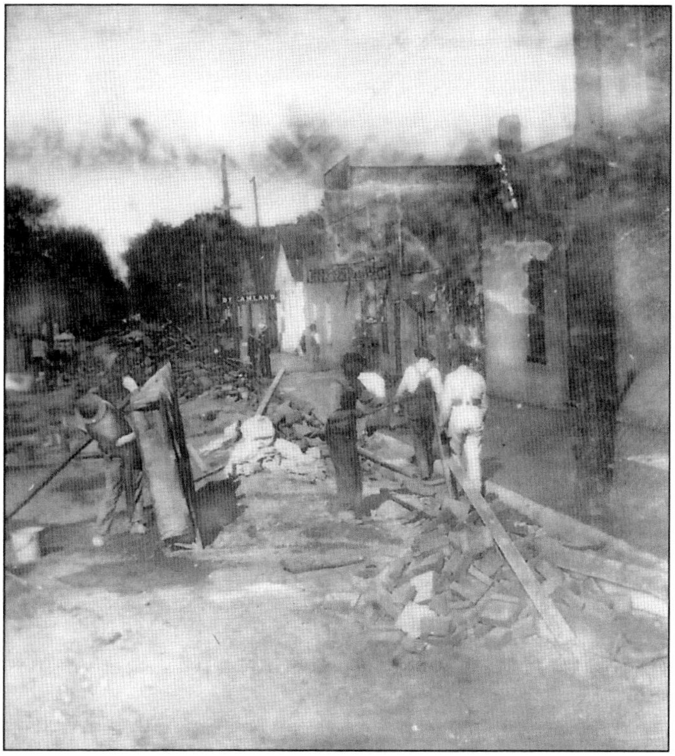

This image shows the paving of Second Street east of State Street.

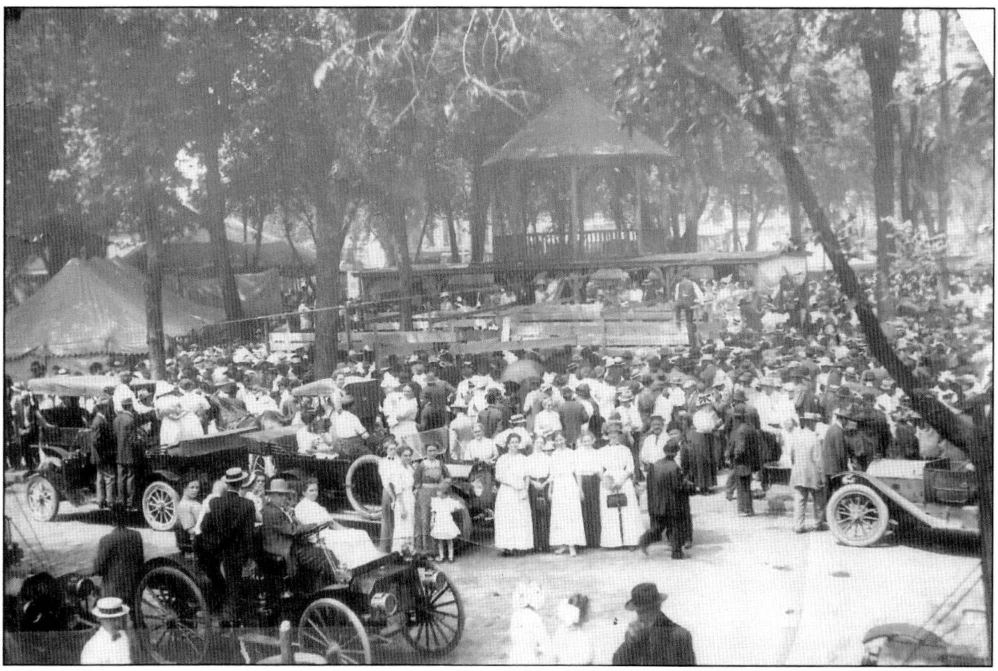

Around 1900, the annual Beardstown Free Fish Fry was moved to the end of Washington Street behind the Arrow Tavern. This photograph was taken when the fish fry was still on the square, so probably in the 1890s. At the fish fry, dinner was free and the fish and oil were paid for by the taverns in town. It was an all-day family gathering.

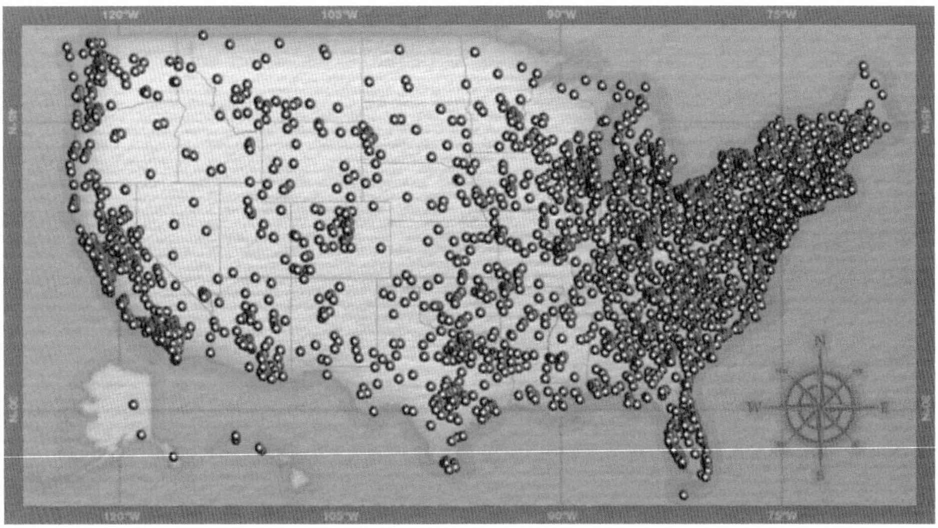